ROGER COOK'S

TEN GREATEST CONMEN

ROGER COOK AND TIM TATE

ROGER COOK'S

TEN GREATEST CONMEN

JB

JOHN BLAKE

Published by John Blake Publishing Ltd,
3 Bramber Court, 2 Bramber Road,
London W14 9PB, England

www.blake.co.uk
First published in hardback in 2008
ISBN: 978-1-84454-646-6

British Library Cataloguing-in-Publication Data:
A catalogue record for this book is available from the British Library.

Design by www.envydesign.co.uk

Printed in the UK by CPI William Clowes Beccles NR34 7TL

1 3 5 7 9 10 8 6 4 2

Papers used by John Blake Publishing are natural, recyclable products
made from wood grown in sustainable forests. The manufacturing processes
conform to the environmental regulations of the country of origin.

Images p1 © National Portrait Gallery, London, p2 © Getty Images, p3,
p5-8 © PA Photos. Other images from the authors' collection

CONTENTS

Introduction   vii

1: Gregor MacGregor: The Crown Prince of   1
Never-Never Land

2: Victor Lustig: The Man who Sold   23
the Eiffel Tower

3: Philip Morrel Wilson: The Bogus Bank of Sark   49

4: Doctor Savundra: The Swindling Genius   79

5: Michael Jeffery: The Great Rock'n'Roll Rip-off   135

6: Frank Abagnale Jr: Catch Me If You Can!   155

7: Barry Gray and Joe Flynn: The Kings of Sting   183

8: Peter Foster: 'Trust Me – I Can Make   199
You Slim!'

9: Robert Hendy-Freegard: The Spy Who   229
Conned Me

10: John Palmer: Goldfinger!   253

Afterword   285

Bibliography   287

INTRODUCTION

There's something about a clever con.

In the anthropology of criminal activity, the confidence trick is a long-term survivor: for more than five hundred years con artists have been creating ever more inventive ways to part gullible victims from their cash.

The scams they have created have proved universal and remarkably adaptable: they cross language and national boundaries with some ease and even the extraordinary speed of modern communications has made little impact on the essential elements of the con.

A variant of one of the very first ever confidence tricks – the Elizabethan-era Spanish Prisoner Letter scam[1] – is alive and thriving today in the instantly connected age of email, text messages and video conferencing.

And the public at large seems to have a sneaking respect for the twisted genius of some of the more intricate scams.

This is despite the fact that the crooks who perpetrate these scams are typically unrepentant rogues, arrogantly living the high life of fast cars, even faster women and extraordinary but undeserved luxury – while their victims lose their savings, their homes, their self-respect and sometimes their free will and even their lives. Nevertheless, it is also true that there is a certain guilty pleasure to be had from hearing about a well-worked con.

The popularity of Hollywood blockbusters such as *Ocean's 11* or *The Sting* – not to mention the extraordinary success of BBC's drama series *Hustle* – attests to this phenomenon.

So just what *is* it about a 'good' con? Perhaps the answer lies in the mythology and the vocabulary that have grown up around confidence trickery. More than any other type of crime, cons have developed their own vocabulary: a unique language has been created around the scams and scammers, growing into a colourful argot that serves to hide the shabby reality beneath the pre-*Minder* clichés.

In this patois conmen are 'grifters', victims are 'marks' and historic scams have the equivalent of a 'play book' – set moves that lovingly detail the well-tried script according to which the trick should be played out.

The mythology of scams feeds into this rich tapestry by reassuringly proclaiming to the outside world that a truly innocent man can't be conned: that the reason the 'marks' have been taken in and cleaned out is that they believed they could get something for nothing (or at least at an absurdly cheap price) – and that they weren't overly scrupulous about the strict legality of doing so. Sadly, this is generally rubbish.

We have spent – individually and collectively – a lifetime dealing with con artists and their victims. We have investigated a large number of scams – from straightforward short frauds to the most elaborate of international long-term operations.

And the truth is that they are – almost without exception – no more than glorified thefts. They may be overlaid with the conman's pleasure in taking someone down, or with his desire to control his victims – but thefts they remain. Yes, the conmen are clever – gifted in some regards. But, when all is said and done, they have still stolen someone's savings. Often those savings turn out to be all the 'mark' had in the world. Too often they don't stand a prayer of getting any of it back.

We've met hundreds of such victims: tearful, torn between anger, incredulity and frustration at the ease with which they have been gulled. Yet still the con artists get a remarkably benign press. You wouldn't give a burglar or a mugger this sort grudging respect: so what makes these (often) huge and heartless scams so different?

It's a question that has exercised us over more than a quarter of a century. And, in truth, we are not immune to the false glamour of a well-crafted con ourselves. The best answer we've come up with is that the stories are just so extraordinary – so involving and so eye-wateringly vivid – that they just cry out to be told.

Unfortunately, so common is the species these days that no one will ever agree on their Top Ten British Cons (much less those perpetrated by foreign-based scammers). Even we had trouble in picking our favourite runners and riders: how do you decide between the competing claims of the bogus 'Fessenden Charles Rex Morley-Morley, Vicompte de Borenden' (or plain Rex Morley as he was more usually and prosaically known to officers of the Metropolitan Police for his repeated and very profitable property frauds) and those of Eric Hebborn, the master forger who conned the art world into buying thousands of his fakes before dying mysteriously in a darkened Italian backstreet? We couldn't decide, so we left them out, leaving room for even bigger fish. Even then, the list of candidates ran to more than a score.

In the end we chose those who had exhibited the most ingenuity – sometimes even style – but who had (usually) eschewed force, either psychological or physical.

It is a sad commentary on the times in which we live that this last proviso became more difficult to follow the more contemporary our stories were. However, the most successful conmen have had their 'marks' on a string by deploying no more than verbal persuasion or a swift sleight of hand.

Writing their stories has been an interesting project involving, as it did, a determined attempt to separate myth from fact. Some of the cases we had dealt with personally and could write about from first-hand knowledge. In other cases we faced the uphill task of evaluating swathes of contradictory documentation and sometimes trying to create something factual but original from multiple sources that repeat each other, almost to the word. And on occasion, précis and paraphrase is as far as you can go without losing the plot.

We hope that we've succeeded n our efforts and that you 'enjoy' the results.

Just not too much.

Roger Cook and Tim Tate, October 2008

1

GREGOR MACGREGOR: THE CROWN PRINCE OF NEVER-NEVER LAND

On Wednesday 22 January 1823, more than 200 men, women and children gathered on the dockside at Leith, a small port just a mile down the Firth of Forth from Edinburgh.

It was the first fine day in almost a fortnight of vicious gales and snowstorms, and, as they picked their way across a narrow gangplank and stepped on board a flotilla of little boats to take them out to the good ship *Kennersley Castle*, the travellers were in high spirits. They were doctors, lawyers, civil servants, farmers and even a professional banker. And they were bound for an earthly paradise.

As they settled – according to rank and status – into their cabins or communal living quarters, with their relatives and friends waiting patiently on the quayside to wave them goodbye, a carriage drew up alongside.

A handsome and imposing man, elegantly dressed and with a distinctly military bearing, stepped from it and boarded a rowing boat before being swiftly transported to the *Kennersley Castle*. Once on deck he hoisted a large flag – a green Cross of St George on a white background – and ordered a six-gun salute to be fired from the ship's 9-pound cannon.

He then addressed the assembled voyagers, congratulating them on their decision to exchange Scotland's windswept shores for the certain fortunes and bounteous delights of their intended new home, and announced – to widespread delight – that, since this was the first and pioneering voyage to 'the new El Dorado', he had generously decided to give free passage to all the women and children.

As he stepped back down into the little dinghy and was rowed back to shore, his audience, lining the railings on board the *Kennersley Castle*, broke into spontaneous and rapturous cheering.

The focus of their approbation, their benefactor and proud unfurler of the green Cross of St George banner, was the Cazique de Poyais – and the promised land to which they were sailing was the Territory of Poyais, 'a free and independent state' situated on the exotic 'Mosquito Coast', along the Atlantic seaboard of South America.

It boasted a cultured and elegant capital city, complete with an opera house, banks, government mansion and a wealth of fine housing. In its surrounding hinterland were unclaimed resources of silver and gold; and its soil and climate were so propitious that farming here was both profitable and pleasurable. To cap it all, the indigenous Indian population was staunchly pro-British.

Little wonder, then, that the two hundred voyagers had so eagerly bought parcels of land and queued in the Edinburgh rain to purchase their tickets for a passage to paradise. Nor that they cheered the charismatic Cazique de Poyais as they sailed off down the Firth of Forth.

A month later they landed on an empty and swamp-infested coastline with no sign of any solid buildings – much less a fully functioning modern city – under the puzzled gaze of a handful of rather bemused natives.

It took them less than twenty-four hours to discover that the land they had been sold was non-existent; that the banknotes and guidebooks they carried with them were forgeries; and that all their documents were worthless. They were forced to realise that they had been the victims of one of the most elaborate hoaxes in history.

There was only one small problem with the Territory of Poyais and its widely promised delights: not a single word was true.

It was Adolf Hitler who first defined the principle of 'The Big Lie'. This, he wrote in 1925, was a lie so huge that anyone hearing it would be forced to believe it on the simple grounds that '[no one] could have the impudence to distort the truth so infamously'.[2]

Sixteen years later, Hitler's propaganda chief, Joseph Goebbels, refined the idea and pointed a shamelessly accusing finger at England.

'The English', he wrote in a 1941 newspaper article, 'follow the principle that when one lies, one should lie big, and stick to it.'[3]

His Royal Highness, Brigadier-General Sir Gregor MacGregor, Cazique de Poyais, followed the Goebbels principle in every regard but one: he was Scottish.

MacGregor's Big Lie has passed into legend among con artists around the world. Where others of his time were content to sell plots of worthless or inaccessible land to gullible prospectors, no one before or since has invented an entire country and proceeded to raise millions by selling its land rights, share issues and even its own currency.

That he managed to do so for more than fifteen years – despite the death of many of his victims and widespread exposure in the press – is a testament to the artistry of MacGregor's con. It is also a sign of the times in which he operated.

The early 1820s saw the beginning of a boom in the London financial markets. The Napoleonic Wars had convulsed Europe since 1803 and laid waste to the economy of Spain just as the French army had devastated its cities. Money had flowed out of Europe and into the growing number of private or merchant banks that had opened in the City of London.

After the Battle of Waterloo brought the wars to an end, the banks' coffers were further swelled by an increase in the wealth of Britain's new middle class – the merchants and factory owners who had grown rich on the fruits of the Industrial Revolution. The immediate post-war years laid the foundations for some of the most famous names in banking today: Barings, Hambros and Kleinwort grew fat on the tides of money flowing in and out of London.

Simultaneously, the wealthier sections of the British public developed an obsessive taste for investing in stocks and shares.

Until the turn of the century there had been only a small handful of companies in which people could invest, but the exponential growth of industrial production – coupled with the emergence of a dedicated and regulated Stock Exchange and the surfeit of European money swilling around in

London's merchant banks – led to a fevered climate in which investors fell over each other to sink their savings in almost any promising new venture. And, much like the dotcom boom of the 1990s, some of these ventures were built on seriously shaky foundations.

The daily newspapers in those times tended to have very few pages. By the early 1820s at least one of those pages would be devoted to news from the City, including the tipping of fancied shares. And, equally typically, one other full page would be devoted to Britain's other apparent obsession of the period: South America.

Napoleon's assaults on the Iberian peninsula had weakened Spain's grip on its colonies – South America, in particular, proved very vulnerable to wars of liberation. The struggles for independence from Madrid spread like wildfire across the continent – Colombia, Bolivia, Peru and Venezuela would all throw off the Spanish yoke within a handful of years – and many British army officers signed up as mercenaries, fighting with the liberating forces.

These wars of independence may have been taking place several thousand miles away from London, but they were faithfully and extensively chronicled in British newspapers. And the leaders of some of these armies of revolution became both household names and romantic popular figures – chief among them was the dashing figure of Simón Bolívar.

From 1808, Bolívar had led the fight against the Spanish, eventually establishing an independent federation covering much of modern Venezuela, Colombia, Panama and Ecuador. He gathered around him an international band of experienced and very successful military campaigners. Every one of them basked in both the reflected glory of the glamorous Bolívar and of the widely disseminated dispatches of their own impressive campaigns.

In 1820 the name of a previously unknown officer – apparently of Scottish descent – began to crop up in these dispatches. Brigadier-General Sir Gregor MacGregor had – apparently – distinguished himself in battle at such exotic-sounding locations as Onoto, Chaguarames and Quebrada-Honda. That the British readers of his exploits were highly unlikely to be able to locate these places on a map – much less to know whether they were as romantic as they sounded – mattered little: the dashing Scottish soldier had been given his rank by the great Bolívar himself.

Furthermore, he claimed to be a descendant of Rob Roy – the so-called 'Scottish Robin Hood' – who had recently been immortalised in Sir Walter Scott's eponymous novel. In the eyes of the press, therefore, MacGregor was unquestionably a copper-bottomed hero.

And so when, in the late summer of 1821, the Brigadier-General arrived in London, accompanied by his beautiful wife Josefa – the niece, no less, of Simón Bolívar himself – fashionable society was ready to welcome him with open arms. And Gregor MacGregor was equally ready to be welcomed. He had come to London not simply as a military adventurer returning home after a great career, but as the self-declared ruler of 8 million acres – 12,500 square miles – of some of the most wondrous and profitable land in the world.

And, while he was anxious to play down his heroic exploits on the field of battle, he was rather less modest about the title by which he wished to be known: His Highness, the Cazique of Poyais.

According to MacGregor, the Territory of Poyais lay in an

area of South America known as the Mosquito Coast. This was a huge and very real swathe of land, situated on the Atlantic seaboard of what today is Nicaragua. Its name was derived not from a pestilential insect but from the Miskito Indians who inhabited it.

Since 1660 Britain had claimed the area as a protectorate, but had never quite got round to turning it into a fully fledged colony. Instead the region was ruled by local royalty: George Frederick the Second, King of the Mosquito Shore and Nation. MacGregor claimed that in April 1820 George Frederick had given him the Territory of Poyais and appointed him its 'Cazique'. He readily admitted that there was no exact translation of the word, but humbly allowed that it essentially meant 'Prince'.

And, as he was at pains to point out, he took seriously the responsibilities of his new regal position. Not merely was Poyais a fertile land with untapped resources, a wonderful climate and cooperative natives, it also had a small number of settlers of British origin. From these, MacGregor said, he had created a civil service, army and democratic government.

But, if Poyais was such a Garden of Eden, what could have brought its new ruler back to the somewhat more earthy streets of London? It was, MacGregor explained, a question of duty.

He had promised all his loyal citizens that he would return to Britain in search of new settlers and investment, and he was able to produce an elegantly printed copy of the impressive speech which he had given to the Poyers (as inhabitants of Poyais were apparently called) just before setting sale for England.

Dated 13 April 1821 and certified as a true copy of the original speech by one Thomas Strangeways, a captain in the

'1st Native Poyer Regiment', MacGregor's 'Proclamation to the Inhabitants of the Territory of Poyais' was an extraordinarily grandiose and self-important declaration.

> Poyers! It shall be my constant study to render you happy and to exert myself in improving your situation by every means in my power... Animated with the hope of... procuring you religious and moral instructors, the implements of husbandry and persons to guide and assist you in the cultivation of the valuable productions for which our soil and climate are so well adapted, I have determined upon visiting Europe ...
>
> Poyers! I now bid you farewell for a while... and I trust that through the kindness of Almighty Providence, I shall be again enabled to return among you and that then it will be my pleasing duty to hail you as affectionate friends, and yours to receive me as your faithful Cazique and Father.

London Society quickly took the dashing Cazique and his glamorous wife to its collective bosom. He and the Princess of Poyais (as Josefa was to be known) became almost instant celebrities, receiving scores of invitations to soirées. The Lord Mayor of London even organised an official reception at the Guildhall in his honour.

And the previously modest brigadier-general became distinctly less reluctant to detail his exploits in the wars of South American independence: tales of high courage and derring-do swirled around the party season. MacGregor was also pleased to receive enquiries from journalists and press reports were both frequent and fawning.

There was, of course, a reason for MacGregor's courting of the newspapers and high society: he had something to sell, and he knew that the City was ripe and ready to buy.

On 23 October 1822, acting in his official capacity as Cazique and backed by the cash-rich merchant-banking houses, MacGregor proposed a governmental loan issue for £200,000. This loan, guaranteed by the government of Poyais, took the form of two thousand bearer bonds, each worth £100. It was a scheme of simple but cunning beauty.

Bearer bonds differ from normal stocks and shares in one key particular: they are completely unregistered. No records are kept anywhere of the owner, or of any transactions involving their ownership. Whoever physically holds the bearer-bond papers owns shares or stock to their face value.

It was this lack of any record of who might own what in the Poyais issue that must have appealed to MacGregor. It would have been difficult enough for any suspicious investor or snooping journalist to discover how soundly based were the Cazique's claims about Poyais, a country halfway round the world in the days before telephones or telegraph. But the anonymity of the bearer bonds would have erected another impenetrable screen.

And the bond issue was fully subscribed in very short order. MacGregor was able to bank the very considerable sum of £200,000 – the equivalent of at least £11 million today. An office for the Legation of the Territory of Poyais was opened at Dowgate Hill in the City and its credentials as an official governmental mission were accepted by the court of King George IV. Meanwhile, the Cazique and Princess Josefa graciously allowed one of their new society friends to put his country mansion at their disposal.

From these two bases, Gregor MacGregor worked steadily to enhance his reputation as the farsighted ruler of an enticing and exotic land. Using the funds from the bearer bond issue – funds that were supposed to be earmarked for the greater development of his Territory – he staged elaborate banquets, inviting foreign ambassadors, government ministers and senior military officers to celebrate the glory that was Poyais.

But the bond issue wasn't MacGregor's only money-making venture. After all, he had promised his people that he would bring settlers to Poyais – talented men and women each with a skill to offer – and what better way to fulfil his pledge than to sell them some of the Territory's rich and plentiful land? He was – naturally – motivated only by duty and so set the price at the very modest level of 3 shillings and 3 pence per acre.

This apparent bargain price was the mark of a gifted con artist. First, it was affordable: in 1821 the average weekly wage of a worker was around £1, and an artisan seeking escape from the stifling atmosphere of industrialised Britain might, without too much hardship, be able to afford a few Poyaisian acres on which to start a new life.

But, more crucially, the price also made official scrutiny much less likely. It has been a pattern of frauds since time immemorial – and one that is repeated today – that the best way to make a dishonest fortune is to con a relatively small sum of money from rather a lot of individuals. We have investigated or reported on any number of scams in which the victims are scattered over a widespread geographical area, and dealt with by a patchwork of different police forces.

Without the critical mass of a single pool of complainants,

the cost of each force investigating its own small constituency of low-value individual claims is generally deemed to outweigh the potential public benefit of doing so.

And, even though the total value of the con may be many millions of pounds, the very fact that each fragmented claim is relatively small ensures that it doesn't fall within the remit of the national major-fraud investigation teams. The result is that it generally languishes in what we have come to think of as a notional 'too hard' tray inside police HQs up and down the country.

Was Gregor MacGregor that calculating? Did he market his land parcels at a knockdown price to lessen the risk of detection? After all, in 1821 there were no real police forces at all (much less a unit such as the Serious Fraud Office) and the Metropolitan Police would not come into existence until September 1829. But the truly enormous effort he put into marketing the sale of plots of Poyais land does suggest a man who knew exactly how to run a scam.

First, he took out a series of adverts in the national and regional press, extolling the wonders of Poyais:

The climate is remarkably healthy and agrees admirably with the constitution of Europeans... the soil is extremely rich and fertile... and produces not only all the necessities of life in profusion but is also well adapted for the cultivation of all those valuable commodities which have rendered the West Indies so important – especially sugar, coffee, cotton, tobacco, cocoa, etc. ...

And there was more: a wide variety of commercially valuable timber was easily accessible, while native livestock, including horses, cattle, deer, hogs and poultry, roamed freely throughout this earthly paradise. Even the rivers could make a man's fortune: 'many of them produce, by washing the sand in fine sieves, globules of pure gold'. And, as if the prospect of precious metals drifting through these crystal waters was not tempting enough, why there were also 'many very rich gold mines in the country'.

To support these adverts, MacGregor published a 350-page illustrated guidebook grandly entitled *Sketch of the Mosquito Shore, including the Territory of Poyais: Chiefly intended for the use of Settlers*. It claimed to have been written by the energetic Captain Thomas Strangeways, still – apparently – of the 1st Native Poyer Regiment, but now elevated to the rank of Knight of the Grand Cross.

And Captain Strangeways was evidently determined not to undersell the glories of 'this unsurpassed Utopia'. Poyais was extravagantly described as a land of cathedrals, grand public buildings and wealthy banks. Its capital, St Joseph, boasted a fine opera house among many other equally impressive buildings – both public and private. Meanwhile, the land itself was described as having unimaginable fertility and beauty on a land where gold nuggets and diamonds and pearls were as 'plentiful as pebbles' and where grain could grow without even the need for sowing.

Finally, as the icing on the cake, MacGregor ladled a large dollop of Scottish patriotism on to the hard sell. In addition to trading on his supposed direct lineage to Rob Roy (a claim as lacking in evidence as was his alleged knighthood), he announced that he wanted the majority of his new settlers to be Scottish as a way of compensating the nation for its losses in an earlier national catastrophe: the ill-fated Darien Scheme.

In 1698 and 1699 the then King of Scotland had dispatched more than two and a half thousand would-be settlers to establish a Scottish colony on islands in the Bay of Darien, on the Panama peninsula. The scheme had been an unmitigated disaster: agriculture proved almost impossible and the plan to trade trinkets and combs for food foundered on the perfectly reasonable reluctance of the local Indian tribes to exchange precious commodities for the tatty little baubles offered by their would-be colonists.

Thanks to malnutrition and disease, the settlers died off at a rate of ten a day – despite the generous care and assistance of the natives. By the time the King of Scotland abandoned the attempt just a few hundred survivors were left. The dismal failure of the plan led directly to the end of Scotland as an independent kingdom and its absorption into the United Kingdom.

Like the Highland Clearances and the subsequent Battle of Culloden, the Darien Scheme was burned into Scotland's psyche – a bitterly remembered and greatly resented national tragedy. And so, when Sir Gregor MacGregor pitched the land sales on Poyais as the balm for this still open wound. He found a very ready audience.

The price of plots steadily rose from the initial 3/3d to 4 shillings an acre. At Poyais's newly opened offices in Glasgow and Edinburgh, people queued with their entire families to sign up for a piece of the Promised Land. Those who could not afford to buy land for themselves signed up for passage on the ships MacGregor was chartering, secure in his promises that they would find instant employment as shoemakers, shopkeepers, jewellers, teachers and clerks – all skills apparently much needed by the booming new state.

By the end of 1822, the bond and land sale schemes were making MacGregor, in today's terms, a multimillionaire. He had also sold commissions in the nation's army (a common practice in nineteenth-century Britain) and even commissioned his own currency – the Poyais dollar – from the printers who supplied notes to the Bank of Scotland.

These were emblazoned with the crest of the Bank of Poyais, the Cazique's own personal coat of arms, and bore the reassuring promise that 'On demand or Three Months after Sight in the option of the Government of Poyais, One Hard Dollar will be paid to the bearer at the Bank Office.'

The starry-eyed colonists were advised that the Poyaisian dollar was the only legal tender in their new home and so, before departing, they exchanged their old Scottish and English pounds for this exciting new currency. What did they care for old money from the old country, anyway? A wonderful new world of plenty awaited them. All they now had to do was get there.

MacGregor announced that the first ship was to set out from London, carrying a relatively small advance party of seventy professional men – doctors, lawyers and the future head of the Bank of Poyais. A second, larger, group of less elevated settlers would leave a month or so later from Scotland. Five further ships were chartered and made ready to leave in the early spring of 1823. Sadly – and much though he wished to – the Cazique himself would not be travelling with either party, because there was still far too much to be done in London to allow himself the pleasure of returning in triumph to his very own nation.

And so, on 10 September 1822, the *Honduras Packet* set sail from the Port of London. Its voyage was expected to take a little more than a month. There was, of course, no prospect of any communication with the ship while she was at sea; nor did the emigrants' relatives expect to receive news of a safe passage and joyous landing for many months.

The second group of settlers arrived in Edinburgh and Leith at the turn of the year. Their departure had been postponed several times – the ship on which they were to sail, the *Kennersley Castle*, needed a complete refit and a further delay was occasioned by the inclement Scottish weather. Despite this – and despite the fact that they had been forced to wait in overcrowded boarding houses for several weeks – the 240 men, women and children were in good heart when finally, on 22 January 1823, the ship sailed up the Firth of Forth and off towards a wonderful new life.

On 20 March the ship anchored off the coast of Poyais in what MacGregor's personally prepared maps depicted as the mouth of the nation's chief port, Black River. Captain Henry Crouch was certain he was in the right place – at least geographically speaking – but was somewhat puzzled that a boat crew he had dispatched into the natural harbour itself had returned reporting no signs of life. Not even a canoe was tied up in what the Cazique had described as a busy trading port, much less any merchant vessels. And where, for that matter, was the *Honduras Packet*?

It took less than forty-eight hours for the truth to sink in. Instead of the civilised and vibrant nation-state MacGregor had sold them, what the settlers found was an untouched and thoroughly unwelcoming jungle. The elegant 'capital city' of 'St Joseph' consisted in reality of a handful of ruined buildings – the legacy of a previous unsuccessful attempt at settlement that had been abandoned sometime during the previous century.

But what of the much-vaunted civil service, the judiciary and the army – the 1st Native Poyer Regiment of which Captain Thomas Strangeways (KGC) had been such a proud officer? The settlers could find no trace of any population except a few native Indians and – bizarrely – two American hermits. The latter disappeared very shortly afterwards; the former seemed thoroughly bemused by the settlers' repeated attempts to find the mansions, the banks and the opera house that MacGregor had promised them.

When they finally located their fellow emigrants who had sailed on the *Honduras Packet* they discovered that only a handful had survived. The ship itself had been swept away by a storm.

The settlers were effectively stranded. They had sold everything they owned to buy their parcels of (evidently worthless) Poyais land and to pay MacGregor for the price of their passage.

While some of the more practical labourers began to build rudimentary shelters for themselves, many of the hoodwinked families begun to argue with each other and some who had been promised lavish houses in St Joseph refused to do anything. Meanwhile, the *Kennersley Castle* sailed away.

The next few months were desperate. Tropical diseases – to which the settlers had no natural immunity – began to take their toll. Malnutrition set in. Even some of the previously amicable local Indians turned hostile. At least one settler committed suicide.

In April, the *Mexican Eagle*, an official ship from the neighbouring British colony of Belize, accidentally found the hapless pioneers. Belize's chief magistrate, Marshal Bennet, happened to be on board, *en route* to a meeting with the local King of the Mosquito Coast, George Frederick II.

Bennet and his clerk listened in some astonishment to the settlers' story. They knew nothing of any plans for any British settlements on the Mosquito coast, had never heard of Poyais – much less its enterprising 'Cazique' – and patiently explained that, sadly, the land they had been sold still belonged, unquestionably, to George Frederick II.

Days later the King himself turned up to investigate. Yes, his majesty told the settlers, he had met Gregor MacGregor; and, yes, he had given him some limited rights over some of the land hereabouts. But, no, he had not bestowed upon the Scotsman the title of 'Cazique' (whatever that might be) and MacGregor had absolutely no right to sell any land in the Territory to anyone.

In fact, now the King came to think of it, the settlers were squatting illegally on the King's lands – something to which he took great exception. And unless they were prepared to swear an oath of allegiance to him – an act that appeared to require them to renounce British citizenship and any protection that might go with it – all of the settlers must leave forthwith.

Later that day, the *Mexican Eagle* took sixty settlers to Belize. The rest were evacuated a few days later. But many of them were suffering from yellow fever and malaria. Even the short sea voyage to the British colony proved a step too far – many died in Belize's makeshift hospitals.

By the time the superintendent for Belize, General Edward Codd, fired off a detailed account of the Poyais debacle to London, 180 of its first 250 would-be settlers had died. Codd's primary concern, though, was somehow to stop the five ships that had already set out from Britain, fully laden with hundreds of new victims of MacGregor's con.

Happily, his letter arrived at the Admiralty in London just in time for naval vessels to be dispatched to intercept and bring back the would-be settlers.

On 1 August 1823 the survivors from the *Kennersley Castle* and *Honduras Packet* set sail for London in the *Ocean*, a ship chartered by the British government. More of them died during that journey, and, when the ship docked in London seventy-two days later, there were fewer than fifty of the original Poyais settlers left alive.

But those survivors had a story to tell – and a conman to expose. The following day the national and London press devoted huge swathes of their pages to the great Poyais swindle.

But where was the dynamic and dashing 'Cazique'? Enquiries at the Legation of the Territory of Poyais on Dowgate Hill drew a blank. Nor was he to be found at Oak House, the elegant Essex country mansion he and his 'princess' had graciously deigned to honour with their long-term presence two years previously.

In fact, Gregor MacGregor had, a few days earlier, followed a tried and trusted procedure for British villains of the period: he had fled across the Channel to France.

He had learned that the *Ocean* was ploughing its way towards London and knew that, when his victims disembarked, not just they, but the City banks through which he had sold the now worthless bearer bonds, would come looking for him. And so he had announced to staff at the Legation that 'Princess Josefa' was unwell and that the medical advice was unequivocal: she must be taken to the warmer climate of southern Italy before the English winter arrived. It was, of course, a matter of great regret, but what could he do? Pausing only long enough to collect the remaining funds from the Poyais government's various bank accounts, the 'Cazique', his 'princess' and their two young children set sail for Boulogne.

In theory, the French port was merely a stopping point *en route* to Italy. In reality, it was the first stage in an escape route MacGregor had meticulously planned the previous year. The real destination was Paris, and the real purpose was to start the entire Poyais scam all over again in the French capital.

Within weeks of arriving in Paris, MacGregor had managed to hold meetings with bankers, lawyers and the French Prime Minister. As a visiting head of state, the colourful Cazique was accorded full diplomatic privileges. And he wasted no time in petitioning his new hosts for their help – both financial and political.

He explained to the Prime Minister that the small but proud nation of Poyais needed French help to persuade the Spanish government to renounce all and any claims to sovereignty over the territory. Naturally, any such claims were spurious, for he, Brigadier-General Sir Gregor MacGregor, was the sole lawful owner and ruler of Poyais.

Within eighteen months, though, that story had changed slightly. In August 1825, MacGregor published a new constitution of Poyais. It was now, apparently a fully fledged republic (although he remained its tireless head of state).

But in every other respect the scam was a carbon copy of the one that had yielded such rich rewards in London. A new bearer-bond issue was announced and French would-be settlers were sold parcels of incredibly fertile land. A sturdy ship, the *Nouvelle Neustrie*, was chartered to transport them to a new life in this South American El Dorado.

Fortunately, French government officials noticed that a large number of people were applying for passports in order to travel to a country no one had actually ever seen. They impounded the ship in Le Havre and launched an enquiry. But, when the investigators turned up at the official premises of the Poyais government in Paris, they discovered that the Cazique himself had mysteriously disappeared.

It would take another year before he was arrested and brought to the first of two ultimately abortive trials. Although the Poyais scheme was declared a fraud and one of MacGregor's French assistants was sentenced to thirteen months in prison for making false promises; the man himself walked free from the court.

A lesser con artist might have called it quits at this point. But Gregor MacGregor was made of sterner stuff. There was only one place go to and only one thing to do. In 1826 MacGregor returned to London. Seeing that the furore over the first Poyais scam had died down, he set about creating a new one.

This time he claimed that the (entirely nonexistent) native population had democratically elected him as the head of state and asked him to obtain finance of behalf of 'the Republic of Poyais'. To support his efforts, he republished a shorter version of Captain Strangelove's colourful panegyric to Poyais under the new and (presumably) ironic name W R Goodluck. Next, using the proceeds of the French version of the fraud, he opened official offices just down the road from the Bank of England in Threadneedle Street.

Although his new legation had to make do without any of the lavish diplomatic trappings of its predecessor, MacGregor managed to obtain the support of a merchant bank to issue bearer bonds for a loan far in excess of anything he had attempted before – £800,000 (£44 million today).

But shortly after the bond issue was announced, in the summer of 1827, an anonymous handbill was circulated throughout the City of London. Entitled 'Take care of your Pockets: Another Poyais Humbug', it rehearsed MacGregor's previous indiscretions and denounced the latest scheme as a 'swindling concern'. The result was predictable: ordinary investors largely shunned the new Poyais issue, leaving MacGregor with a bundle of seemingly worthless bonds.

It is a tribute to the extraordinary greed of the City's nineteenth-century speculators – a rapaciousness that has continued unabated to this day – that he was able to find a group of investors willing, despite all the evidence that the self-styled Cazique of Poyais was an unrepentant charlatan, to buy them from him, albeit it at a reduced price. Once again, the money poured in.

Nor was this the last time he would stage the same con. Between 1828 and 1837 MacGregor set up at least four new Poyais-based scams, selling investment bonds and land certificates to gullible banks or would-be settlers. He also managed to write and circulate yet another new constitution for his republic – despite widely available evidence that he had no right to any land anywhere in the area and that the sovereign territory of Poyais itself was a complete fiction.

And yet, except for a brief scare when he spent a week in prison over a completely unrelated (but equally unpaid) fraudulent debt, the law never once troubled Gregor MacGregor. When he finally left Britain, he did so as both a free and relatively affluent man.

It would be pleasingly romantic to report that when he set sail from the Port of London in 1839 he was bound for the Mosquito Coast and the never-never land that had sustained him for so long. Sadly, romance rarely intruded on the unrepentant venality of Gregor MacGregor's career. Instead of the Republic of Poyais, he landed in Venezuela – and promptly claimed a government pension for his efforts as a general in its war of independence. He died on 4 December 1845, three weeks short of his fifty-ninth birthday, and was buried with full military honours in Caracas Cathedral.

Close to that cathedral stands the Monument of the Liberators. Into its stone surfaces are carved the names of all those heroes who fought to free Venezuela from the rule of its imperial oppressors. And in the middle of that impressive roll call is the name of a solitary Scottish army officer: Brigadier-General Sir Gregor MacGregor.

Though of the Republic of Poyais and the unique title of 'Cazique' there is strangely no mention.

2

VICTOR LUSTIG: THE MAN WHO SOLD THE EIFFEL TOWER

A mong connoisseurs of the breed, when the conversation turns to confidence tricksters, 'that man who sold the Eiffel Tower' is often cited as the prime example of the enterprising confidence trickster. 'That man' was Victor Lustig – or Robert Miller, or any one of the ten aliases that he assumed over the years – but the con for which he has gone down in history was by no means his only, nor necessarily even his most imaginative, fraud. However, it does illustrate perfectly his preferred method of working.

Victor Lustig – or Count Lustig, as he styled himself – was a professional confidence trickster of rare, not to say unique, talent. Other men may well have cheated their victims out of larger sums of money, but few have been so imaginative or so stylish as the man born into an ordinary middle-class family in Hestinne, Czechoslovakia, in 1890 and who died, uncharacteristically, in prison in Springfield, Missouri, on 9 March 1947.

At the age of nineteen, Lustig collected a distinctive scar that ran from the edge of his left eye to the lobe of his left ear. He had been attacked by a man who objected to Lustig's flirting with his girlfriend, but was later to say that he had acquired the scar in a duel. He became highly skilled at games – particularly billiards, bridge and poker.

As a gambler, Lustig took to the high seas. The luxury liners that constantly crisscrossed that Atlantic were loaded with wealthy passengers – a magnet for opportunist crooks and conmen. It was on one of these cruises at the beginning of the twentieth century that Lustig met up with professional gamblers such as Nicky Arnstein (who later gained fame for marrying *Ziegfeld Follies* star Fanny Brice) and learned the ropes.

World War One put an abrupt end to all transatlantic pleasure cruises and Lustig's career was brought to a halt almost overnight. He then decided to head for the United States, just as the roaring twenties were about to unfold. This was the time of Prohibition and the stock market boom. It seemed as if everyone was getting rich and Lustig was right there to take advantage of it. He pulled off a number of highly profitable confidence tricks, perhaps the simplest (and boldest) of which involved the purchase of a derelict farm in Missouri in 1922.

He offered the bankers who had repossessed it $22,000 in Liberty Bonds to take the farm off their hands – and they gladly took it. Lustig also persuaded them to exchange an additional $10,000 in bonds for cash, as he said, 'to give him some operating capital until the farm became productive'.

The bankers readily obliged. They were so excited to be rid of this near-worthless property that they failed to notice that Lustig had switched envelopes and made off with both the bonds and the cash.

Lustig made no attempt to hide his escape. The bankers hired a private detective, who, in company with bank officials, finally cornered him in a New York City hotel room. During the long train ride back to Missouri, Lustig convinced his captors that, if they actually did press charges against him, the publicity would trigger such a run on the bank that it would be forced out of business. And Lustig then convinced them that they should give him $1,000 compensation for the inconvenience that the arrest had caused him. The audacious Count Lustig was set free – with an additional $1,000 of the bank's cash in his pocket.

However, Lustig's best-known con sprang to his fertile mind in Paris on 8 May 1925. He and his then accomplice, 'Dapper' Dan Collins, were taking their ease at what was then the best hotel in town – the Hôtel de Crillon. Lustig picked up the afternoon paper, in which appeared a short news story that reported that the Eiffel Tower was in dire need of repair. The estimated cost was apparently so high that the government was considering the possibility that it might be cheaper to dismantle the Tower rather than maintain it.

Dan Collins protested, however, that the likelihood that the French government would actually tear down an edifice that had become a national icon was extremely remote. That was not the point, Lustig patiently explained. As long as people thought demolition was a possibility, he would make money from it. He would sell it for scrap.

Contrary to popular foreign opinion, he went on, the Eiffel Tower was only ever intended to be a temporary symbol, created for the Paris Exposition of 1889. Even at the time of its construction, there were many indignant protests at the 'crude structure' that had 'desecrated' the skyline of Paris. Alexandre Dumas called it a 'loathsome construction', Guy de Maupassant had asked 'what will be thought of our generation if we do not smash this lanky pyramid?' It was by no means so beloved of the Parisians as cartoonists and foreigners would have thought, said Victor. To prove his point, he added that the newspaper report had not provoked any negative reaction.

However, whether the average Parisian liked the Eiffel Tower or not, the report in the paper was precisely the kind of trigger that Victor Lustig was waiting for. It would give his nascent con real credibility. From that afternoon on, he worked busily to add more. He visited a contact in Paris, who produced for him some fine forgeries of the letterheads of the Ministère des Postes et Télégraphes, the official authority responsible for the Eiffel Tower.

He carefully researched all the major iron-and-steel stockholders and scrap-metal dealers in the Paris area and found one who fitted his bill perfectly. Nonetheless, five invitations to a 'confidential meeting' were sent out, including one addressed to the planned 'mark', an unfortunate man whom the papers later nicknamed André Poisson (a French joke).

Each invitee was a man in the scrap-metal business, each was extremely wealthy and each was invited to an urgent private meeting with the deputy director general of the Ministère des Postes et Télégraphes at the Hôtel de Crillon.

Victor Lustig had met his partner in crime, 'Dapper' Dan Collins, while they were both 'playing the boats' between New York and Europe and was particularly attracted (in a professional sense) to his good looks, his striking air of innocence and especially his perfect French. Although Lustig himself was an extremely good linguist (he had mastered five languages in his early years in Czechoslovakia), for this particular swindle he needed an accomplice. Dapper Dan fitted the part perfectly and became, temporarily, 'Monsieur Dante'.

As the five men sat down in Lustig's impressive suite at the Hôtel de Crillon, they could hardly help but be impressed by the man who sat at the head of the table. Lustig, in his role as assistant to the director general, with his immaculate suit, his handsome, chiselled face and his clipped moustache, looked every bit the successful government official. Drinks were served by Monsieur Dante, who then made considerable play of closing the door of the hotel suite and ensuring that was no one around.

Then, in the cultured tones that had already helped him fleece others of a fortune, Victor Lustig began by telling them that they had been invited on a matter of extreme secrecy and national prestige. They had been chosen because they were thought to be discreet as well as successful businessmen, and invitations had been restricted to them alone. The five men were now all ears.

The come-on was perfect. Lustig became even more conspiratorial and confided that the secret he was about to share was known only to his immediate superior, the director general of the Ministère des Postes et Télégraphes, to the Prime Minister and of course the then President, Gaston Doumergue. When what is proposed becomes public, he assured them, it will create an enormous furore – but by that time it would be too late because their business arrangements would have been legally completed. At this stage, the five businessmen were hanging on his every word.

Pausing for effect, Lustig told them in hushed tones that the government was going to have to scrap the Eiffel Tower. There was a stunned silence. Lustig now had them eating out of his hand and continued earnestly to outline the plan. He referred to the newspaper report about the extremely high cost, not only of the upkeep, but also of necessary repairs to the Eiffel Tower. The men nodded sagely – indeed, there had been such a report in the papers.

Lustig continued ruefully that the state of the nation's finances was not at the moment at its highest, and that the government had decided that the structure, which, in any case, was intended only as a temporary symbol for the International Exposition of 1889, would have to be demolished. In fact, doing so would remove what many people considered to be an eyesore from the Paris skyline.

Lustig then moved to the setup. He invited them to tender for the scrap metal involved, and handed each a folder containing an 'official' government specification – the main points of which were the height of the tower (984 feet), the base (142 yards in each direction) and the fact that the interlaced iron girders were made of 12,000 sections joined together by more than 2.5 million rivets. The total amount of salvageable high-grade iron ore was calculated to be some 7,000 tons.

Victor then proposed to the spellbound scrap dealers that they take one of the official cars that had been put at their disposal that afternoon to view the Eiffel Tower. He further proposed that they return to their businesses, consider the value of 7,000 tons of high-grade iron ore, deduct the considerable cost of dismantling the edifice and then put their bids in sealed envelopes to be delivered to the Hôtel de Crillon.

Victor Lustig concluded by explaining that the reason for conducting the meeting, and, indeed, all subsequent negotiations, from the hotel rather than from his office was that, in a matter of such extreme delicacy, the ministry could not be officially involved. To distance him still further, the bids should be addressed to Lustig in the name of his colleague, Monsieur Dante. With that, the count and 'Dapper' Dan Collins swept majestically from the room with the five dazzled businessmen in tow.

On arriving at the Eiffel Tower, Victor Lustig flashed an official-looking set of credentials at the guards – done brusquely enough to avoid close inspection – told them that the party were guests of the Ministère des Postes et Télégraphes, and were duly admitted to the Tower. After some refreshments on the observation platform and a short sight-seeing tour, the five were dismissed and asked to submit their bids within four days.

Victor had chosen his 'mark' perfectly. The other businessmen had been invited only to create a sense of competition. André Poisson was destined to be the successful bidder. He was a self-made millionaire from the sticks, and, despite his wealth, had never managed to gain a foothold in the society to which his money, though not his background, qualified him.

He therefore looked on the project not just as a means of increasing his wealth, but as a means of achieving the recognition that he thought his abilities and his success should have brought him. He could see himself going down in history as the man entrusted with the demolition of the Eiffel Tower. He did, indeed, go down in history, but not quite in the way he had intended.

Poisson's bid was submitted on time, but it is the mark of the professional conman not to rush things, and Victor Lustig let him dangle for a few days. Eventually, there was a knock on the door of André Poisson's apartment and outside stood Monsieur Dante.

He announced that Poisson's bid had been successful and that within the next forty-eight hours he was required to bring a certified cheque representing a quarter of his bid price to the same suite of rooms at the Hôtel de Crillon. Once the cheque had changed hands, he would receive the necessary documents confirming his ownership of the Eiffel Tower and the terms and conditions under which he would be demolishing it. Monsieur Dante then took his leave and returned to the hotel.

André Poisson was overjoyed. For the first time broke his vow of secrecy and told his wife of their good fortune. She queried why it was necessary for the negotiations to be taking place in a hotel rather than at the ministry.

Although Poisson dutifully repeated the reasons given by Count Lustig, seeds of doubt had been sown in his mind, and so, while he arrived on Wednesday, 20 May, with the certified cheque in his pocket, he was in no immediate hurry to turn it over to the urbane deputy director general.

Lustig immediately sensed the hesitation and, on the spur of the moment, conjured up the sort of embellishment that had marked him as such an artist in his chosen profession.

He turned to his assistant – Monsieur Dante – and told him that it would be better if the negotiations were finalised between himself and Monsieur Poisson alone. Dante bowed his way out and, when he had gone, Lustig's attitude, which until then had been slightly supercilious, changed subtly.

The count looked at his watch and noted that the time was ten minutes past two. The time was crucial, because the banks in Paris would be closing in twenty minutes, and it was essential for his plans that the certified cheque that he was about to receive should be cashed and the two conmen be on their way that afternoon. So he leaned forward to Monsieur Poisson and, somewhat nervously, began to explain that one of the problems of being an official in a ministry such as the Postes et Télégraphes was that, while one must conduct important negotiations with influential men such as Monsieur Poisson, one's salary hardly matched the style that one's job demanded.

Lustig hesitated and feigned embarrassment. It was, he continued diffidently, customary for an official, in this case himself, to receive, er, 'a commission'. 'A bribe, you mean?' asked Monsieur Poisson.

Now he relaxed visibly and assumed the dominant role for the first time during their negotiations. Poisson's nervousness and suspicions instantly disappeared and were replaced by a feeling of superiority. A bribe! This was a situation he really did understand. One had to oil the wheels of business. At last he knew the deal was genuine. Poisson was at pains to emphasise he was not unsophisticated in the ways of business and, had Lustig only hinted at such a convention earlier, days could have been saved on the project.

With a studiedly careless gesture, Poisson removed a

wallet stuffed with bank notes from the inside of his pocket and tossed it over to Lustig. Victor smiled at him, removed what must have totalled several thousand pounds' worth of francs, returned the wallet – and held out his hand out for the certified cheque.

The 'sting' that was to go down in history as, perhaps, the definitive con trick had been completed. By the end of the afternoon, Lustig and Dan Collins had boarded the train for Vienna. From the sanctuary of their plush hotel, over the next ten days they bought and studied every French newspaper. Not a word of the hoax ever emerged in any of them.

Clearly they had selected exactly the right victim. André Poisson had obviously decided that his dignity and his pride were worth more than the several hundred thousand francs that he had lost.

A fortnight later, Lustig decided that he could breathe freely and that the operation would never be reported to the police. So it was that, within three weeks of his arrival in Vienna, he cheerfully informed 'Dapper' Dan Collins that it was time for them to leave Vienna and return to Paris.

'We are selling the Eiffel Tower again,' he grinned.

It is a matter of record that Victor Lustig and his accomplice did indeed return to Paris and they did indeed sell the Eiffel Tower again. This time, however, when the 'mark' discovered the deception, he created so much fuss that the two were forced to flee across the Atlantic in haste, rather than return to America at leisure, as they had originally planned.

The Eiffel Tower sting had significantly boosted Victor Lustig's resources and a healthy reserve of ready cash is one of the primary requisites of a really good confidence trickster.

In presenting himself and his business proposition, he should appear to be totally without need of money himself.

Only in this way can he gain the confidence of the people who represent the easiest pickings – the rich and especially the *nouveaux riches*. As with André Poisson, it was the latter's greed for status as well as money that made them such attractive 'marks'.

Victor Lustig's next caper continued his role as the European count, dispossessed of his family fortune, castles and feudal rights, but nevertheless with considerable residual wealth and, above all, family background.

The following incident is well documented from newspaper reports and from first-hand accounts. If it reads like high farce, remember that it is strictly factual and that a hard-headed businessman involved eagerly parted with $25,000 for a piece of equipment that not even an eight-year-old would have taken seriously. Such is the magic of the true conman, however, that he can give credibility to even the most far-fetched of schemes, provided only that the victim is avaricious enough to suspend disbelief.

Victor Lustig sailed from France to New York in the summer of 1926 and by the winter had made his way down to Palm Beach, Florida. At that time, Palm Beach was the playground of the very wealthy and to create a big impression there – something that was essential to Lustig's plan – required a display of head-turning style.

On a December afternoon at precisely the time at which the majority of the guests at the best hotel in town would be sipping pre-dinner cocktails on the veranda and gazing out along the beach, a stately and discreet Rolls-Royce purred to a halt outside the hotel. But it was not the car so much as the chauffeur who turned heads. Contrary to contemporary expectations, he was Japanese.

From the car alighted a handsome, elegantly dressed man with a cane in one hand and a briefcase in the other. Having caused something of a stir, he checked into the hotel and one of the penthouse suites. That he was not seen again for days only served to heighten the curiosity of his fellow guests. His next appearance saw him strolling regally down to the beach, where he sat in solitary splendour, reading a book.

Shortly afterwards, the Japanese chauffeur, in a state of some agitation, came sprinting across the sand waving a telegram. The count read it without any sign of emotion and stuffed it into his pocket. Minutes later, another telegram arrived, was read and discarded. This performance was repeated throughout the day and into the next.

By the end of the second day, the telegrams were arriving at frequent intervals and the count was no longer even bothering to read them. This extraordinary sequence of events had the desired effect.

It made Lustig the focus of attention among the moneyed guests at the hotel. They were not to know, of course, that the telegrams were completely blank. Over the next week the count allowed himself to relax a bit and was seen swimming and playing a little tennis, but nobody was able to engage in more than a few words of polite conversation with him.

However, while they were watching him, he was quietly assessing them, in order to select the right target. At the end of the first week, he found precisely the right 'mark'. Herman Loller was a self-made man who had begun his career operating a lathe and was now operating a sizable engineering company. It irked him that, despite having acquired the trappings of considerable wealth, he had not been accepted as an equal by the 'old-money aristocracy' of America. Loller was staying at the hotel with his wife and rather plain daughter, and his whole bearing, particularly the way in which he extravagantly overtipped, told Lustig that he was one of the newly rich.

One afternoon of the second week, Lustig contrived to bump into Loller at a news vendor's kiosk and to be drawn into conversation by him. Loller was completely captivated by the cultured manner of the man, who spoke with only the merest trace of a foreign accent.

When he got round to asking Lustig's profession, Victor politely explained that as a count, albeit one dispossessed of his real family wealth and fortunes, he still had sufficient funds to live in some style and, in fact, did not have to work at all. European aristocracy, even today, impresses in America. In those days, to meet and befriend a 'true-life' count was a real social coup.

Loller could not help betraying his excitement and tentatively asked the count to dine with him that evening. To his surprise and delight, Lustig accepted almost immediately. Their relationship blossomed, with Lustig maintaining just the right amount of distance, while still encouraging fairly frequent meetings at dinner and drinks time. Loller was flattered and his increased status among the other guests in the hotel as the only man to capture the attention of the count was proof enough to him of Lustig's worth as a friend. And so it was that one evening, when the two men were alone and taking a drink together, Loller felt sufficiently bold to tell Lustig of his current problems.

His engineering business, which had been extremely successful, was currently in difficulties, because the market for the products upon which his fortune was based appeared to be shrinking fast. He had been supplying parts to the motor industry when there had been many makes on the market. Now, however, with a consolidated group of large manufacturers in Detroit making the majority of their own components in-house, he faced the prospect of seeing his wealth evaporate entirely.

Lustig nodded sympathetically. When Loller suggested that a man in Count Lustig's position was hardly likely to appreciate such potential financial difficulties, Lustig was quick to rejoin that his own life had by no means been problem free. He had already mentioned the fact that his family's country estate had been confiscated back in Europe and he now chose this moment to confide in his new friend that his own money difficulties had been solved by what could only be called a 'moneymaking machine'.

Loller looked at Lustig, incredulously. 'You mean you actually counterfeit notes?'

The count explained patiently that he did nothing so crude. He merely had a secret chemical process that would duplicate any paper currency, of any denomination, with unerring accuracy. A dollar bill was inserted into the machine and after a period of time it automatically processed blank paper of precisely the right size and specification to produce two identical bills. In other words, he was duplicating genuine dollar bills. They were certainly not counterfeits, because it was impossible to tell the new bills apart from the originals.

The banks accepted them and nobody got hurt. Indeed, said Lustig, warming to his theme, he could almost claim to be doing his bit to prime the country's economy.

The semantic difference between counterfeit and self-reproducing bank notes and Lustig's novel view of economics were lost on Loller. He could only gaze in bewilderment at the count and protest that it was impossible.

'You may think so,' concluded Lustig, 'but nevertheless that is the main source of my current wealth.'

Loller took the bait – and nothing would satisfy him but to see this incredible machine with his own eyes. Lustig appeared reluctant, but eventually allowed himself to be persuaded and promised to reveal all that afternoon. Before Victor Lustig demonstrated his moneymaking machine, he fed his mark some seemingly credible background detail.

He explained how the device was produced, how a Romanian friend of his in New York – also a nobleman who had been left penniless by the Revolution – had perfected the process, but had died within weeks of its development, leaving the prototype to him. Victor explained to Loller that his friend was not the creator of the duplicator, and that its real inventor was a certain Emile Dubré, who had been captured by the central powers in Yugoslavia after the assassination of the Archduke Ferdinand in Sarajevo.

Dubré, he went on, was known to be working on a top-secret duplicating process, and as such was installed by the Germans in a modern laboratory with the most up-to-date equipment and told to get on with it. The result was a foolproof method of duplicating foreign currency with which the Germans had originally planned to flood the economies of enemy powers, thereby undermining them. (Interestingly, this story, which was of course a complete fabrication, does predate an actual operation that the Nazis undertook towards the end of World War Two.) The duplicator, Lustig emphasised, was the only one of its kind in existence. However, why would the owner of such a machine want more than one?

And so came the demonstration. Victor Lustig brought out the dollar duplicator, which was a beautifully crafted mahogany box, festooned with dials and knobs. It had a pillar-box slot at one end and a crank that, when a dollar bill was inserted into it, wound the bill into the interior. Into this slot, Lustig inserted a piece of bank-note specification paper, cut to precisely the size of the dollar bill he was about to duplicate.

In this case, it was a $100 bill. He explained that the bill and the blank paper were now pressed together within the machine and immersed in a chemical bath, which transferred all the images from the $100 bill to the blank paper, without losing any of the definition of the original. The process would take some six hours, after which they would return to examine the results.

At the end of the six-hour period, Lustig returned with his eager victim. With a theatrical flourish, Lustig adjusted all the knobs and then turned the crank again. Out came two damp $100 bills. They were identical to the last detail. They should have been, because they were both, in fact, completely genuine bills. Prior to the whole performance, Lustig had concealed the second bill inside the machine.

By carefully selecting bills with similar numbers and by skilfully altering the threes and the eights, he was able to ensure that even the serial numbers of the bills appeared to match. At this point, Lustig again demonstrated his complete mastery of the art of deception. He held out both notes, suggesting that, when they were both dry, Loller might like to take them to the bank and ask them for their expert opinion.

Somewhat diffidently, Loller accepted both notes and, as Lustig had instructed, took them the next day to a nearby bank, where he explained that he had won the money in a poker game and was anxious to validate the bills. The bank official examined one of the bills and gave his technical assurance that it was indeed genuine.

Loller went to another bank to validate the second bill, which, because it carried the same serial number, could not have been authenticated at the same bank – and received an identical reassurance.

The mark was now completely hooked.

He hightailed it back to Lustig's suite in a state of great excitement, almost overcome with the news that the bills had checked out. The machine was fantastic, he said.

Lustig nodded calmly (he could now afford to relax and underplay his duplicator's magical properties). He admitted that it had served him well for many years and had guaranteed that he had never had any money problems. Loller rushed headlong into his own trap. He demanded to know whether there was another machine; whether it too could be duplicated; and were any plans available? Lustig pondered the questions, then, with a show of reluctance, confided that he thought it would be unwise to have more than one machine in existence. Despite their friendship, said Victor, Loller might be tempted to sell the second machine to somebody else, and it was, after all, worth a considerable fortune.

Loller protested vehemently that he would guarantee never to reveal its existence to anybody. He then offered to pay Victor $25,000 for a copy of the machine. Victor Lustig considered the offer with an inward smile. Now he had his mark trying to convince him! He turned up the pressure another notch. He suggested that it didn't really matter what Loller paid for the machine – $25,000, $50,000, even $100,000 – because he would soon recover the cost by duplicating his own dollar bills.

Then Lustig came to an apparent decision. He said that, in view of their very pleasant relationship, he had concluded that he would like to help Loller. So he extracted the eager victim's solemn word that he would not pass the money duplicator on to anybody or reveal its existence to a soul. The fish had been landed.

Loller was quick to make the promise and such were the count's powers of persuasion that even when the money had changed hands, even when Victor had checked out of the hotel (which he did within four hours), and even when the machine patently failed to work, Loller was convinced for months and months– not of Lustig's duplicity, but that somehow he had the chemical balance wrong or that he had failed to set the knobs in the correct sequence. Indeed, it was almost a year before he dug up the courage to tell the whole story to the police, after which it became public knowledge and part of the incredible legend of Victor Lustig.

To those readers who feel that the whole story is too fantastic to have fooled anybody but the most gullible, we should stress that it is a matter of historical fact that Victor Lustig not only devised yet more exotic and very profitable confidence tricks, but actually pulled this identical hoax, the so-called Romanian Box Caper, on a Sheriff Richards of Remsen County, Oklahoma, a few years later.

He used the same story on Sheriff Richards as he had on the equally gullible Herman Loller, but with rather more impressive results. He sold the sheriff the machine for $10,000 – and the chance to walk unhindered out of jail. At the time, Lustig was a guest of the county while awaiting trial on another offence.

Sheriff Richards soon found that the magic box wouldn't work and that he'd been conned out of $10,000 and into releasing Lustig (quite illegally) from jail. Furious, he eventually tracked the conman down to a hotel room in Chicago. By all accounts, the meeting was dramatic. There was a knock on the door early one morning and Victor Lustig opened it to be faced with the barrel of a gun and an extremely irate sheriff on the end of it – promising there and then to kill Lustig because the 'son of a bitch' had sold him a machine that wouldn't work. Lustig was equal to the crisis. He feigned puzzlement and then launched into a highly technical stream of gobbledegook, totally confusing the sheriff, who began to waver in his conviction.

Sensing victory, Lustig offered to refund the sheriff's money on the spot, and promised to visit him in Oklahoma to make sure the machine was working properly. Only when the sheriff was satisfied would Lustig get the $10,000 back again.

Thinking he couldn't lose, Richards agreed to the proposal. From his wallet, Lustig counted out one hundred $100 bills and handed them to the sheriff, with the parting advice that, in the light of all the trouble and inconvenience that he had suffered, he really ought to take a couple of days off in Chicago and have himself a good time.

The sheriff hardly needed any encouragement. For the next few days Victor Lustig, rather as he had done some years before in Vienna, bought every paper in Chicago. At the end of the week he found what he was looking for – a small report that a Sheriff Richards from Oklahoma had been arrested for passing counterfeit notes in a local nightclub. The sheriff was charged, tried, convicted and dispatched to the Federal Penitentiary in Pennsylvania. He didn't trouble Victor Lustig again – and we can safely surmise that Victor Lustig's conscience was not unduly troubled.

One particular escapade of the Cavalier Count – although simpler than many of his other bizarre con tricks – provides another good illustration of the way that a sting can be set up, given the necessary avarice in the target. Lustig's scheme was the forerunner of the telephone 'boiler-room' scams of the past few years. The venue was Texas, where, by reputation, everything is bigger, bolder, brassier and richer. As always, his setup was as meticulous as was his researching of his mark.

For the execution of the con, he recruited an ambitious but unprincipled young clerk in a stockbroking house in New York, which specialised in selling stocks and shares by mail. His other confederate was a local counterfeiter. With his associates well briefed, he headed south for Texas and to the house of a certain Mr Ray Murdoch.

This time Victor Lustig dropped the count title and became – for the purposes of the Texas take – Mr George Simon. He telephoned Ray Murdoch, who was a customer of the New York stockbroker, and offered to see him personally to impart advice that he said would be of considerable financial advantage to the millionaire Texan. Mr Murdoch accepted with alacrity, and over dinner Victor gradually steered the conversation around to the subject of 'insider dealing' and 'inside information'.

He had hit the Texan on a particularly sensitive spot. It

was apparently precisely what the Texan resented about the big stockbroking houses in New York. He felt, probably with some justification, that, at his distance from the Big Apple, he never got to know the really hot inside tips. 'George Simon', he was skilfully led to suppose, did have the hot inside information.

Lustig was in his familiar self-created role – the 'innocent' being pursued by his victim. Reluctantly, he admitted that he did get to know things but – and he fell silent.

The Texan encouraged him to continue. Victor hesitantly explained that the problem was that he didn't have the capital to make a real killing. And without the capital, he couldn't really exploit the information. The Texan was hooked. Why, he had the capital and the problem was solved!

Lustig avoided arousing his suspicions by agreeing too easily. He said that in the interests of fairness, he did not wish to enter any business relationship where he did not put up at least half of the capital. This, of course, was precisely the sort of equity deal the Texan wanted to hear about. 'Mr Simon' was proving to be a man of integrity and reliability. The Texan then asked conspiratorially whether there was any particular deal that 'Mr Simon' currently had in mind.

Again, Lustig let himself be drawn. There was a particular gold-mining company whose shares had long since been languishing on the floor of the stock market. They were considered virtually worthless because the mines it owned had been well worked out, but he happened to know that very recently a rich new gold seam had been discovered and that the stocks were due for a very rapid takeoff in the next few weeks.

The opportunity 'Mr Simon' saw involved persuading some existing holders of the shares to sell at a slight premium on the basis that the stocks were near worthless and that a small profit was better than a loss. He and Murdoch could then reap all the benefits of the considerable appreciation when it came.

That was precisely what the Texan called inside information – and he was eager to hear more of the plan. Lustig grudgingly allowed himself to be pumped. He eventually admitted that his visit to Texas was not solely to see his client, but because the biggest single holder of the stock in the gold-mining company lived within fairly easy reach. In fact, he confided, his plan was to see the man and persuade him to sell – although he was afraid that he didn't have the capital to buy the whole block.

Murdoch was immediately anxious to join him as a partner and Lustig agreed it was sensible to join forces than risk losing the deal. Nonetheless, Victor was at pains to point out that he was by no means without funds. He had some government bonds, which were of significant value – around $20,000 – but he was not anxious to pay the penalties involved in cashing them in before maturity. (His reluctance was not surprising, because the bonds were forged.)

The Texan saw no problem. He would be happy to take these bonds as security and in that way they could go into a true partnership. He suggested he would put up £20,000 in cash and Victor would put up his bonds. The next day, Murdoch and Lustig drove down to Brownsville, Texas, to visit the 'stockholder' who controlled the biggest single block in the gold-mining shares.

The 'stockholder', of course, was a confederate hired by

Lustig (in fact, he was the New York counterfeiter). He had prepared not only the government bonds that Lustig was using as security, but also the shares in the gold-mining company – which was actually quoted on the New York Stock Exchange at the time, though not on a daily basis.

The setup was perfect. As they arrived at Brownsville, they found that the supposed owner of the shares was in a hotel room, very ill and apparently on his deathbed.

After an hour or so of gentle coaxing, it was agreed that Lustig and Murdoch would buy the gold-mining shares from their weak and dying owner. They promised to return the next day, when the 'owner' had obtained the share certificates from his local bank. That evening, Lustig agreed with the Texan to send a cable to the stockbroking company (addressed to the sales clerk in the conspiracy) to ask what price the mining shares were selling at. Back came the cable: 'Your stock selling $78 and rising.'

Lustig turned to the Texan and turned up the pressure. He suggested they get back to the hotel quickly in the morning because, if the old man found out that the shares were going up, he was hardly likely to sell. They just had to hope that he hadn't access to the same share information as they did. When they returned to the hotel the next day, Murdoch feared he might have. They found that the old man was in noticeably better health and in an aggressive mood.

'I've been thinking it over,' he said, 'I am not so sure if your original offer yesterday was all that fair. I am not going to part with this block of shares for under $40,000.'

Lustig and Murdoch exchanged glances. They knew that at the prices quoted on the telegram the block of shares was worth at least $90,000. After a further hour's haggling, the price of $40,000 was agreed – £20,000 in Lustig's negotiable bonds and $20,000 in the rancher's cash. The gold-mining stock was handed over and the deal completed.

As soon as they were outside the hotel and in the street, Victor Lustig gave the whole of the stock to the rancher and told him to take it to New York and cash it, whereupon they would split the proceeds. Murdoch could only admire the fact that 'George Simon' trusted him with the stock and to return to split the proceeds. So the venue for the share-out was set and the two men parted – though the Texan wasn't to know it was for good.

Not all conmen get their just desserts but, if taking a moral stance, you could say that retribution did come to Victor Lustig eventually. Throughout his career, as is almost inevitable in the case of a man dedicated to making his living through fraud, Lustig had been arrested many times – in fact a total of 47 times – but never convicted.

His downfall came perhaps through pride – ironically, the self-same weakness as had enabled him to con so much from so many people. He became involved, as one of the principal characters, in a record-breaking fraud. It was so large that, in 1934, a special department of the American Secret Service was formed to deal with it. The fraud was for him a little untypical – it involved counterfeiting money – but in this case the counterfeit notes were so good and were flooding into the economy in such quantity that they were thought to represent a genuine threat to the nation's finances.

By this time, Victor Lustig's exploits had become well known in police reports throughout America and, via the newspapers, rather well known to the public. Yet for nearly three years little or nothing had been heard of him, and initially the steady flow of high-value counterfeit notes circulating from New York did not seem to be connected to him.

However, thinking he'd really hit the big time, Lustig had put himself in the firing line by becoming the main distributor of the counterfeit notes. He was no longer relying on having conned a single wealthy victim who would probably be too embarrassed to complain. Doggedly, the special squad followed the paper trail that led, inevitably, to Lustig. He was arrested in early 1935 and eventually jailed on 10 December of that year.

Even in what must have been his most dangerous hour, Lustig managed to react with characteristic bravado. Although the West Street Detention Center was one of America's maximum-security facilities, the day before he was due to go on trial he managed to escape.

Several weeks before, and shortly after he was locked up, Lustig had noticed that, when the attendants brought clean bed sheets to the cells, they would simply ask how many beds were occupied and hand over the required number of replacements.

When they came around to collect the soiled sheets, they never counted how many were returned. Lustig simply added a notional one to the number of occupied bunks and accumulated nine sheets, which he stored in a slit in his mattress. At night, while the other prisoners were asleep or listening to the radio, Lustig tore the sheets into long strips and made himself a makeshift rope.

As part of their daily routine, the prisoners were taken to the prison roof at noon for exercise. On the day of his escape, Lustig claimed that he was ill and stayed behind.

When he was confident that it was safe to do so, he went down the hall to the washroom and cut through the wire screening with a pair of wire cutters previously smuggled out of the prison workshops. He then securely fastened the rope to the bars of a third-floor window and stepped outside onto a narrow ledge.

In the blink of an eye, he had deployed his knotted strips of sheet and abseiled to the street below. Having reached the ground, Lustig apparently bowed politely to a small group of amazed onlookers, before sauntering down the road and out of reach of the law – for another six months. It was only by sheer ill luck that he was apprehended half a year later in Cleveland, Ohio, but this time his luck had run out for good.

On 10 December he was found guilty and sentenced to fifteen years plus another five years for his escape from the Federal penitentiary. After ten years in Alcatraz, where he probably came into contact with Al Capone – whom he'd had the nerve to con out of $5,000 in Chicago – Lustig fell ill, contracted pneumonia and died in Springfield jail on 9 March 1947.

It is reported that on his death certificate, a clerk had written under the heading 'Usual Occupation', the laconic entry, 'Apprentice Salesman'.

3

PHILIP MORREL WILSON: THE BOGUS BANK OF SARK

The Bank of Sark wasn't really a bank. But, then again, it wasn't on Sark, either.

The bank that wasn't was actually based in two rooms over an optician's shop in St Peter Port, Guernsey. However, to its overseas clients, it was made to look very much more substantial and became the instrument by which a notorious 'paperhanger' called Philip Morrel Wilson fleeced real banks and other financial institutions of millions of dollars.

These days, the Channel Islands – Jersey, Guernsey and Alderney – are famed for their sophisticated offshore banking facilities. Thirty years ago, Sark, the smallest of the four main islands, became infamous as the apparent source of staggering quantities of 'bad paper', as Wilson, his friends and associates papered the world. It's an interesting, but rather convoluted story and, like most such stories, this one requires a little scene setting.

The term 'bad paper' once referred exclusively to bad cheques, and a 'paperhanger' was someone who passed them. The growth of the trade in stolen securities gave these expressions a wider application. Now, 'bad paper' is also the term used for stolen or counterfeit shares or securities, and a paperhanger is a conman who specialises in 'hanging', or passing, this paper on to banks, brokerage houses, insurance companies and individuals.

Once accepted at face value, these worthless securities are used to back loans or overdrafts taken out by the paperhangers.

Stolen securities are not the only kind of bad paper passed by the paperhangers. They also handle counterfeit stocks, bonds, treasury bills and other government paper. A securities counterfeiter will first purchase a legitimate certificate. He then takes it to his printer, who, using sophisticated techniques, makes a series of exact reproductions, limited only by the quality of the paper.

The only drawback to these counterfeit securities is that they all bear the same serial number. If a paperhanger tries to pass too many over a short period of time, he will alert the transfer agent at the bank where they are registered. Enquiries about identically numbered certificates from several brokerage houses within a short time span are a sure sign that the certificates in question are counterfeit.

A friendly printer is also an important asset to paperhangers who create their own bad paper rather than stealing or counterfeiting it. Fraudulent securities have a number of advantages over other types of bad paper. They are cheaper than stolen ones, since most of the latter end up in the hands of organised criminals. So a paperhanger who makes his own can avoid paying a Mafia-style supplier of stolen securities a large percentage of their face value. Even counterfeit ones can cost 20 per cent of face value because of the time and the skills required to reproduce the original seals and source suitable paper.

Fraudulent securities cost practically nothing. Any cooperative printer can produce fake letters of credit, certificates of deposit, cheques, bonds and share certificates, which are then issued by a bogus bank or mutual fund. To lend an aura of legitimacy to this worthless paper, impressive-looking stationery, annual reports and promotional literature are manufactured simultaneously.

The biggest capital outlay involved in opening the kind of offshore bank or mutual fund that issues this bad paper are the printers' bills, the price of incorporation in a tax haven – typically, a few hundred pounds – and perhaps rent for a room, telephone and post office box.

Fraudulent paper is also less dangerous. A paperhanger who uses it does not have to worry about being gypped or threatened by his organised-crime suppliers. Moreover, the mere possession of counterfeit or stolen securities is a serious crime and one that is relatively easy for law-enforcement officials to prove. This is not the case with fraudulent securities.

Often, it is even difficult to establish that they are worthless. They can appear to be backed by seemingly legitimate foreign institutions. The difficulties involved in penetrating layers of bureaucratic insulation may postpone the discovery that the paper is fraudulent for months or even years. In the meantime, a paperhanger can construct a convincing explanation that his bank or mutual fund was merely the victim of a series of regrettable but unavoidable financial setbacks.

Some paperhangers deal in fraudulent paper for the excitement and the challenge of doing it. By his own admission, Phil Wilson trafficked almost exclusively in fraudulent paper. We know this, and much more, because, in 1973, roughly midway through his career – and following one of the few occasions when the law caught up with him – he turned state's evidence and testified before the McClellan Committee on Organised Crime. You might think that in such circumstances it would be wise to minimise the extent of your skills and experience. Not so with Wilson, whose ego drove him to boast:[4]

From 1964 to 1972, I was involved in at least 150 paper frauds using offshore insurance companies, offshore banks and offshore mortgage companies... my practices in the field of fraud have extended from St Louis, Missouri, to the capital of Mongolia, to the reaches of Moscow, to Buenos Aires, Argentina, Panama, Australia and even to the far reaches of East Africa...

My dealings have led me to do business with first-class banks, merchant banks and government banks in many corners of the world.

Wilson went on to detail his preferred method of operation:

I found that it was a lot better to create my own securities than it was to deal in stolen securities. Quite frankly, it took a lot of long hours when we did it. We worked at it very extensively.

I went to the printing shops. I sat with printers while

they made the balance sheets... so we had our own do-it-yourself balance sheets. When we did a new [financial] statement, all we had to do was fill in the blanks.

Like many paperhangers, Wilson was outwardly nondescript. Usually dressed in a modest, off-the-peg suit, he was a short, stocky chap, with soulful eyes, a weak chin and a strong sense of humour. He had the tastes and appearance of a Middle American insurance salesman, which, before he turned to big-time fraud, is exactly what he was.

Wilson was born in 1937 in St Louis, Missouri, where he attended elementary and high school, and, for a short period, college. He had originally planned to become a schoolteacher, but succumbed to the lure of money, dropped out of the University College of Washington University and took up selling car insurance instead. Within a year, he was running his own business – the Bel Air Agency. He soon found that taking premiums without actually issuing proper insurance certificates was very profitable. And two years later, in 1964, he diversified into offshore fraud with something called the Buckingham Insurance Company, registered in Nassau.

By his own admission, from that time until 1972, he was instrumental in perpetrating at least 150 sizable frauds involving bad paper, domestic and offshore insurance and mortgage companies, banks and mutual funds. He was arrested more than a dozen times, but convicted only twice – for contempt of court and mail fraud. He obviously took encouragement from this.

Phil Wilson loved his work, and it showed in the results. While his notorious Bank of Sark was in operation from 1968 to 1972, it printed $300 million in worthless paper, enough to fleece business concerns and individuals of $40 million – or $240 million today, as measured by relative purchasing power. And all this was apparently generated from a tiny island that was then little more than a bird sanctuary.

Sark is located about 80 miles south of the English coast. It is barely 3 miles long, and a mile and a half wide, with a resident population that varies between six hundred and a thousand. It has no airstrip, no cars or proper tarmac roads, and until recently was the last remaining feudal fiefdom in the Western world. In the late sixties and early seventies, its arcane banking rules and the lax financial controls in neighbouring Guernsey were an absolute gift for a skilled financial fraudster like Phil Wilson.

Sark was, perhaps, a little too isolated, so Wilson's bank just took its name and then took advantage of neighbouring Guernsey's banking regulations. The bank's 'headquarters' were nothing more than a small upstairs office in St Peter Port with a desk, telephone and telex. To establish the bank's credibility, Wilson had printed a financial statement, which made the bold but totally false claim that it owned $72.5 million in assets. It was an impressive and outrageous document, which included a letter from a Dr Samuel J Wilkinson Sr, a certified public accountant, who gave his address as Post Office Box 4253, Nassau, Bahamas. The letter concluded:

I have examined the records, vouchers and documents for the Bank of Sark for period ending December 1, 1969... In my opinion and to the best of my knowledge and information given me by the Officers and

Directors, the balance sheet reflects a true and fair position of the affairs of the Bank of Sark Limited as of 31st December, 1969.

Some years later, while testifying to the McClellan Committee, Wilson admitted that this financial statement was utterly fraudulent and that the obliging Dr Wilkinson had prepared at least ten others. He had met Wilkinson in Nassau, where the latter worked for the Bahamas Electricity Corporation, though he was not exactly well qualified.

He had failed to complete even his first lesson with the UK Chartered Institute of Secretaries, for example, and had to make do with a worthless diploma bought from something called the Metropolitan College. Nevertheless, Wilkinson listed a remarkable string of letters after his name – AAI, ACPA, AMBIM, FCBI and so on. As a certified accountant, his chief merit was that he would certify absolutely anything.

He helped make the Bank of Sark's balance sheet look very impressive indeed. On the front cover was an embossed heraldic shield supported by two sword-brandishing knights in armour. Below them was the bank's motto, '*Nulli Secundus*' (Second to None). Wilson, not yet thirty years old, was clearly taking the Mickey – and enjoying it.

Besides the balance sheet, Wilson's most important props were his telex, bank code and listing in *Polk's World Bank Directory*, the banking industry's bible.

Any banker who doubted the bank's validity was reassured by the Polk's listing, which included an address and telex number. When one of the many paperhangers who traded in Wilson's worthless paper encountered a suspicious banker, he would tell him to check his Polk's and telex the bank to confirm that his funds were on deposit. Wilson's Guernsey office manager immediately replied that the paperhanger was a wealthy and respected customer.

Wilson said that getting listed in Polk's presented no problem. He wrote to the Chicago publisher, Rand-McNally, and requested an application form. He filled it out, enclosed his fraudulent financial statement, paid the fee and was listed in the next edition. In the wake of Wilson's activities, Polk's embarrassed proprietors revised their procedures.

The existence of a telex machine on its premises was also helpful in giving an aura of legitimacy to the Bank of Sark. At the time, such machines were seen as pretty hi-tech. Wilson ordered his from Western Union, which promptly installed one, having no reason to suspect anything was amiss.

He persuaded a St Louis bank treasurer to let him copy the code that bankers use when they communicate by telex. 'He was having his own problems and we were trying to help him out,' Wilson later explained. 'It was one of the most valuable tools that we acquired.'

The variety and quantity of bad paper issued by the Bank of Sark was prodigious. It was grafted onto the balance sheets of Wilson's numerous other offshore enterprises. He sold it to other paperhangers, who passed it on or used it to bolster the balance sheets of their own offshore swindles. By propping up other fraudulent enterprises, Wilson's $300 million in bad paper produced a ripple effect amounting to at least another $200 million (more than $1 billion today).

Wilson also printed up thousands of international cashier's drafts – basically cheques drawn against the issuing bank – and sold them to other paperhangers, who agreed to pay him a percentage of their earnings. When they cashed the drafts, they notified Wilson which bank had been stung and for how much, and paid him accordingly.

Apart from his immediate associates, he worked with a loose network of other paperhangers, some of whom used his natty pink paper, while others used their own – often in combination with paper from the Bank of Sark. Typical of the breed were Allen Lefferdink and Louis (the Doc) Mastriana.

Persuading a bank to accept a Sark draft presented few problems to an accomplished paperhanger such as Mastriana, a man with serious Mafia connections. He had an extensive repertoire of wardrobes, business cards, identifications and personalities, which he tailored to the locale in which he operated.

To prepare the ground, Mastriana would first visit one of the leading real-estate agents in his target town. In a small conservative town, he would wear an Elk's or Mason's pin and a modest suit. In a larger city, he allowed himself a flashier image. Mastriana would tell the estate agent that he wanted to make a large property investment and would transfer the funds for this purchase to a local bank. Hoping to close the sale, the estate agent would call the local bank and, as a courtesy, recommend Mastriana. Moreover, he would probably do so in the hope that bringing in such a potentially lucrative account would make a favourable impression on the banker.

Mastriana would then go to the bank and open an account with a Bank of Sark cashier's draft. If the bank wanted, it could refer to Polk's and, using their telex and code, verify the cheque. Within minutes, Wilson's Guernsey manager would telex back that Mastriana was a longstanding and cherished customer with millions on deposit.

The local bank would accept his cheque and open an account. Many banks apparently did so without even bothering to check out the Bank of Sark. A day or two later, Mastriana would return to the bank and make a large cash (or cashier's cheque) withdrawal from his new account.

One of the many banks on which Mastriana executed this simple but effective swindle was the Dallas Bank and Trust Company. He deposited a $250,000 Bank of Sark draft, returned to the bank the same day, withdrew $10,000 and skipped town. The Dallas Bank was naturally unable to collect the original $250,000 draft. The Guernsey office manager had already forwarded it to Wilson's St Louis headquarters.

The Bank of Sark may not have had any assets, but it was well equipped with a variety of form letters useful for stalling banks that had been duped into accepting its cheques. Wilson had sent such a letter to the Dallas Bank claiming that the Bank of Sark had never received Mastriana's original $250,000 draft and therefore could not make any payment against it.

The bank tried to sue Mastriana for the $10,000 he had withdrawn. Mastriana promptly demanded that the bank return his original $250,000 Sark draft, knowing, of course, that since it was with Wilson in St Louis, the bank would be unable to do so. He then accused it of losing his cheque and countersued for a million dollars. The bank dropped the action. According to Mastriana, he and the other paperhangers counted on the bank's reluctance to take them to court and thereby make public that it had been swindled. Such negative publicity would put it in a very embarrassing position and 'the depositors will start to worry what kind of bank they are putting their money into, if they are just going around giving out these $10,000 cheques, so they backed away from [a law suit].'

PHILIP MORREL WILSON: THE BOGUS BANK OF SARK

On one memorable occasion, Mastriana transformed two Bank of Sark cheques totalling $75,000 into three Lincoln Continentals and $15,000 cash. In more relaxed mood, he beat a Vegas casino for a $40,000 cheque and sportingly lost it back again. 'The Italians have a wonderful saying,' he remarked philosophically. 'Money makes the blind see and the lame walk.' But he was nearly always ahead of the game.

Employing variations on this core swindle, Mastriana estimated that he had passed millions of dollars of bad Sark paper. He was not alone. Many other paperhangers were faithful Wilson customers, and the cashier's drafts were only one of a variety of Sark paper.

Others included letters of credit, certificates of deposit, and personal cheques. There were also other offshore ventures that closely followed the Bank of Sark; among them, according to Wilson, was Allen Lefferdink's Atlantic Trust Bank, which also traded in Sark paper.

Allen Jonas Lefferdink, a tall, handsome American who could charm all four legs off a donkey, was perhaps the world's unluckiest financier – though personally he doesn't seem to have suffered much as a result. After commanding a US Navy submarine chaser in World War Two, Lefferdink started his business career in 1945 by setting up an agency for the Northwestern Mutual Life Insurance Company in Boulder, Colorado. Starting with a $200 loan, within a year, he had broadened his base and become Allen Enterprises.

He then branched into consumer credit and founded Colorado Credit Life Insurance. It was a low-risk, high-profit operation, guaranteeing department stores, car dealers and banks that payments on instalment credit contracts would be completed if the customers died before paying up.

It was a roaring success. By 1955, Colorado Credit had more than $100 million worth of insurance on its books.

Even in the early days, though, he displayed a characteristic that both escalated his fortune and accelerated his downfall. Lefferdink preferred to do business with himself. If someone bought a car with finance from Allen Enterprises Loans, for example, then Allen Enterprises would handle the motor insurance and his Northwestern Mutual agency would tackle the driver about life insurance. There is nothing much wrong with that. Many keen insurance salesmen would do the same. Two commissions are better than one, after all, and three commissions are better still. The trouble was that Allen J. simply didn't know where to draw the line – or didn't care.

By 1959, Lefferdink was operating out of a swish $2 million headquarters in Boulder and in control of an empire comprising forty different firms worth roughly $30 million. Money rolled in at the rate of more than $150,000 a month. But in 1960, the Securities and Exchange Commission (SEC) put the skids under the Lefferdink boom by charging that there were financial irregularities in his brokerage house.

They couldn't make the charges stick, but then Internal Revenue Service presented him with a bill for $100,000 in back taxes, and the government indicted Lefferdink and five associates for fraud for allegedly diverting $2.4 million worth of funds. Trading blow for blow in court, the state accused Lefferdink of trying to bribe the SEC and Lefferdink accused the SEC of extortion. Twelve months later, the case went to trial. It lasted four weeks and the jury acquitted each defendant on every count.

Allen Lefferdink was free to go, though the bad publicity surrounding the trial had dealt his US enterprises a mortal blow. The man himself simply shrugged it off. Ever the entrepreneur, he set sail for Bermuda, where he would be out of the reach of the SEC and other American regulatory and law-enforcement agencies.

He arrived just before Bernie Cornfeld, creator of the largest crooked mutual fund of all, Investors Overseas Services.

Lefferdink was well situated in Bermuda to take advantage of the offshore boom once it started. Using borrowed money, he organised a number of offshore mutual funds, among them the World Investment Fund. It cost Lefferdink very little to set up these funds – a few hundred dollars for the paper formalities. Their portfolios consisted largely of stock in other Lefferdink-owned mutual funds and companies. He soon had salesmen dotted round the globe from South America to the Far East. Millions of dollars rolled in.

In the late 1960s, Lefferdink decided that a bank would add class to his growing string of offshore enterprises. When he first opened the Atlantic Trust Bank Limited, Guernsey had no law that defined exactly what a 'bank' was. Anyone could just turn up, rent an office, and advertise himself as a bank. He had seen how this almost total lack of control had been exploited by Phil Wilson.

To promote his bank, Lefferdink placed advertisements in the *International Herald Tribune* and in the international editions of *Time* and *Newsweek*. Those who answered them received literature promising 11 per cent interest on savings accounts and 6 per cent on cheque accounts. To sweeten the bait, the cavalier Lefferdink threw in a free double-indemnity life insurance policy issued by his Bermuda-based World Insurance Company.

Meanwhile, squads of salesmen, some graduates of his

Rome-based International College of Finance, promoted the Atlantic Trust Bank and the Lefferdink mutual funds. One of the bank's greatest selling points was its secrecy. Its literature promised complete and impenetrable secrecy. No government authorities would ever be allowed to see the records of the Atlantic Trust Bank. Little did depositors know that this secrecy was soon to be extended to include the location of their money, the headquarters of the bank and the whereabouts of Lefferdink himself.

The Bank's depositors ranged from the gullible to the furtive. Because of the Guernsey location, many foreign investors believed that they were dealing with a reliable British bank. Failing to see that 11 per cent interest violated the 'too good to be true' rule, they surrendered their money willingly. The majority of the bank's depositors were undoubtedly violating one or many of the laws of their own countries.

Lefferdink was now truly offshore in his floating head office, as the aptly named 100-foot yacht *Sea Wolf* cruised the Caribbean.

Like most offshore operators, Lefferdink did not care where the funds came from so long as they arrived. Black, white or anything in between, it was all money. Highly paid American expatriates keen to share in the US economic miracle, European businessmen intent on evading their tax inspectors, South American landowners desperate to get their money out of the country and into hard currency – they were all eager to buy dollar funds without too many questions asked. It was only later that they realised that a PO box number did have one potential snag: it could protect the seller as well as the buyer.

Lefferdink had one additional quirk. Whereas Phil Wilson

had relied on compliant accountants such as Dr Samuel Wilkinson to give financial credibility to his fanciful corporate accounts, Lefferdink relied on himself. In other words, he preferred not to use auditors at all. Stuffy conventional financiers, of course, would regard some 'outside' audit – however cursory – as essential to reassure investors that the figures were correct. But he had an answer to that. 'The appeal of offshore funds', he once remarked, 'is confidentiality.'

From time to time, Lefferdink got together with Wilson and other offshore buccaneers in particular deals. He provided bank references, insured and reinsured. But whereas the others swapped their 'securities' around with gay abandon, melding one company into another so fast that it was almost impossible for any outsider to keep up, Lefferdink had enough weight to 'rent' his fake securities out for a cash return. 'Renting' forged and made up securities was a stroke of evil genius.

Thus, a trading company with an unhealthy balance sheet could, by injecting, say, $1 million of such shares into its 'assets', transform its apparent liquidity and company worth.

This was a trick pulled 'countless times'. 'Renting' stocks to plug a hole in some hard-pressed (and previously straight) company's balance sheet was one area in which the mercurial Wilson and the more methodical Lefferdink collaborated. It was highly deceptive, of course, because everyone normally assumes that such securities are actually owned and not merely hired for the duration. But many desperate corporate executives, hoping against hope that their financial embarrassment would be purely temporary, were prepared to bend the rules to stay in business. And Wilson was prepared to move the stock halfway round the world and back to cover up.

In Asia, a Lefferdink agent did a booming business among Americans and other foreigners eager to get their money out of Vietnam. He speedily sold a total of $300,000 in Lefferdink mutual funds and deposits in the Atlantic Trust Bank. In Latin America, Lefferdink had a team of agents who pulled in over $400,000 in deposits for the bank, much of it in cash, thereby avoiding exchange controls. As affairs soured, the Latin American depositors proved to be a thorn in Lefferdink's side.

One enraged Peruvian travelled all the way to Guernsey to withdraw his money. He kicked down a door and terrorised the office staff. Another agent in Georgetown, Guyana, sold over $3 million in Lefferdink investment plans. 'I am unable to satisfy policyholders and investors with any explanation of the company's whereabouts,' he told a *Business Week* reporter. 'I was arrested and now I am penniless.' One determined Ecuadorian did bring a successful legal action in Guernsey, but he recovered only a fraction of the fortune he had deposited in the bank by attaching Lefferdink's office furniture.

A few depositors managed to withdraw their holdings from the bank. Many did not. But, because of the illegal origin of much of this money, it is doubtful that anyone will ever ascertain exactly how many depositors lost how much money. Nor is it entirely clear what happened to it.

By early 1969, the bank had begun to experience real difficulties. Depositors found that their cheques were being returned and that it was impossible either to make withdrawals or to reach Lefferdink. By mid-1969, they received a letter informing them that their bank had relocated and been renamed the Atlantic Trust Bank SA, now of Panama. The move from Guernsey, it was explained, had delayed all payments.

Later, new cheques were sent to each depositor. On the back of each was printed, 'To any Bank or banker, mail this check direct to Capital National Bank of Miami, P.O. Box 4141, Miami, Florida, for collection. This check is payable at par in the currency indicated by the maker.' On the front of each cheque Lefferdink had emblazoned a picture of his yacht, the *Sea Wolf*.

In early 1969, Lefferdink had begun to acquire stock in the respectable Capital National Bank of Miami. To buy the shares, he borrowed from one of his many mutual funds, the Universal Bank Stock Fund SA of Panama. He then used the newly purchased Capital stock as collateral to obtain yet more loans, which enabled him to buy more of the bank's shares. By early 1970, Lefferdink was on the board of directors. His new position was instrumental in reassuring Atlantic Trust Bank depositors that their money was in competent hands.

Fortunately, his tenure at the Miami bank was a brief one. Under pressure from federal banking officials, Lefferdink was forced to resign, and not a moment too soon. Already the Capital National Bank was being inundated with cheques drawn on the Atlantic Trust Bank and hopefully presented to it for payment. Capital returned the cheques with a letter denying all knowledge of Lefferdink and his companies.

Doors everywhere began to close on Lefferdink. The Guernsey legislature rewrote the island's banking laws and as a result the Atlantic Trust Bank was forced to eliminate the word 'bank' from its title. In Bermuda, information from Lloyd's of London about his so-called World Insurance Company was enough to persuade the Bermudans – who at the time were trying to build up their offshore insurance business – that Lefferdink must leave the island. Meanwhile, his prized yacht had fallen into the hands of a Miami boatyard, which had impounded it to settle a repair bill he had neglected to pay.

By 1971, the depositors of the Atlantic Trust Bank had become militant. They were outraged by letters from Lefferdink, which informed them that, 'Our bank decided to discontinue publishing our financial statements... in order that we may give depositors maximum protection.' In a later communication they were told that their bank had moved to yet another offshore tax haven. Some depositors were told that they could correspond with their bank through a post office box on the Cayman Islands; others were told to write to one in the Netherlands Antilles. The latter group never had a chance to reach Lefferdink. The Dutch authorities had received an avalanche of complaints and impounded the mail.

Some of the depositors formed vigilante groups and spent thousands of dollars hopping between obscure Caribbean islands on small planes trying to track down Lefferdink. One man, who got closer to the quarry than most, caught him on the phone.

Lefferdink reassured him that the bank was only experiencing some 'temporary' difficulties and would soon be solvent. He then hung up. Another depositor, who by chance made contact with Lefferdink, claimed that he was threatened with physical harm and legal action for defamation.

How much he got away with, Lefferdink only knows. In 1969 and 1970 alone, he passed $3.5 million in foreign currencies through Deak National Bank in New York. One Swedish investor claimed losses of $1 million; a South American monastery in Bogotá dropped $4,146 and 47 cents. It was enough to keep him going for quite a while, but the federal authorities eventually collared him. In March 1976, he was found guilty in Miami on seventeen counts of wire fraud, mail fraud and conspiracy involving upwards of $5 million, three foreign banks and twenty-six other companies. He was sentenced to eight years' imprisonment the following month, but stayed out on $100,000 bail, pending appeal.

A particularly apt summary of Lefferdink's business philosophy was actually quoted in a sermon by Dr Norman Vincent Peale, protestant preacher and author of *The Power of Positive Thinking*. He said that he had once asked Lefferdink why his 'business troubles' did not dull his enthusiasm. 'He said to me a priceless thing: "A disaster is only an incident in a business career. It is something to forget, to bypass, and go on." '

Lefferdink had amassed more than enough cash to 'go on' and live out his retirement in comfort, but apparently couldn't resist the temptation to dabble now and again and to pass on his skills to others, as he had done with his school for scammers in Rome – the International College of Finance. He died in Carson City, Nevada, in September 2003, at the ripe old age of eighty-five. At the considerable expense of others, he had enjoyed life enormously.

'I only have two kinds of day,' he was once heard to say: 'happy and hilariously happy.'

Another notorious Wilson associate was Ernest Shinwell, whose position as the son of Lord Emanuel 'Manny' Shinwell, a much-respected member of the House of Lords, gave him a unique entrée to bankers and brokers all over the world. Shinwell capitalised on this advantage. A one-time business partner of the Kray twins, he operated out of Panama City and from a palatial English estate with a twenty-five-room manor house, spacious grounds, lawns, swimming pools, and a fleet of Jaguars and Rolls-Royces.

Bankrupt three times, he kept bouncing back – always at other people's expense. In 1965 he was jailed for three years for fraud. He was also indicted in New York for trafficking in $18 million in Bank of Sark paper and was jailed for four years in Luxembourg in 1972 for attempting to pass off stolen securities on the Investors Bank of Luxembourg.

The Luxembourg authorities refused to extradite Shinwell to New York since he was already in prison there on stolen-securities charges. In 1976 he was back in the UK, beginning a three-year sentence for another fraud. He died in 2001.

Wilson, exhibiting his affinity for the grandiose, believed that in the late sixties there were enough of his crooked confederates to make up an army. 'It is my estimation that there are approximately, in the whole world, 10,000 people operating in white-collar fraud as an organised criminal activity,' he told the McClellan committee, and continued,

In the United States alone, there are approximately 2,500 people involved in this kind of activity. Many of the operators of this kind of fraud in the United States know each other by reputation, by references, or by dealing with each other directly or indirectly on a peripheral basis in this field.

For the remainder of the world, with the other 7,500 estimated people with the same system – that of knowing a reputation or being referred to or having operated with the people directly or indirectly – a person is able to move to any part of the world to conduct this type of business.

Phil Wilson used Bank of Sark and other worthless paper to incorporate a succession of American and offshore insurance companies. He formed one of his first in 1966. Included in its balance sheet was $400,000 in blue-chip securities stolen from a rural Missouri bank. Wilson, who claimed that the thieves were friends of his, agreed to place the securities 'as a favor' in his Bankers Security Mutual Insurance Company of Kansas City, Missouri.

Wilson wrote Bankers Security policies in New York and California and re-insurance for brokers at Lloyd's of London. (When an insurance company takes on a risk, especially a sizable one, it will often prefer to spread it around on other insurance companies. To do this it has them re-insure the original risk. This prevents one company from being solely responsible for paying a claim on a large, catastrophic loss. Lloyd's of London is the centre for this business.) A year later he dissolved Bankers Security almost overnight and went on to form more fraudulent insurance companies.

The experience had been valuable. It had served to introduce him to the Lloyd's brokers. Until 1971, his group of insurance companies went on to earn $20 million in premiums by writing reinsurance. Lloyd's eventually blacklisted him and as many of his companies as they could identify. However, Wilson continued to prosper by using three clever techniques to neutralise the blacklist.

He made himself easily available to the Lloyd's brokers – instead of asking them to reinsure him, he went to them and said, 'Let me sell you some reinsurance.' He created more credibility for his insurance group by getting a British 'bank' to give him a glowing testimonial. The institution in question was none other than Lefferdink's Atlantic Trust Bank. Finally, he specialised in reinsuring risks in communist countries that were shunned by the other companies. Wilson was a true pioneer in the field of East–West trade, albeit an unsavoury one.

He was also a patriot. Since his insurance group wrote reinsurance for risks in Mongolia, the USSR, Communist China, Poland and other Eastern European countries, he learned a certain amount of strategic economic and military information, including the details of the shipment of Russian warplanes and helicopters to the Middle East. Wilson instructed his St Louis attorneys to make this information available to the Central Intelligence Agency.

The only communist losses his insurance companies actually had to cover involved the Polish Airline LOT. LOT claimed, somewhat suspiciously, that two of its planes had crashed into the same Polish mountain within one ninety-day period. Wilson did pay the first claim, but slipped the Poles a dud Bank of Sark cheque to cover the second.

Oddly enough, Wilson did not actually set up the Bank of Sark. It was innocently 'founded' in 1966 by John Christian Konig, a twenty-two-year-old inheritor who rather fancied himself as a banking and insurance tycoon. Unfortunately, Konig lost £80,000 on his very first venture, Southern Counties Insurance, and found himself strapped for cash. Bank of Sark wasn't doing anything; its £1 million nominal capital had cost him £1,700 in stamp duty and the name had to be worth something. So he advertised in the *Financial Times*. Initially, there were no takers, but then a solicitor's letter arrived, offering £3,000 on behalf of a Jersey farmer Charles Howeson. It was accepted.

More than two and a half years later, Howeson denied that he had ever 'bought' the bank, but had merely signed a paper for an insurance broker friend, in a five-minute meeting at Jersey Airport. He was told that the bank was being purchased on behalf of American clients, who needed someone with Channel Islands residential status to be a director and had naively accepted it.

But thousands of miles away in St Louis, Missouri, master-swindler Philip Wilson and his associates – having secretly bought control of an offshore bank that appeared to have capital of £1 million for an outlay of £3,000 – planned to hit North America with a positive blizzard of bogus worthless securities. Personal cheques, bank drafts and certificates of deposit would be cashed, injected, pledged, substituted, transferred and used every which way to relieve banks, corporations or individuals of their actual cash.

It would be 'paperhanging' as nobody had ever hung paper before, not just on a grand scale, but on several levels from retail cheque-writing to wholesale asset removal.

The Bank of Sark could hardly be made to look like a normal commercial bank to any passer-by in Guernsey's Smith Street. With some ingenuity, however, it could easily seem authentic to anyone 3,000-odd miles away. And Wilson and his St Louis cronies, though not exactly authentic, were certainly ingenious. International banking, stripped to essentials, revolves around credibility, figures, paper and trust.

Wilson, together with the Bank's ever-helpful manager B Green (a.k.a. Bernie Greenberg), managed the credibility, Dr Samuel Wilkinson certified the figures, one Ralph

Sonneschein arranged the printing and the bank's luckless customers provided the trust. It was appearances that counted. The Bank's heraldic device, featuring knights in armour with drawn swords, looked quaintly but properly British. Its slogan was arrogantly vague: 'In the Highest Tradition of Merchant Banking'.

Wilson gave the McClellan Committee a quick lesson in how to use 'created' securities: 'We used them in our balance sheet so that we could get statements, item one. Item two, we used them as collaterals to guarantee other purchases. We used them as securities for other purposes. We used them as trading devices with other people in the business', he told Senator Gurney. 'Maybe they had a group of securities – it was like Monopoly. You would lay them out on the table and say, "I need one, two, three of those and I will trade you some of this." '

Dozens of American swindlers and quite a few desperate businessmen were ready, willing and able to deal in the Bank of Sark's natty pink drafts. Houston tycoon William Shepherd, whose conglomerate interests in electronics, paint and insurance were already borrowed up to the eyeballs, bought a swatch of Sark drafts for $100,000 from one Robert Ostrander in Chicago.

With a little bit of help from a chap called Wesley Alexander, he took the Mercantile Bank of Dallas for $320,000 and private bankers W L Moody & Co. of Galveston for $185,000. By the time he had finished, Shepherd had converted this bargain bundle of bogus paper into $1,290,000 of genuine cash by using Sark 'bad paper' as security for genuine bank borrowings.

To avoid the premature demise of the Bank of Sark,

Wilson and his college chum Bernie Greenberg not only attempted to ensure that such 'take-downs' were spread throughout North America, but also devised several ingenious methods to stall indignant bankers.

The 'vanished-cheque' procedure was one option. Another was the 'irregular-signature' gambit, which Mercantile National Bank experienced ('The drafts in question are signed by a depositor, not an officer of the bank, and we feel we definitely do not have liability in this matter'). And then there was the 'Sark stand-off', where the draft was merely returned with the enigmatic message, 'We thank you for your continued co-operation.'

Swindler-in-chief Philip Wilson was apparently having the time of his life. In autumn 1969, his St Louis group teamed up with Michael Strauss and several others in the mighty Cumberland Insurance Investment Corporation. Such an important event, naturally, required some hectic asset shuffling.

Cumberland emerged with national assets of $53.8 million, consisting largely of paper from Trans-Continental Casualty and other largely fictional businesses. And in November these imaginative fraudsters dreamed up the super-colossal Tangible Risk Insurance Co.

To spell out the full cross-linked ramifications of the Bank of Sark, Cumberland Insurance, Trans-Continental Casualty – plus others too numerous or nefarious to mention – and the aptly named Tangible Risk would be both bewildering and a waste of time. Which is exactly what Philip Wilson, his partners and his associates had in mind.

'To complicate matters when you commit fraud is one of the prerequisites,' Wilson told McClellan, but there was a downside risk. 'It gets so confusing that you even get confused when you are doing it.'

He did his best to keep it all together, though. When he moved to a luxury flat in Fort Lauderdale, one bedroom was cleared for a filing area, the dining table was shifted round to make room for the Telex and multi-line telephones were installed everywhere, including the two bathrooms. The place was later described as 'a residential swindling parlour'.

Though Wilson was collecting an untaxed income of 'several hundred thousand a year', his personal lifestyle was relatively modest. He dressed casually, drove a mid-range Pontiac and his only concession to a luxury lifestyle was an elderly 135-ton yacht (*c.* 1923) owned by First Liberty Fund. (It didn't make sense to alert the tax inspectors.)

And he apparently got his kicks from little tricks, such as kissing off the Polish air insurance claim with a Bank of Sark draft, or cheekily informing UK immigration control that he would be staying at the Sherlock Holmes Hotel – having booked in somewhere else.

By now considerably embarrassed, the Guernsey authorities decided that they would have to do something about their problem banks – not just the mysterious Bank of Sark, but also Allen Lefferdink's so-called Atlantic Trust Bank. They had passed the Prevention of Fraud Act in 1969, which forbade any company to call itself a 'bank' unless it actually was. The Bank of Sark was struck off the Guernsey register in March, 1970. And in May they announced that all 'banks' would have to satisfy the Finance Committee. But rumours of Sark's imminent closure were denied. 'The bank is still right here,' announced B Green. It kept going for some time.

Nobody realised at the time quite how dangerous some of those offshore sharks were. Even in his testimony to the McClellan Committee, Philip Wilson played down his connection with the likes of the Mafia-connected Louis Mastriana. White-collar fraudsters dealing in stolen securities, he admitted, were liable to be taken over.

'The end result is that the white-collar fraud individual ends up being dominated and owned by the Mafia-type criminal.'

But he (Wilson) claimed to have avoided this problem because he always fabricated his own securities.

Talking himself out of trouble, Wilson had named five other banking operations, similar to the Bank of Sark 'but not as sophisticated', that were in business at about the same time. Two rate special mention, one to conclude the saga of Phil the Flam and the other to highlight a different approach to illegal banking.

By 1971, Philip Wilson and an associate called Michael Strauss had moved to Fort Lauderdale, then the swindle centre of the Western world, and for a while concentrated their attentions on Canada – probably on the basis that it is more difficult to hit a moving target. An operation called Anglo-Canadian Group, which seemed to have taken over the mighty Tangible Risk, opened a small office in Montreal. Its front man was one Herbert Lion Singer, who was formerly with the Bank of Sark.

Anglo-Canadian's specialty was to induce would-be borrowers to part with brokerage fees (advance commission) for loans that they would never receive. The company was shut down by the authorities in fairly short order, but a new enterprise was already up and running.

Normandie Trust of Panama was even more super-colossal than Anglo-Canadian or Tangible Risk. It also specialised in the advance-fee racket, and boasted assets of $170 million, including $63 million in Tennessee real estate – actually worthless land grants – and $40 million of 'platinum certificates'.

Normandie's auditor wanted to disclaim this fanciful balance sheet, but said that a thug had come up from Florida and intimidated him. The phoney front stayed intact and the money kept on rolling in.

For a man accustomed to earning upwards of $200,000 a year, the present-day equivalent of around $1 million (or, as he quaintly put it 'enough money to live on'), Philip Wilson was ostensibly in a very poor financial condition when he went before the McClellan Committee in September 1973. 'No, I don't have any money in a safe-deposit box,' he told Senator Gurney. When pressed to reveal his current worth, Wilson conferred with his counsel and declined to go further, indicating that it would be inappropriate to continue the discussion because he had done a confidential deal with the Fraud Section of the Department of Justice in exchange for information.

It was arguably his best ever deal. What he had to offer the US Justice Department was not restitution but records, neatly stored in a Fort Lauderdale warehouse. His sentence was reduced from eight years' hard labour to a few comfortable months, the Internal Revenue Service forgot about his back taxes and he was provided with a brand-new (Italianate) identity. But in 1976 he was back at the Justice Department asking for another name. Someone had apparently taken out a contract on him.

'For Christ's sake, you've got to do something,' he pleaded. 'My mother will never forgive me if I die an Italian.'

However, he was determined not to die poor, and soon resumed his criminal career. He kept a relatively low profile for a number of years, but in 1999 he teamed up with a former stockbroker turned fraudster called Ralph McNamara, for one last big sting. Unfortunately for them, the stingers were themselves stung.

In November 2007, McNamara was convicted of multiple charges of racketeering, fraud, grand theft and money laundering and was sentenced to fifteen years in prison to be followed by ten years of probation and the obligation to fulfil a massive restitution order.

The co-conspirators promised their victims they had access to millions of dollars for venture capital funding and used fraudulent letters of credit purporting to be from reputable banks to support these claims. Six 'marks' were enticed to part with more than $1,167,500 in advance fees and expenses. But co-defendant Philip Morrel Wilson escaped any penalties at all. He died shortly before charges were filed in March 2003.

There are those who think that Bernie Cornfeld of Investors Overseas Services made more money than Wilson, but it's difficult to tell. However, Wilson started first, his activities were much more varied and, for the most part, well concealed – while the publicity-hungry Cornfeld was pretty much a one trick pony.

4

DOCTOR SAVUNDRA: THE SWINDLING GENIUS

Emil Savundra was born in 1923 into a prosperous middle-class family in the northern town of Jaffna in what is now Sri Lanka, but was then known as Ceylon. His father, Anthony Savundranayagam, was a self-effacing, highly principled lawyer. Sadly, Emil did not take after him.

So sensitive was Savundra Sr, and so prone to fall for the most improbable stories, that he rarely sent anyone to prison and was eventually removed from his post as a judge and became an academic instead.

Young Emil was educated at the Benedictine College of St Peter in Colombo, the capital, where he was remembered as 'erratically brilliant' and also as someone who enjoyed being the centre of attention. His forte was mathematics. He could solve complicated equations in his head far faster than could his classmates using pencil and paper. Doing so became a childhood hobby, as did tinkering about with mechanical and electrical devices with an eye to 'improving' them. He became a lifelong ham-radio enthusiast and a devotee of speed.

Emil's older brother Aloysious was destined for a high-flying career in the civil service, but tragically succumbed to hepatitis, while his two equally intelligent sisters went on to achieve prominence at universities in America.

Emil did not want to follow in the family tradition and become a lawyer: his preference was to become an entrepreneur. However, his father insisted, and on his sixteenth birthday, perhaps in order to soften the blow, gave him something on which he had set his heart: a powerful Norton motorcycle.

This was not a wise choice for someone of Emil's temperament. Within weeks of acquiring it he'd had two serious accidents and had broken both his legs. A few months later, weaving drunkenly through the night streets of Colombo with two friends clinging to the pillion, he came a cropper again. This time, his arm was so badly damaged it required extensive reconstructive surgery – and his two friends were killed.

That was the end of the young Savundra's motorcycling days, but, like Mr Toad, he remained addicted to speed regardless. Bizarrely, his parents continued to indulge that addiction by giving him a de Havilland Tiger Moth biplane. He soon became an accomplished airman whose speciality was heart-stopping stunts, usually with a terrified passenger on board.

When the war came in 1939, Emil was desperate to join the air force, but was still too young. By the time he was old enough, his father, showing a belated concern for his safety, had got him into the Royal Engineers instead. He rose to the rank of captain, but his escapades – usually involving attractive women – eventually saw him demoted.

At one stage, in order to facilitate his nocturnal visits to the local WRNS hostel, he'd had a self-designed, automatic extending ladder fitted to the boot of his Cadillac.

Ceylon escaped the attention of the Japanese during the war, and Emil saw no action – at least of a military sort. He carried on with his serial womanising and with taking friends and acquaintances on terrifying Tiger Moth joyrides.

After the war, though his father had now died, Emil complied with his wishes and returned to law school. But he took little interest in the course. As he'd told a schoolfriend years earlier, he wanted 'to be someone' and a business career rather than a legal one now seemed the best and fastest way forward.

He abandoned his studies in 1947 and joined a Ceylon-based, English-owned trading company called Taylor Mackay. In a time of postwar shortages, Emil demonstrated a genius for playing the black market and acquiring desirable goods at affordable prices. His contacts were impeccable and his way with a bribe irresistible. Taylor Mackay made him a director.

Six months later, at a party organised by friends, he met the woman who was to become his wife. But it was not to be an easy process. Pushpam Aloysius was beautiful, aristocratic and rich, and her family were the largest landowners in northern Ceylon – descendants, they claimed, of the Kings of Jaffna.

Emil Savundra was not considered a suitable candidate, but he rose to the challenge. He bombarded Pushpam with flowers by the vanload. And, when her family moved her upcountry to the estate of a rich uncle in order to escape her suitor's amorous attentions, he took to the air in his faithful Tiger Moth to buzz her as she lay by the pool and to flower-bomb her with yet more bouquets.

Eventually, Pushpam was worn down and won over by the sheer persistence of this 'chubby charmer', and her family reluctantly followed. To please them, Emil returned to law school. The marriage and a champagne reception for three thousand followed in June 1949. Such a strange courtship may not have seemed the best foundation for a lasting marriage, but Pushpam remained devoted to Emil for the rest of her life, and he – in his own odd way – to her.

When required to impress, Emil was a man of some style, with a permanent glint in his eye, a persuasive tongue and a near-professional ability as a jazz pianist. As Pushpam later recalled, 'He had the energy of twenty men. He had ability, imagination and drive and dominated any company he was in. In his way, he was a genius. Other men walked in his shadow and talked in tens, while Emil talked in tens of thousands.'

Figures like this would not easily come through the law – or by legal means – so Emil again abandoned his studies and plunged into a round of business deals that were as diverse as they were dubious. But they were relatively small beer and fell far short of Emil's soaring aspirations.

Just four months after his marriage, Emil's luck improved. He formed the grandly named Trans-World Enterprises Limited (paid-up capital, just £7) – the first of the many companies he would create in his career – and he met an enterprising American wheeler-dealer called H E Renfro.

Over a drink in a bar in Burma, the two men struck up a friendship and conjured up the outline of a really big deal. Renfro explained that Red China was in desperate need of strategic materials, particularly oil. The Korean war was imminent and, because the Western powers believed that China would support Korea, they had imposed a strict trade embargo that would prevent the import of oil and petroleum, some of which might be passed on to the enemy.

Renfro boasted that he had business contacts in China senior enough to order oil on behalf of the government and inside information about several oil companies that would be willing to break the embargo on supplying China – if it could be done discreetly. For his part, Savundra had the ideal vehicle for this deal in Trans-World Enterprises, based as it was in Ceylon, where trading regulations were elastic to say the least.

Savundra and his brother-in-law then set up a subsidiary company to Trans-World, Eastern Traders Limited. This company had no more in the way of assets than its parent, but from the outside it looked good. Savundra had persuaded some of Colombo's great and good to become directors – including the son of the then Prime Minister.

In August 1950, Renfro turned up in Colombo as the accredited representative of Hwa Shih Company of Tientsin with a mandate to negotiate an oil-supply contract. Two months later, Savundra wrote to Renfro in the latter's capacity as Hwa Shih's representative:

Dear Sirs,

We confirm our conversations of these last weeks and confirm our acceptance of your order for 45,000 drums of lubricants of various specifications to be shipped direct to Tsingtao, China at a C.I.F price of $1,230,000. It is agreed that you will open Letters of Credit in our favour with a bank or banks nominated by us in Ceylon

and/or India and/or Switzerland to cover the cost of this shipment and that this credit will be in favour of our subsidiary firm Messrs. Eastern Enterprises Co.
Yours faithfully,
Trans-World Enterprises Ltd.

Eastern Enterprises was yet another subsidiary company, owned 50:50 by Trans-World and Eastern Traders and typical of the intercompany webs that Savundra would weave throughout his career. Apart from its imposing list of directors, Eastern Enterprises enabled Savundra to disguise successfully the fact that the two shareholders were 'straw' companies, without assets.

A letter of credit was duly opened at the Eastern Bank and later transferred to the Union Bank of Switzerland. So far, so good. But now Savundra had to source – or appear to source – the specified oil. He set off for Europe, having borrowed the money to cover his expenses, which would be considerable. He took his wife Pushpam and baby son with him and set up headquarters in the luxurious Mayfair Hotel in London. From a target list of four oil companies agreed with Renfro, Savundra chose to write to one, the Société Méditerranéen de Produits Pétroliers (SMPP):

Dear Sirs,
We have been given your name as a firm of petroleum dealers who are out of the 'ring'. There is a large order for approximately 1 million US dollars worth of petroleum products for the Far East, which we are in a position to obtain for you. Should you be interested, please contact the undersigned immediately.

The SMPP were apparently very interested and replied within days. Company director Pierre Duval met Savundra in Zürich, London and Paris to negotiate the deal. There followed a nerve-racking six weeks while Savundra said he was waiting for the documentation to be produced, and several of his eminent board of directors considered bailing out of what was, after all, an illegal transaction.

By 10 January 1951, Savundra announced that all the documentation was now in hand: (1) affidavit signed by the agents; (2) certificate of Lloyd's survey; (3) bill of lading (a guarantee that the correct cargo has been loaded, signed by a representative of the relevant shipping company); (4) export licence; (5) certificate of sailing; and (6) analysis of cargo report.

Savundra's meeting with the manager of Union Bank in Zürich, scheduled for 16 January, was postponed at the last minute due to the manager's ill health. A nervous Savundra telegrammed the mother superior of the Carmelite convent in Colombo asking her to pray for him and the success of his venture. It must have worked, because, twenty-four hours later, Savundra was, as they say, in funds. He had a banker's draft for $825,552 to pay Pierre Duval for the oil, a further draft of $169,447 to the credit of Trans-World at the bank of Ceylon, and $255,000 in crisp, new $50 and $100 bills.

Savundra did not immediately return to Ceylon. Instead he flew to London, where, from the comfort of the Grosvenor House Hotel in Park Lane, he began to create a smokescreen, an art at which he was to become increasingly adept as his career progressed. He claimed to have been interviewed by an American secret agent who told him that they were on to his embargo-busting scheme and would not allow the oil through – even if it meant torpedoing the tanker and terminating Renfro and Savundra.

The worldly-wise Mr Renfro didn't seem to be unduly worried. He cabled Savundra, then back in Colombo. In part, his message read:

NCONCERNED YOUR INFORMATION STOP MY INTEREST PROFIT ONLY AND I AM PERFECTLY HAPPY IF SHIP NEVER ARRIVES STOP DID YOU ALL PULL A FAST DEAL AND NEVER INTEND ARRIVAL STOP THIS OK WITH ME BUT DID SHIP ACTUALLY SAIL OR WERE DOCUMENTS FORGED STOP MUST HAVE MORE INFORMATION TO DECIDE NEXT MOVE STOP PLEASE OBLIGE.

Mr Renfro's intuition had served him well. The whole oil deal was bogus. There was no oil, no ship and no Société Méditerranéen de Produits Pétroliers. Pierre Duval – and that's unlikely to have been his real name – was a stooge recruited by Savundra to help dupe everyone – including Renfro.

All the documents produced by Savundra and examined by the Union Bank were forgeries, albeit skilful enough to be convincing at first sight. And there was no ship of the name given in the documents.

Though it is clear from Renfro's cable that he would not have been surprised if Savundra had pulled off a huge confidence trick, he was unaware just how big it was. He continued to believe that there was a ship with a cargo of oil, but that the Chinese would not now be getting it. Desperately trying to pull a stroke of his own, he cabled with an offer of $100,000 to be divided between Savundra and the captain if the ship was diverted to a 'safe island' where the cargo could be profitably disposed of. However, and by then under pressure from the Chinese, he soon cabled again, withdrawing his offer and insisting that the shop should proceed to its original destination.

This prompted a barrage of smoke-screen cables from Savundra, which left Renfro increasingly frustrated. He eventually made enquiries of his own and discovered that there was, after all, no ship and no oil. The Chinese also discovered the truth – and that Renfro had been made a fool of – and so turned their fire directly on Savundra.

They accused him directly of being a crook and a swindler. Savundra fired back that all the irregularities were on their side and demanded an immediate apology.

The Chinese threatened legal and other unspecified sanctions. Savundra calmly pointed out that it was their appointed representative, H E. Renfro, who had dealt with SMPP and that it wasn't his (Savundra's) fault that they had turned out to be crooks. At this stage the Chinese still hadn't realised that SMPP was just a figment of Savundra's fertile imagination.

Claiming that he had made almost nothing out of the deal, he replied to their demand for the return of their money:

It is not possible to get blood out of a stone. We suggest you treat this as a gamble which you took and lost, or alternatively, that you take it out of the hide of the bankers whose negligence has caused you this great loss and us so much unnecessary worry.

The threats subsided when the Chinese realised that it was they who would suffer most from violating an international embargo and also that they would probably lose face on a grand scale. C Y Fang, Hwa Shih's general director, sent the following, cap-in-hand cable:

GENTLEMEN, WITHOUT ALTERING OUR RIGHTS TO OUR CLAIMS FOR $1,250,000, WE BEG TO REQUEST TO INFORM US HOW MUCH YOU WILL BE PREPARED TO PAY AND HOW SOON YOU WILL PAY. A GRAIN OF RICE TO A STARVING MAN IS BETTER THAN A BOWL OF RICE THE NEXT DAY.

Though there was to be a great deal of further correspondence, this must have been the moment when Savundra knew he had won. As for Mr Renfro, there is no evidence that Savundra ever heard from him again. All of which leaves the question: whatever happened to the $825,552 that was supposed to have been paid to the mysterious Pierre Duval, representative of a nonexistent French oil company? It seems that the money was split between the co-conspirator playing the part of Duval and Savundra, with the latter retaining around $500,000.

Strangely, that is about the sum the ever-religious Savundra subsequently donated to the Roman Catholic Church, via his friend Monsignor Asta. This generous gift was to be used to found a Carmelite convent in Kandy. Perhaps Savundra regarded it as insurance. He would thenceforward have ties with an institution that could intercede on his behalf with the Almighty.

The aftermath of the phoney Chinese oil deal, combined with his dubious postwar black-market dealings, severely dented Savundra's reputation among Colombo's small, tight-knit business community. Nobody wanted to deal with him and eventually even the banks turned him away.

This bothered Savundra not at all. He'd already set his sights on Europe and before long, with the financial backing of his uncle, he and his family were ensconced in the prestigious Georges Cinq Hôtel in Paris.

His business cards announced him as the chief executive of a Colombo-based conglomerate called Modern Industries Limited. Though the name was purely a façade, Savundra's luxurious lifestyle proclaimed him to be a successful businessman. This, coupled with his charm and apparent generosity, soon had his chosen circle eating out of his hand.

He was soon plotting his next big scam, hand-picking his team and planning every last detail. It is a measure of how cleverly he did this that the operation he had under way is still remembered by Interpol as one of the most baffling cases they had ever been called upon to investigate.

The Chinese oil deal left Savundra convinced of two things: first, that the best way to maximise your profits is to sell a product that doesn't exist; second, that the Achilles heel of the European banking system was its implicit trust in pieces of paper. Provided the paper looked right, the most preposterous fraud could be perpetrated with minimal risk of being detected – at least in the short term. Savundra's paperwork was always immaculate.

In April 1954, about a year after Savundra had set up his headquarters in Paris, the Kreditbank in Antwerp received a request from the Banco Nacional Ultramarino of Lisbon to open a line of credit for $865,000 on behalf of the government of Portuguese Goa. The money was to be for the credit of the well-known Belgian shipping firm of Hantra.

The purpose of this entirely ordinary banking transaction was to finance the purchase and shipping of 8,000 tons of

Italian and Burmese rice to the Goan port of Mormugao, where it was urgently needed for famine relief. The documents required to support this transaction – bills of lading, insurance policies, consular invoices and the like – would be forwarded in due course by a Ceylonese company called Modern Industries Limited, which was handling the whole deal on behalf of the Goan government.

When all the necessary documentation had been handed over, the insurance underwriters and the shipping agents were to receive (legitimately) $15,140 between them, whereas the vast majority of the remaining money – some $669,860 – was to be diverted to Switzerland and the Banca Report of Lugano for the account of a Mr George Kaufman.

Early in the development of the scam, Savundra had received a sample of rice from the Goan government as an indication of the quality required. Savundra stuck it in a drawer and never gave it another thought. His main concern was how to ensure that the Kreditbank swiftly transferred $669,860 to Lugano, from where it could be diverted directly into his pocket. So far, Savundra had transacted what looked to the institutions involved like a perfectly normal business deal. Once their confidence was secured, the transaction turned fraudulent.

In May 1954, a Swiss forwarding agent called at the Kreditbank and asked to see the managing director. The agent was Herr von Hornung, the head of Hantra's shipping office in Basle. He explained that he had been instructed by Modern Industries to handle personally the Goan rice deal and that he knew the bank would understand his client's reason for wanting to transact it via the Swiss banking system. Von Hornung handed over copies of the correspondence with Modern Industries in Ceylon, which confirmed what he had said, and, crucially, an invoice that showed the rice had been purchased and shipped.

The clock was now ticking and it was only a matter of time before the plot was discovered. Savundra and his cohorts had to work fast. Within hours of von Hornung's leaving the Kreditbank, a messenger arrived bearing an impressive-looking invoice, apparently signed and sealed by the Portuguese Consul in Antwerp, which certified that the rice had left port in a Norwegian-owned freighter, the *Trianon*.

In the meantime, a man called Mayers, representing another shipping firm called Marinex – appointed to act on behalf of Modern Industries – had purchased a perfectly genuine insurance policy for the cargo from the respected firm of Outschoorn and Landau. This was presented to Kreditbank, which then had all the necessary documentation assembled and airmailed it to the Goan government. The $669,680 could then be transferred to the Banca Report in Lugano and thence into the account of a Mr Kaufman.

Shortly after the transfer had taken place, the money was on the move again. Herr Kaufman turned up at the bank in Lugano and asked for $366,860 cash in Swiss francs and for the remaining $303,000 to be transferred post haste to the Hofman Bank in Zürich for the credit of one Andre Klotz. Accustomed to the wheeler-dealings of their wealthy customers, the bank happily complied.

The $303,00 had barely reached the Hofman Bank when Herr Klotz identified himself to the manager and instructed him to convert almost the whole of the amount into gold, to be held by the bullion dealer until they were presented with an Italian 1,000-lire note bearing the serial number

6/85/18364. Within minutes of this cloak-and-dagger procedure being organised, an unknown caller presented the note, collected the gold and disappeared. In the nick of time, it would seem.

The Kreditbank received a cable from the Banco Nacional Ultramarino in Lisbon asking for the name of the ship carrying the rice, and for its estimated time of arrival in Goa. This prompted a phone call to the owners of the *Trianon* in Oslo, and a severe shock in Antwerp. Kreditbank was told that the *Trianon* wasn't calling at Goa, and, what's more, wasn't carrying any rice. When the awful truth had sunk in, the police were called and Interpol was alerted. The Banca Report in Lugano was ordered to freeze the relevant funds, but it was twenty-four hours too late.

Initially, Interpol thought they were dealing with a large but relatively simple fraud. The first to be interviewed was Mr Mayers of the shipping agents Marinex, who protested his innocence long and loud. All his dealings had been with legitimate firms of unimpeachable reputation and he had no reason to suspect anything was amiss. He had also dealt in person with Mr von Hornung from Hantra. Mayers was arrested, but later released.

When he was tracked down, von Hornung opened up almost immediately. He knew he'd helped facilitate an illegal currency transaction, but that was nothing unusual. He denied all knowledge of anything else. In the course of a vigorous and protracted grilling, he appeared genuinely surprised that the Goan rice export deal was a complete fraud and was eventually allowed home under strict surveillance.

By the next morning, he was dead, having shot himself through the head.

Unfortunately for Savundra, that wasn't the end of the trail. Von Hornung had left a signed confession. He was an innocent party in a complicated business arrangement that he didn't fully understand. Modern Industries in Ceylon had asked for his cooperation in setting up an export deal that would aid Goa, while at the same time earn Modern Industries much-needed Swiss francs to finance an expansion of their European operations.

In Paris he had met the company's top man, a Mr Emil Savundranayagam, who had given him precise instructions about what he should do and had provided him with all the necessary documentation. Only now had he learned that it was all forged.

All this was something Savundra could not have anticipated, but he had already sent Pushpam to London to prepare a bolthole for use when the balloon eventually went up: a flat in St James' Court. Within hours of the police seeing von Hornung's suicide note, Savundra was back in London, but without the usual smoke screen to hide behind.

The Belgian Police applied for his extradition, and Savundra found himself in the dock at Bow Street. He was, he said, an innocent businessman whose name had been misused by unscrupulous Continental financiers to perpetrate a gigantic fraud. As a member of one of Ceylon's wealthiest families, he had no need to stoop so low. Nevertheless, having heard all the evidence, the magistrate was unimpressed and found that there was a serious case to answer. Savundra was asked if he wished to testify further or call witnesses. He wished to do both and the case was adjourned for two months.

In the meantime, Savundra resorted to a tactic he would

use time and time again whenever his back was against the wall. He had a heart attack.

It was probably not a real one, but, as the possessor of a genuinely weak heart, Savundra was in a position to make it look convincing and could afford to hire medical experts to back him up. The court was convinced that he was unfit to face extradition and Savundra booked himself into the plush London Clinic. Here the catering was of such a high standard that the Duke of Windsor once remarked that he wished the food was half as good in the West End's best hotels.

Savundra had a very superior room on the second floor and at one stage had no fewer than fourteen of the country's leading heart specialists advising on his case. Endless delays and legal adjournments eventually infuriated the magistrate, Mr Bertram Reece, who decided that, if Mr Savundra could not come to court, then the court would come to him.

In February 1956, a cavalcade of cars drew up outside the clinic, disgorging the magistrate, a gaggle of barristers and solicitors, the clerk of the court, shorthand writers and numerous other officials. They were followed by a bevy of reporters. Savundra's sick room was filled to overflowing and the whole affair became something of a circus. Nevertheless, the magistrate granted the extradition order, and Savundra subsequently lost an appeal against it.

Soon afterwards, he was stretchered onto an aircraft at Heathrow, flown to Belgium and transferred by ambulance to Antwerp prison. Within days he'd managed to get himself transferred to the luxurious St Elizabeth Catholic Hospital. The parlous state of his health made this essential, he said.

It was six moths before the case came to court – at which point Savundra, the man at death's door, became Savundra the showman. Immaculately turned out, he exuded confidence and glowed with good health. He dominated the proceedings and vigorously challenged every piece of evidence, often giving Pushpam a wink or a thumbs-up when he thought he'd done well. The trial had been scheduled for ten days, but Savundra's efforts ensured that it dragged on for months.

Predictably, he claimed that he was only an innocent middleman, acting for the sole owner of Modern Industries Limited, a Mr Perera in Colombo. Perera had instructed him to find the most profitable way to ship the rice. Savundra, emboldened by his perceived success so far, couldn't resist remarking that the most profitable course would have been to ship no rice at all. Even the court president smiled at that.

But, unusually, Savundra had misread the situation. He was found guilty and sentenced to five years in prison together with a fine of 40,000 Belgian francs.

Pending an appeal, he was returned to the St Elizabeth hospital, where one of his regular visitors was his clerical friend from Ceylon, Monsignor Asta. Savundra, you'll remember, had given the monsignor $500,000 to build a Carmelite convent in Kandy.

Two months later, Savundra was on a plane to Italy a free man. The purpose of his trip was to pay his respects to Cardinal Montini, later to become Pope Paul VI, before returning to his family in England.

How was this miraculous reversal of fortune achieved? Immediately after his appeal had been dismissed, Savundra fell ill again and it seems that he prevailed on Monsignor Asta to intercede with the Belgian Minister of Justice. One can only surmise what was said, but Savundra would probably been portrayed as a good man ill-used by others, a generous benefactor to the church, and someone whose dying wish was to spend his final days in the bosom of his family.

Whatever was said, the minister bought it and authorised the prisoner's release.

Back in England, Savundra had his obituary published in the Belgian press. This had the effect of silencing any criticism from the Portuguese and Goan governments about his excessively lenient treatment, and also meant that all the files on the case were removed from active consideration and archived.

To those who knew him to be still very much alive, Savundra gave a typically grandiose explanation of his part in the affair: his motivation had not been personal profit, but was purely political and at the behest of the Prime Minister of India, Pandit Nehru.

Goa was then in a state of near revolt against Indian domination and an invasion by Indian troops. It had been decided that Goa's defenders should be starved out. No food was allowed across the border and the only other possible entry point was the port of Mormugao. Savundra claimed that his mission, ultimately successful, was to ensure that no food ships ever got there.

The next country to become the focus of Savundra's attention was Ghana. Together with an entrepreneur called John Dalgleish, he planned to acquire the exclusive mineral rights to the entire country, newly independent under President Kwame Nkrumah.

Dalgleish was a burly former army officer whose books about his wartime exploits had made him enough money to become a City investor. His first big deal was to acquire control of an ailing group of companies called Camp Bird, named after the gold mine in Colorado where it had come into being. By the time Dalgleish took over, the mining company had diversified into a number of unprofitable, non-mining activities. Dalgleish had turned the group round and was seeking new opportunities.

Savundra had the political skills and the Third World business knowledge and Camp Bird would provide the right sort of front and the mining technology. The two men agreed to work together and flew to Ghana to meet the President, with whom Savundra seemed to be on very friendly terms. Dalgleish was not to know that Savundra had met Nkrumah only once before, at the latter's birthday celebrations, which had been held at the fashionable Mirabelle restaurant in London. Savundra had managed to book himself an adjacent table and introduce himself to the President.

That they then greeted each other effusively in the Ghanaian capital Accra certainly impressed Dalgleish. Convinced by Savundra's bold plans and bowled over by his contacts, he returned to the UK. Shortly afterwards he announced that Camp Bird had formed a new subsidiary called Ghana Minerals Corporation. Camp Bird's worldwide reputation, the million dollars set aside for geological surveys and the promise of huge inward investment to follow sealed the deal for the Ghanaians. With an economy on its knees, it was an offer they couldn't refuse.

In the meantime, Savundra had parlayed up his own reputation. He was a devout Christian and a fervent anti-colonialist, he said. He was one of the first businessmen to deal successfully with the People's Republic of China and had actually been thrown into prison for his anti-colonial sentiments by the Belgians, the oppressors of the Congo. He was saved only by his Christian connections, in the person of the Apostolic delegate in Brussels.

Further, at a time when many of the companies owning mineral rights seemed to be in a dubious financial state, Savundra and the Ghana Minerals Corporation appeared to have money and mean business. The company had been registered with an authorised capital of £50 million 'to cover the company's immediate needs', and another two Camp Bird-backed companies were registered with a capital of £100 million each.

This looked good and clearly dazzled the Ghanaians, but it had cost very little. By contrast with the UK, where to register companies with such substantial authorised capital would have cost a colossal sum, in Ghana any size of company could then be registered for a flat fee of around £7.

When details of the new venture were announced in London towards the end of 1958, there was uproar – primarily among the companies that already owned mineral rights in Ghana – but Savundra pressed ahead. A few months later, he and his family arrived in Accra in a blaze of publicity and took over an entire floor of the plush Ambassador Hotel. The *Ghana Times* hailed him as a saviour with £350 million to spend, a man who could put paid to poverty in the region.

To supplement this, Savundra began a massive advertising and PR campaign. Champagne flowed and politicians were entertained on a lavish scale. Nobody queried the fact that only £14 had been subscribed – as registration fees – for two companies claimed to be worth £100 million each.

Savundra promised far higher wages than his rivals and

that he would build hospitals and provide free electricity for the areas around his various mining operations. All he wanted in return was a guarantee of exclusive rights in all new mining areas for fifty years and a requirement that the companies already operating in existing mining areas should pay him a levy of 10 per cent of all their proceeds. This would cost the country nothing.

Just about the only person not caught up in the general euphoria was Geoffrey Bing QC, who had been appointed by Nkrumah as his Attorney General. Bing became suspicious when he discovered that only a tenth of the 50 million authorised shares had been issued for cash and that the remainder had been issued as so-called bearer warrants, in contravention of Ghanaian exchange-control law.

He sent his officials to examine the three companies' books, only to discover that there weren't any – and there were no bearer warrants, either.

What they did eventually find were copies of cables sent to the mother superior of Savundra's convent in Kandy, asking for prayers to be said on his behalf. They were pinned to copies of correspondence referring to crucial meetings.

There was a cable and a subsequent letter from the mother superior, confirming that a black bag of documents had been destroyed unopened and that prayers had been offered. Most revealing of all was a copy of a letter to a British MP, explaining how easy it was to hoodwink the Africans.

All this was very interesting, but hardly damning evidence. Eventually a bundle of receipts was discovered, for four packages deposited in the vaults of a Ghanaian bank. Bing was convinced that they contained the missing bearer warrants and ordered that they be seized and delivered to his office. While the formalities to achieve this were under way, Savundra got wind of it and visited the bank himself to inspect his packages.

Whatever they had previously contained, when they were opened in Bing's office they were found to be full of torn-up magazines, toilet paper and obscene poems about Bing's wife – in what appeared to be Savundra's handwriting. But, once again, there was nothing illegal in any of it.

The collapse of Savundra's Ghanaian enterprise, when it did come, was not primarily his fault. Shortly after his arrival in the country, and as part of his promotional efforts, Savundra had persuaded a junior minister to write a letter, which said that the government had approved his mining proposals in principle.

As the minister concerned had no connection with mining and no authority to make any commitments, Savundra knew it wouldn't stand up as a binding document, but in the interim he could use it to impress people with.

To convince his business partner, John Dalgleish, that he was making good progress, he sent him a copy of the letter. Dalgleish, annoyed at official denials from Ghana that any agreement had or would be reached with Camp Bird, impulsively published the letter in retaliation. That really put the cat among the pigeons.

Bing immediately seized upon this to make public his distrust of Savundra and to declare that his continued presence in Ghana was 'not conducive to the public good'. He began legal action against Camp Bird, Ghana Minerals Corporation and Savundra himself, alleging various infringements of company law. When the police raided his suite at the Ambassador Hotel, they were told that he had taken to his bed and that his severe and recurrent heart problems meant that he could not be moved or taken into custody.

Back in Britain, the press turned on Nkrumah for his 'unfair' treatment of foreign investors, but the City and disgruntled Camp Bird shareholders took another view. The stock exchange suspended dealings in Camp Bird shares, despite the fact that the company had, by now, issued a statement withdrawing its mining proposals and dissociating itself from Ghana Enterprises.

The Ghana government then issued a statement of its own, in which it asserted that Savundra had lied about the financial position of Ghana Minerals when he stated that it had a fully paid-up share capital of £5 million. It went on to say that Savundra was at no time about to be granted exclusive mineral rights to the whole country – and it disowned the letter to that effect, written at Savundra's behest by that hapless junior minister, who was then summarily sacked.

As for Savundra himself, it was decided that, as he was in such poor health and his business affairs had become so tangled, it would be easier to deport him than prosecute him. Put on a plane for Ceylon, Savundra left behind a commercial mess that was never to be cleaned up – and dozens of cases of empty champagne bottles.

Surprisingly, John Dalgleish, Savundra's erstwhile partner in this ignominiously failed enterprise, now sprang to Savundra's defence at Camp Bird's annual general meeting, where he sang the man's praises long and loud. The shareholders were singularly unimpressed. Tens of thousands of pounds had sunk without trace in Ghana, and Camp Bird's once-proud reputation had been sullied for ever. It was the beginning of the end for the company and its chairman. Within a couple of years, an annual profit of £1 million had turned into a £1 million loss. In 1963, Dalgleish finally threw in the towel and called in the Official Receiver, unable to explain the disappearance of some £2.4 million.

A friend remembers Savundra's reaction to the Official Receiver's report: 'The poor dim British,' he spluttered, before dissolving into peals of helpless laughter.

After his involuntary departure from Ghana, Savundra applied his fertile mind to other possible ventures. An acquaintance brought to his attention a newspaper article highlighting a problem then facing the government of Costa Rica. This tiny Central American country, bordering on the Caribbean, was almost totally reliant on coffee production, but was in the embarrassing position of having produced more than it could sell. A massive sales drive was being contemplated to increase exports.

Not long after the newspaper article appeared, Savundra was knocking at the door of the Costa Rican Consulate in London. Rather as he had done in Ghana, he presented himself as a wealthy international financier with Vatican connections and a philanthropic interest in helping underdeveloped countries.

The Consul was impressed with Savundra's apparent credentials and subsequently introduced him to the chairman of the Costa Rican Coffee Brokers' Association. Savundra then revealed his plan to rescue the country's finances. He claimed that he had a buyer for a considerable amount of Costa Rican coffee – almost all that embarrassing surplus – for distribution throughout Europe.

His partner this time, introduced as the broker, was a once-rich, self-styled Indian prince called Shiv Kapoor. A wheeler-dealer whose specialty was scrap metal, he had fallen on hard times, but had not yet had to vacate his palatial home in Ascot. He was just what Savundra needed – someone who looked the part, but was nevertheless desperate enough for money to be malleable. Although he only knew Savundra socially, the coffee deal seemed to be his way back to prosperity.

The chairman of the Costa Rican Coffee Brokers' Association, Charles Vincent, was flown to London and travelled down to Ascot in Savundra's Rolls-Royce. He was instantly impressed by the grandeur of the venue and the emollient charm of Shiv Kapoor, who said that he had already found a buyer for 6,000 tons of coffee at the then very generous price of £359 per ton. It was to be Costa Rica's biggest ever export order, amounting to one-tenth of the annual crop and an anticipated revenue return of over £2.1 million.

A month after signing the deal, Kapoor 'contracted' to resell the coffee to a Savundra associate, a French count called Maxim de Cassan Floyrac. As part of the contract, Kapoor agreed to an extraordinarily onerous penalty clause of £271 per ton for any shipment that failed to arrive on time. The coffee was to be dispatched in twelve monthly instalments of 500 tons each to three different European ports. The first shipment left the Caribbean for Europe in January 1960.

But all was not as it seemed. The coffee wasn't to be sold to Floyrac, but was to be disposed of cheaply in East Germany. What's more, there was to be no payment for most of it. It was to be one of Savundra's classic phantom shipments in reverse. Instead of there being money and no goods, this time there were to be goods and almost no money.

Since Floyrac obviously didn't receive any coffee, the penalty clause was invoked and the majority of the money from the sales to East Germany was diverted to a friendly bank in Tangiers. After the second shipment had arrived and been sold, the sum of £137,000 for the first shipment was remitted to Costa Rica. The delay in payment initially raised no eyebrows there, because they were so desperate to sell that they had agreed 180-day settlement terms. The shipments continued, but the payments alas, did not. When the debt had reached £1.7 million, a worried Charles Vincent ordered that the shipments should cease.

Under the Floyrac penalty clause, the money had already been paid into the American and Foreign Bank in Tangier. The bank and its proprietor subsequently vanished, and Kapoor's Swiss banker, also embroiled in the deal, shot himself. Charles Vincent, who had given guarantees over the coffee shipments to Costa Rica's state-run bank, was ruined when the deal went sour and the guarantees were called in. 'Prince' Shiv Kapoor was tried on fraud charges in London and sentenced to six years' imprisonment. The Costa Ricans took years to recover from what they described as 'a paralyzing blow to our economy'.

Yet Savundra, the man who arguably aimed the blow that Kapoor delivered, got away scot-free. Indeed, while the coffee deal was still in train, he was trying to interest the Costa Ricans in another deal: the purchase of the country's British-owned Northern Railway. Nothing came of it, and, with the coffee scam over and Kapoor still in prison, Savundra embarked upon another scheme, which was to dwarf all his previous efforts. But, before he did so, he set about brushing up his image.

On 10 February 1960, he became a naturalised British citizen. Shortly thereafter, he announced that he had been granted two doctorates and henceforth should be known as Dr Emil Savundra, PhD, DCL. The degrees weren't real, but Savundra had always worked on the principle that the bigger the lie you told, the less likely people were to question it. Man of letters, rising tycoon – Savundra certainly looked the part, with his wavy, iron-grey hair, black-rimmed glasses and an immaculately cut suit that almost disguised his thickening waistline.

The late fifties and early sixties marked the beginning of the era of the big business fraud, in both Britain and America. Insurance was a particularly fertile field, because is was a business in which the customer paid upfront, and, provided that he or she had not made a claim, never expected in return anything more than a fancy piece of paper. And even those who did have the temerity to claim could be stalled, argued with or fobbed off.

Basically, all you had to do was to borrow enough 'working capital', usually on the strength of phoney securities, buy a company off the shelf and reward yourself hugely while at the same time milking the company of its premium income and stripping it of its reserves. The one big problem was that when the day of reckoning came – as it surely would – the man seen to be in charge would have a lot of explaining to do.

As usual, Savundra's plans sought to ensure that man would not be he. The man in the firing line was to be one Stuart de Quincey Walker, former public-school boy, bar owner and smuggler who had previously met Savundra when seeking his backing for one of his many abortive business adventures – a failed arms deal. Walker had what might best be described as 'a reverse Midas touch', but neither that nor his total lack of experience in the insurance business mattered at all.

At the time, London was the world's insurance capital and the industry was run more along the lines of a gentlemen's club than of a business. Walker looked the perfect gentleman, but would play, as instructed, by Savundra's rules. The only qualification required to set him up – in this case as a motor insurer – was that he could show he had available capital of £50,000. What's more, once this capital had been 'shown', it did not have to be deposited or invested in gilt-edged securities. Once shown, it could be spirited away.

A very sensible rule, which required that all insurance companies had to be able to show in their annual accounts that they had liquid capital in excess of £50,000 or 10 per cent of premium income, was effectively invalidated by a clause that inexplicably stated that this rule did not apply to companies in their first two years of trading. Membership of the trade body, the British Insurance Association, was not obligatory and there was no requirement to abide by its rules either – and the Board of Trade's invigilation of the industry was actually circumscribed by law.

For a man heard to boast, 'When you English see a loophole in the law, you drive a Mini through it; I, Savundra, drive a Rolls-Royce', the temptation to set up as an insurer was irresistible.

His first step was to convince the Board of Trade that he had £50,000. He would not have dreamed of using his own cash, so turned instead to his old friend, Count Maxim de Cassan

Floyrac. He would put up £48,000 and both Savundra and Walker, in order to become shareholders, would put up £1,000 each. Floyrac used a Liechtenstein-based trust to provide him with a note of credit for his £48,000 share.

This impressive-looking document was not actually worth the paper it was printed on, but it served to convince the Board of Trade. Formalities having been completed, the impressive-sounding Fire, Auto and Marine Insurance Company (FAM) was registered on 14 February 1963. Its cynical motto: 'Benefit Though Care'.

Stuart Walker was appointed to be managing director, but the strings were actually pulled by Savundra, even though he was not, at this stage, a director. Until he'd tested the water, Savundra billed himself simply as the company's attorney, representing the interests of an important group of foreign investors.

One of the other contemporary advantages of setting up in the insurance business – for Savundra or anyone else – was that the expensive and time-consuming processes of building a sales force or mounting a national advertising campaign were entirely unnecessary. A network of brokers already existed – all of them hungry for the commissions paid for signing up new business. Savundra paid higher commissions on policies that were also very competitively priced. The brokers went for it in droves.

Savundra also protected himself against claims by taking on only those clients least likely to make them: responsible family drivers with a clean insurance record. As a further protection, his policy conditions were so onerous that, according to a seasoned industry observer, 'They ruled out everything but an act of God.'

Not that prospective clients were made aware of the downside. All they knew was that they were getting what looked like a very good deal, and advertisements in the trade press told brokers that they'd be making fat commissions.

Within weeks of setting up in small offices in Baker Street, neither the premises nor the staff could cope with the ever-increasing volume of business. Stuart Walker bit the bullet and took on a whole office block in Orchard Street, just off Oxford Street. Finding staff with qualifications was not so easy, so Savundra decreed that new recruits didn't need any. The only vetting procedure involved assessing the applicant's astrological suitability. The result was chaos.

Savundra eventually discovered that only one of his appointees had any real insurance experience at all. Reg Sutton was quickly made head of the Endorsement and Renewals Department, where he discovered a logjam of some 60,000 unprocessed endorsements and virtually no staff to do the job. Actually, staffing was adequate, but usually staff were somewhere else. So loose was their job description and so poor their supervision that many of them clocked on in the morning and then popped over the road to Selfridges, where they had second jobs as sales assistants. It took Sutton three months to sort out the mess.

Rising blissfully above it all, Savundra turned his mind to improving the company's image in the close-knit insurance world, where his upstart company was regarded with some suspicion. What was needed, he decided, was a company chairman whose integrity and social standing were beyond reproach.

He settled on a distinguished former naval officer called Cecil H Tross Youle OBE, and began to woo him. The process was made easier by the fact that Savundra had acquired a swish Thames pleasure cruiser and had managed to get membership of a club for ex-naval officers co-founded by Tross Youle.

They were soon socially inseparable, but Tross Youle wavered over taking the chairmanship of FAM, so Savundra offered it to another acquaintance, the inveterate gambler Lord Bingham, later to become Lord Lucan. When Tross Youle found out, he was horrified, and said so. He wanted the job – which would detain him for only a couple of days a month – and the £1,000 a year that went with it.

In fact, almost losing the job somehow increased his determination to take it, despite warnings from friends that this was not a good idea and that Savundra was not a good man with whom to do business. But Tross Youle was mesmerised. In a letter he subsequently wrote in Savundra's defence it is clear that he had swallowed the man's story hook, line and sinker. In his eyes, the convicted fraudster had somehow become a martyred hero.

In May 1964, Tross Youle signed on as chairman of FAM – a business about which he knew little and in which he was allowed even less involvement. He was well and truly sidelined— 'kept out from underfoot', as Savundra put it.

Eventually, this proved to be a good thing, because, when the inevitable crash came, it was crystal clear to the Fraud Squad that he had been kept in complete ignorance of what had been going on. He retained his good name, but not his fortune, and narrowly escaped bankruptcy.

At about the time that FAM's fortunes took off, Savundra became embroiled in what was undoubtedly the biggest scandal of the sixties. By the time it had run its course, the Secretary of State for War had been disgraced and forced to resign, and a society portrait painter and osteopath had committed suicide.

Savundra was introduced to Stephen Ward, the osteopath in question, when in need of treatment for a back injury. Through Ward, Savundra met Christine Keeler and later, Mandy Rice-Davies, who shared Ward's flat. At this point, Keeler had been conducting a simultaneous affair with the Secretary of State for War, John Profumo, and with a Russian diplomat suspected of spying. When this fact emerged, after a failed attempt to cover it up, Profumo was forced to resign.

Keeler was then about to move into a flat of her own in Dolphin Square, and Ward suggested to Savundra that he might be paid in kind if he covered her rent. He could also use the flat for assignations with other women who regularly took his fancy.

However, once he'd met Rice-Davies, this proposition was forgotten. Savundra commenced an affair with Mandy, who was generously rewarded with gifts and money. The affair was relatively short-lived, but, when Ward went on trial at the Old Bailey charged with living off immoral earnings, Mandy Rice-Davies's evidence was damning. 'The Indian Doctor', as she called Savundra, always left money on her dressing table, which she routinely shared with Ward.

Savundra's antics were eagerly followed by the satirical *Private Eye* magazine, and he was one of the first dishonest businessmen to attract its attention. Savundra was also one of the first crooks to exploit UK libel law to gag publications such as *Private Eye* and prevent them from publishing damning allegations about him and his business practices.

Extraordinarily, Savundra came through the trial virtually untouched. He was usually referred to in court simply as 'the Indian Doctor' and, on the one occasion his name was mentioned in the newspapers, it was wrongly spelled. His anonymity was preserved and his luck held.

It almost ran out shortly afterwards, however, during an enquiry into his Swiss bank accounts, which, oddly, arose from his long-running interest in ham radio. Two of his more frequent correspondents were fellow hams, Senator Barry Goldwater and Herbert Hoover Jr, but it was his regular calls to Switzerland, via his call sign G3SDN, that aroused police suspicions. They thought he was milking FAM and siphoning money out of the country.

At the behest of the UK authorities, a Swiss Commission of Enquiry was set up to investigate the source of funds flooding into Savundra's numbered account. This was something he could not afford to have happen, and so he dispatched the long-suffering Stuart Walker to Geneva to assess the lie of the land, and then to Tangier, carrying a £3,000 bribe for a local banker.

In return the latter had agreed to sign an affidavit specifying that the deposits had come from sources outside the UK, thereby legitimising Savundra's international transactions. This document was passed to the Commission, via his Swiss bank. Fortunately for Savundra, it was accepted at face value.

As it entered its second year, FAM had become the fastest-growing car-insurance firm in the country. Rival insurance companies looked on in frustration and one of them, General Accident, took advertisements in the national newspapers, warning the public of the risks they were running: 'There is no cheap insurance. As with everything else you get what you pay for. It is dangerous to seek the lowest price just to hold an insurance certificate. . .'

Sour grapes maybe, but the Board of Trade was watching FAM with equal anxiety. However, the antiquated insurance laws under which it then had to operate made it almost impossible for it to intervene in the first two years of a company's existence.

It was against this background that Savundra pulled what he hoped would be his master stoke. He would market the world's first computerised insurance. Not only would this be a good selling point, but it might also help cope with the huge volume of business the company was now transacting.

In December 1963, he ordered from IBM – at vast expense – the most sophisticated computer system then available. It was to carry out all FAM's main underwriting calculations automatically. Punched cards would be fed in one end and policy documents were to be disgorged at the other. Savundra was told it would take two years to install properly, but by a mixture of charm and arm-twisting he got them to agree on a deadline of just four months.

Immediately the computer was installed and had begun churning out its much-publicised 'instant policies' when Savundra took another very ambitious step. He acquired an eight-storey office block on the North Circular Road near Hendon.

No expense was spared in equipping the place on a lavish scale. The executive lavatory cost as much as a small house. Savundra's own office on the top floor was extremely impressive and accessible only by invitation. On the pale-green wall behind his vast desk hung a photograph of himself, apparently chatting warmly with Lord Mountbatten. The picture was not what it seemed, however. After a *Daily Express* powerboat race, in which the speed-addicted Savundra had competed, he tried to persuade the aviator and yachtsman Tommy Sopwith to effect an introduction to Mountbatten. Sopwith refused, but Savundra was undeterred.

Having briefed a freelance photographer to stand by, he marched up to the distinguished earl, proffering his hand and proclaiming that he had served under him 'out East'. Mountbatten smilingly shook hands. The camera clicked for posterity – and recorded Savundra's entirely stage-managed link with Mountbatten.

The luxurious boardroom next door to Savundra's office was regularly used to wine and dine the great, the good, and selected influential journalists – who, Savundra claimed, would all be slipped a £100 note as they left. When one of his executives protested that you shouldn't attempt to bribe Fleet Street's finest, Savundra replied, 'Don't teach your grandmother to suck eggs. I've bribed Cabinet ministers in my time.'

By this stage, Savundra's ego had got the better of him. He now wished to be recognised as the genius behind the great success story that was FAM. Instead of staying on behind the scenes, where he would have been relatively safe come the day of reckoning, he had himself elected vice-chairman of the company and moved out of his relatively modest family home in Hendon to a very grand house in the Bishop's Avenue, Hampstead, popularly known as Millionaire's Row.

There, Pushpam and their five children enjoyed every conceivable luxury and a succession of Rolls-Royces and

Aston Martins adorned the drive. At home at White Walls, the Savundras were perfect and popular hosts. At the office, Emil was usually charm itself. The sweet smell of success wafted all around him and enveloped his staff – most of whom would have done anything for him. Those who wouldn't saw another side of the man: 'Do as I say!' he would bellow. 'See that cupboard over there? It's full of balls. Do you want yours to join them?'

Now directing the business from out front, he ordered a second computer from IBM. Both machines were directly linked to FAM's provincial brokers and could issue a policy in exactly sixty-seven seconds, which was previously unheard of. Even previously nervous brokers were now convinced and Savundra's mighty money machine rolled on ever faster.

Still a speed demon, and now completely carried away with the glamour of offshore powerboat racing, Savundra spent some of that money on a new boat. In fact, to secure it, he bought the yard that built it as well.

The *Jacquie S*, named after his daughter, had three huge American engines and a top speed of more than 50 knots. With it, Savundra was convinced that he could win the 1962 *Daily Express* powerboat trophy and become 'the greatest powerboat racer in the world'.

Unfortunately for him, Savundra had both the enthusiasm and the ineptitude of Mr Toad. Come race day, the boat was poorly prepared and badly driven, and had never been tested in the kind of conditions it would experience off Cowes.

The *Jacquie S* was subjected to a pounding so severe that one of its fuel tanks split, filling the bilges with petrol. Savundra powered on, missing his turning at the first marker buoy, then hitting the crest of a wave with such force that the boat took off in a spectacular leap, followed by a crash landing that permanently damaged Savundra's back. They limped home last.

In search of yet more speed, Savundra struck up a friendship with Donald Campbell, later to die tragically in *Bluebird* while trying to break the world water-speed record on Lake Coniston. While Campbell cultivated Savundra as a possible backer, Savundra picked Campbell's brains and exploited his contacts, having developed an ambition to break the record himself. He also announced that, once he'd won the powerboat race and taken the water-speed record, he would win the America's Cup.

Nothing came of it of course, but Savundra did have the *Jacquie S* fitted with four engines instead of three in preparation for the 1963 *Daily Express* Trophy race. The boat was now even more uncontrollable than it had been previously. Within minutes of the start it had collided with another competitor, almost swamping them both. Recovering his composure, Savundra floored the throttles and shot off erratically in the direction of the Needles lighthouse, where he managed to run the boat up onto the rocks. Somehow, it survived virtually undamaged. Savundra calmly reversed and resumed the race.

He was next to collide with a 30-foot launch called *Skip Jack*, one of the many pleasure craft that lined the course to spectate. *Jacquie S* cut *Skip Jack* clean in two. 'Everyone all right?' called Savundra cheerily before roaring off again, leaving the two halves of *Skip Jack* to sink and other boats to rescue the shocked and soaked passengers and crew – all luckily unhurt.

By this time, the *Jacquie S* was so badly damaged that Savundra had to hoist the yellow flag, signalling his withdrawal. But the next year he was back again, with a much more powerful boat, the *Jacquie S II*. During this race, Savundra managed to avoid the rocks, other competitors and spectators – but the boat broke down and he trailed home fifth.

For the 1965 race, his last, Savundra had the *Jacquie S II* fitted with even more powerful engines, which he had custom-built at the then considerable cost of £5,500 each. The boat was now so fast, he boasted, that it had broken two speedometers. But once again, when used in anger, the boat broke down. By the following year, Savundra was in no position to compete.

However, two years previously, Savundra had been riding a rising tide of premiums, which financed an extravagant lifestyle for both him and Stuart Walker. Savundra splurged tens of thousands of pounds on other abortive business ventures – such as a laser burglar alarm and a proximity fuse for missiles.

He also created a web of thirty-two companies in order to obscure his complicated financial dealings. The most important of these was a secretive, Liechtenstein-based '*anstalt*'[5] company called Merchants and Finance Trust. Officially, it was a merchant bank with the responsibility of investing FAM's funds. In reality it was little more than a pipeline from FAM's unwitting premium payers to Savundra's back pocket.

The 'bank' consisted of no more than a brass plate in Zürich, a ledger in Liechtenstein and another at FAM's head office in London, but its constitution rendered it virtually impenetrable to outsiders. It is estimated that at least a million pounds in premium income passed through it. At today's values, that's around £30 million. So effective was Savundra's system that nobody noticed – until the claims began to arrive in earnest and, in spring 1965, premium income began to fall.

A trial balance sheet drawn up by the firm's accountant showed that FAM was insolvent. Savundra's solution to this problem was to fire the accountant. External accountants reached the same conclusion, but by then Savundra had conjured up another solution. At a meeting in his grand bedroom he produced for the auditors two documents, which he said had been inadvertently overlooked, but which proved the company was solvent after all. One was a 3 per cent Government Bond with a face value of half a million pounds, and the other was a letter from the Merchants and Finance Trust (MFT), which read:

> This is to inform you that the credit balance of the Fire, Auto & Marine Insurance Company in our books on April 30th, 1965, was £77,660 7s 5d. We also confirm that we have purchased on behalf of Fire Auto & Marine Insurance Company and in their name $510,000 15s 10d value of 3 percent Savings Bonds, 1955–1965, for the sum of £500,000, stock certificate in respect of which is attached herein. This last mentioned item is not reflected in our books as an asset held by us.

The letter was signed by one J S Martin on behalf of the MFT board. J S Martin didn't exist, and the stock certificate may have been temporarily purchased or 'borrowed' for the purposes of convincing the auditors – or it may have been forged.

No one will ever know, because Savundra, having passed round the bond, hastily put it back in his briefcase; but, whatever its provenance, it worked like a magic wand. The balance sheet was duly amended to show a healthy surplus of £400,000 instead of a shortfall of £100,000.

However, smoke and mirrors don't pay the bills. Savundra restricted the amount that could be paid out to claimants, with predictable results. The punters didn't like it, and neither did those in FAM's offices who found themselves in the firing line as a result. Some loyal members of staff, swallowing Savundra's line that this was 'only a temporary blip', offered to help out by taking a pay cut, but morale continued to sink and the company secretary abruptly quit.

By April 1966, as the time approached for the second company audit, Savundra drew up the draft balance sheet himself. It showed that the £500,000 Government Bond had been replaced with an £800,000 portfolio of blue-chip investments in companies such as Great Universal Stores, Burmah Oil and the Distillers Company. FAM's reserves, banked with MFT in Liechtenstein, now apparently stood at £877,606.

Much to the puzzlement of his senior executives, Savundra then embarked on a campaign to raise fresh capital. Why was this necessary, they asked, when the company was sitting on such substantial reserves?

'I have run the financial affairs of governments,' Savundra bellowed in response. 'So mind your own business.'

Unfortunately for him, potential investors wanted no part of his business.

The auditors were now demanding to see the share certificates held by MFT, and, after weeks of procrastination and a string of convoluted excuses, he said he was able to produce them, or at least have Stuart Walker do so. Once again, they were quickly circulated round the meeting room and replaced in a folder that Stuart Walker subsequently claimed was collected by a man he'd never seen before to be taken straight back to Zürich. What is certain is that they were never seen again, but, as before, they served their purpose. The audit went through – but the claims kept coming in.

Savundra's aura of invulnerability began to evaporate, and he tried to sell the company to much larger rivals, such as Vehicle & General and Legal & General, for £1.5 million. His sales pitch left them unmoved because he was reluctant to show them the books or provide proof of the company's reserves. Where are those shares, they wanted to know, and where is the interest on them? And, if you do have such significant reserves, why don't you liquidate some of them instead of asking us to bail you out? They got no answers, and Savundra got no takers. He endured a similar round of rebuffs in America.

Savundra had realised before he went to America that, if he failed to attract more capital, his overblown insurance edifice would surely collapse, but he had no intention of going with it. He formed a new insurance company called Transway, which was to be even more streamlined than FAM. It would issue policies and settle claims in seconds. Directors included Donald Campbell and Lord Lucan and the company was headquartered in lavish offices in Pall Mall. Most of the 50,000 shares were issued to another new business called Interstate Trust, which meant that, in the event of another collapse, those responsible would not be in the front line.

In line with his usual business practice, Savundra needed an offshore bank through which to 'disappear' the expected flood of premium income. This time, he created his own, the Security Bank of London, based in Guernsey. His most pressing problem now was how to disentangle himself from the doomed FAM. He summoned the ever-loyal Stuart Walker to his home.

From his sickbed he told Walker that he was extremely ill and would have to seek treatment at his Swiss clinic. Someone else would have to take the reins of FAM, and that someone should be Stuart Walker. With the expected injection of new capital, Savundra claimed, the company would return to profitability and make Walker a very rich man.

He proposed that Walker should buy him out of his shareholding, and, knowing the man had little in the way of liquid assets, made him the following extraordinary offer. He would sell his entire shareholding for the knockdown price of £2,529 – provided that Walker took on Savundra's debts to FAM of £488,285.

Like a rabbit mesmerised by headlights, Walker fell for it – and was left to carry the can. Savundra immediately resigned from the board and from all related directorships and flew to Switzerland. Pushpam and the children remained behind, holed up in Hampstead. From his five-star clinic in Zürich, Savundra made plans to commence operations with Transway Insurance.

Walker, meanwhile, struggled to keep FAM afloat. He was asked to put up the securities allegedly held on the company's behalf by MFT and flew immediately to Zürich, where he was told that the securities actually belonged to someone else. It transpired that the share certificates were all forgeries – albeit of the highest quality. Walker sent out teams of salesmen to little avail, and, as a last-ditch measure, announced that premiums, while remaining competitive, would rise by 30 per cent. It was too late. He was forced to cease trading on 1 July 1966. What had looked like a company in financial trouble had become one of the biggest ever financial frauds.

The liquidators and the Fraud Squad were in the next day to begin an investigation, parts of which were to last ten years. Overnight, 450 people lost their jobs and 400,000 motorists lost their insurance, 43,000 of whom had outstanding claims – some of them involving death and serious injury.

It soon became clear that Walker had been left holding the baby, and all eyes turned to Savundra. At this point, he did what he always did when in a corner: he had another heart attack. Interestingly, according to the Sri Lankan journalist Nalin Fernando, 'Emil told me that he could induce a heart attack any time he wanted to. He even showed me a pill that you could ingest and within a few minutes you would have a coronary. An ECG would be performed and even the best physicians in the world would tell you that you were suffering a massive heart attack.'[6]

So even his coronaries were forgeries. Days after his latest one, he disappeared. He took a taxi to the airport and caught a BOAC flight to Colombo, where he would be out of reach of the British authorities.

As he walked down the gangway of the aircraft, he noticed

a group of armed soldiers and police waiting on the airport apron. Deeply shocked, he collapsed – with a heart attack – this time for real. He came round, not in jail, but in a bedroom at his sister-in-law's house. The armed posse had not been waiting for him, but for the disgraced commander of the Ceylonese Army, who had led an unsuccessful coup six months earlier.

Several days later, Savundra's whereabouts became known and the house was besieged by reporters. He ignored them, but eventually was unable to resist the urge to justify himself in the public eye. He invited one of them in, read out a statement and then threatened to shoot him. The reporter feigned sympathy with Savundra's cause and was rewarded with a long diatribe on how badly he had been misunderstood and how very poorly he was.

The collapse of FAM could not be laid at his door, and he had been in the process of raising new capital when illness struck him down. He then fell back on his pillows, swallowed a handful of tablets and dismissed his guest with a hoarse, 'I could have done great things for the English people' and a feeble wave of his hand.

The next reporter didn't fare so well. He asked Savundra outright what had happened to the money he stole. This question caused a furious Savundra to overcome his medical condition, leap from his bed and beat the poor cowering chap over the head with a drawer from his bedside table. Apart from a black eye and bruising, the brief message he took away from their encounter was that Savundra believed he had been unjustly persecuted in England – a country to which he would never return. And he would never speak to another reporter.

However, he couldn't resist the chance to air his grievances in public, and it wasn't long before he granted audience to a number of impressionable local reporters. He regaled them with stories of his great business success and subsequent betrayal by trusted associates. He was a pioneering entrepreneur whose noble efforts had been frustrated by envious members of an institutionally racist establishment.

'When the true facts are known,' he declaimed, 'the repercussions will be felt right around the world.'

Perhaps he talked himself into believing all this, too, because he then changed his mind about never returning to Blighty: 'Of course I will go back and fight. How could anyone think otherwise?'

Meanwhile, Stuart Walker spent most of his time with the Board of Trade and the press, when he wasn't burning the midnight oil in his office, wrestling with the problems he'd taken on with Savundra's poisoned chalice. Only slowly did it dawn on him that he'd been totally taken in.

He was advised by some of Savundra's criminal friends to stymie the Board of Trade investigation by 'losing' the books, but couldn't bring himself to do it, despite the fact that he was now desperate and virtually broke. Various dubious concerns made rescue proposals to the Official Receiver, but they came to nothing. Savundra himself, in a cheeky attempt to get himself off the hook, suggested that all car insurance should be nationalised.

The public besieged the FAM office and the press did more or less the same at White Walls. Neither achieved anything. By mid-November 1966, the Official Receiver had passed a damning ten-page report to the Director of Public Prosecutions, but the Fraud Squad were still mired in what had turned into an exceptionally complicated investigation, and were not ready for court action.

Then, having written to the Official Receiver to say he that his health was so very fragile that he should be treated lightly, and attaching a long list of cardiologists he claimed would support him, Savundra set off for England on 17 December 1966.

Always the gambler and always betting on himself, in his vanity he seems to have believed that he would win against the odds. And, after all, he had left FAM before the crash – an unfortunate event that had nothing to do with him.

However, he did not keep his appointment with the Official Receiver, scheduled for 9 January 1967, preferring instead to spend Christmas and New Year in Rome. The press thought his promised return was a hoax, but Savundra then issued a challenge to the BBC. He would appear before a television jury in London to account for his actions. He demanded a fee of £100 per second. An hour-long programme would therefore earn him a massive £360,000, which he generously offered to give to disappointed FAM creditors.

When he did eventually reach Heathrow, strutting across the tarmac in his immaculate Savile Row suit towards the waiting reporters he reviled so much, he was brimming with confidence.

'I am like General MacArthur, who said "I shall return" when the Japs drove him out of the Pacific, and I, the great Savundra, am returning in likewise fashion.'

Several days later, in order to demonstrate his poverty, he was chauffeur-driven from White Walls to the labour exchange in Regent's Park Road, to sign on.

Savundra finally came face to face with the Official

Receiver on 23 January and was served with a writ for £386,534 the following day. Walker received one for £216,762. Both also received volumes of hate mail, the worse of it reserved for Savundra. Much of that was actually racist, and some of it seriously threatening. Nevertheless, still believing that he could outface his enemies, and recalling his challenge to the BBC, Savundra decided that he would confront the broadcaster David Frost.

He'd been watching *The Frost Programme* and seen himself sent up in a sketch about cut-price car insurance. He rang in to say he'd actually enjoyed it and an astonished researcher asked if he'd like to come into the studio to be interviewed. He said he'd have to think about it, but minutes later he rang back again to agree. Instead of the £360,000 previously demanded, he settled for the standard fee of 45 guineas.

News of this clash of titans was big news. Neither could afford to be seen as the loser, but Frost had the advantage of controlling the arena. He filled the studio with FAM victims.

Barely minutes before the programme was due to begin, Savundra arrived in a chauffeur-driven limousine to cries of 'Lynch him, lynch him!' from the angry crowd that had gathered outside.

Police struggled to control the demonstrators. Inside the studio, the atmosphere changed from nervous anticipation to near-hysteria as Savundra, beautifully turned out as usual, stepped onto the set and took his seat opposite David Frost. It was television history in the making.

After a short preamble from Frost, the interview began in a relatively restrained fashion. But it wasn't long before Savundra's arrogance let him down. Prompted by heckling from the audience, he spat, 'I am not here to cross swords with peasants! I came here to cross swords with England's greatest swordsman.'

'Nobody is a peasant,' replied Frost. 'These are people who gave you money.'

Savundra kept cool, but his usual charm deserted him. 'They have given me nothing at all!'

'Oh yes we have!' shouted the increasingly angry audience.

Point followed telling point, as Savundra's denials and obfuscations began to anger Frost too. Two widows in the audience were singled out. One, left with no income and three children to provide for, had been offered just £500. The other had actually received a cheque for £7,000 – but it bounced. Their heart-rending stories elicited a heartless and selfish response: 'All these stories which I have heard make me realise only too well that my selling out was the wisest thing I ever did.'

The anger in the studio was palpable. 'What about us?' yelled the audience.

Now it was Savundra's turn to lose his composure. Frost accused him of being involved in a 'fake deal' and asked how his resignation could have absolved him of all moral responsibility. Eyeball to eyeball, the two men battled it out, and the interview ended with a diatribe from Savundra about the British democratic system, which he blamed for all his woes, including the demise of FAM. This left Frost shaking with anger and indignation and an audience, now on its feet, booing with rage as a furious Savundra strode out of the studio.

It had been riveting viewing, but was roundly condemned as 'trial by television'. A week later, Savundra was arrested and charged, later to face trial by jury.

In fact, he was initially charged on only two specimen

counts of fraud and forgery, because *The Frost Programme* had forced the hand of the Director of Public Prosecutions. It took a further year before the investigations were complete and the case was ready for trial. Start Walker was to join him in the dock.

On 10 January 1968, Savundra, now aged forty-four, stepped into Court Number One at the Old Bailey. After several days of legal argument, the case began. Whereas Savundra's trial by David Frost had been short and devastatingly sharp, his trial by jury was to be a very traditional, almost leisurely affair. Savundra seemed to revel in it, behaving more like the lawyer he might have been than the prisoner. Observers had to keep reminding themselves that this was the accused.

Counsel for the Crown, the aptly named Mr Buzzard, circled and tracked his way through FAM's labyrinthine affairs – the setting up of MFT in Liechtenstein, the conspiracy to steal £600,000 in premiums from motorists, the forging of bonds and share certificates, the false accounting, and so on – documented in some 2,400 pages of evidence.

As the trial progressed, documents and bound transcripts of evidence piled up on Judge King-Hamilton's desk until eventually he could barely see over them.

Witness after witness attested to Savundra's misuse of great natural charm and a powerful personality to get what he wanted, regardless. They spoke of his persuasive powers and his innovative ideas, of his extravagance and total lack of scruples – and they made much of his ego. According to Tross Youle, 'Savundra regarded himself as one of the world's great geniuses.'

The Great Genius eventually took the stand a month after

proceedings had commenced. As reported in one newspaper, 'The podgy figure in the suit of a City gentleman took the rostrum at the Old Bailey and with majestic sweeps of his slender brown hands gave his final performance before the hyper-critical eye of justice.' He boasted of his pioneering use of the computer in insurance transactions, and, thumping the witness box for emphasis, completely denied doing anything wrong.

'Did you knowingly use or utter documents that were not genuine or true?' Savundra thumped the witness box again: 'Under no circumstances at all!'[7]

'Were you ever knowingly a party to putting forward any balance sheet or other record of account which contained a false entry or false assertion?'

With another thump of the witness box, Savundra almost shouted, 'Again, emphatically no!'

He claimed that he'd left FAM on doctor's orders, having been given the alternative of learning to play the harp.

'That is a picturesque way of saying you would put your life at risk?'

'Yes.'

When asked to answer questions more briefly and to the point, he replied, 'It is very difficult to be an Anglo-Saxon when one is not.'

Savundra's treatment of learned counsel alternated between amused tolerance and flashes of anger. Awkward questions – about MFT or his treatment of his co-defendant, or his opinion of himself – would be shrugged off, seemingly with infinite patience. 'I suggest, sir, that the question is not worthy of you,' he would say with a dismissive wave of his hands. Or, with a sad shake of his head, 'I'm afraid that your instructions are hopelessly wrong, sir. I suggest that you must re-inform yourself about this matter.'

He was less restrained when it was suggested that his 'lively imagination' had enabled him to substitute Walker's actions for his own. 'I suggest sir,' he shouted, 'you have been paid to use your imagination yourself.'

Not for the first (or last) time the judge had to intervene, warning him not to be offensive to counsel and that he was not doing his case any good by trying to be too clever. 'Sitting there in court Number One,' wrote one newspaper reporter, 'I marvelled at his cleverness – and his stupidity.'

Of his pre-FAM ventures, Savundra would say little under questioning. He maintained that he did have business dealings with national leaders such as Kwame Nkrumah and Pandit Nehru and had handled monies for the Vatican, but could not say more; nor could he say anything at all about his Chinese oil deal, because he claimed that would be in breach of the Official Secrets Act.

The failure of FAM, he insisted, was all down to Stuart Walker, 'a once decent man who had become dissipated, lazy, greedy and unreliable'. He went on to assert that Walker also controlled MFT and that he, Savundra, got involved only in the latter stages of running the company.

'Walker started coming in later and later every morning and asking for more and more Alka-Seltzer.'

And it was only the sudden death of Walker's mysterious and untraceable friend Sultan Achmed Mohammed Pashsa that prevented MFT from lending money to FAM at the crucial time, because nothing could be done until his estate had been wound up.

Meanwhile, the £10 million pound capital injection

Savundra said he had arranged from First National Bank of Boston inexplicably failed to arrive – and, even if it had, he now realised that Walker was not up to running the company. As he chose to put it, 'Some people are born to sit in the driving seat, and others to ride in the dicky.'

Asked whether he was trying to make his former good friend into the fall guy, Savundra replied, 'If you are suggesting that I am the Big Bad Wolf and Walker is Little Red Riding Hood, you may as well take him back to the Baby Bunting stage.'

All in all, Savundra spent twenty-eight hours in the witness box, being taken through every twist and turn of the FAM story. He held up very well – some say he dominated the proceedings – but by the end of his evidence the strain was beginning to show. He slumped down on the steps of the witness box, buried his head in his hands and began to sob bitterly. A prison officer offered him a handkerchief and a phial of smelling salts. Savundra slowly recovered his composure, inhaled deeply from the phial, swallowed several tablets, and was led from the court.

Towards the end of his last day of evidence, it was suggested to Savundra that, 'you embarked upon this FAM enterprise and conducted its affairs for more than two years to provide yourself with an extravagant living.'

Speaking almost in a whisper, Savundra replied that he had done his utmost to modernise and computerise the insurance business. He then found a new villain of the piece, a new cause for his company's failure, portraying himself as a lonely David facing an army of Goliaths. 'I was bludgeoned out of existence by the giants. I should have known better than to engage in war against the enormous forces ranged against me.'

Stuart Walker, the man whom Savundra had spent most of his time trying to blame, could not have made a more contrasting impression on the court. Thin, balding and bookish, and speaking softly, almost obsequiously, he claimed he knew nothing about the forgeries, little about Savundra's past and nothing about the reality of MFT. He had taken money from the company only because Savundra had told him he could.

Walker didn't entirely convince the court. His evidence was described as 'a skilful mixture of truth and falsehood', but he was generally seen as Savundra's subordinate. Indeed, the prosecuting QC, in his closing address, told the jury that, though both men were undoubtedly guilty of the main charge – conspiracy to defraud – they should consider carefully whether Walker was involved in the first big step in that fraud, the use of a forged £500,000 Government Bond.

The two leading counsel for the defence were now at odds. Mr Shaw, for Savundra, said the evidence showed his client was not an evil genius and that Walker was the man responsible for running MFT. Mr Lyons, for Walker, said almost exactly the opposite.

Eventually, nearly three months after the trial began, Judge King-Hamilton began his summing-up. He carefully led the jury through the whole convoluted case. It took him nearly eleven hours, but in the end, he said, it all boiled down to one simple question: 'In doing what they did, were Savundra and Walker acting honestly, doing what they sincerely believed was in the best interests of FAM and the policyholders, or were they acting dishonestly and not in the interests of the policyholders, but fraudulently and in their own interests?'

It took the jury just four and a half hours to decide that

they were – and that Savundra had been in charge from Day One. Walker was found not guilty of using that forged £500,000 bond.

As the verdicts were read out, Savundra clutched the rail of the dock and closed his eyes; Walker stood stiffly to attention, biting his lip. Neither man ever looked at the other. When it was all over, Savundra remained slumped in the dock. The drive, self-belief and ebullience that had carried him through the trial had completely deserted him. Eventually, a prison officer led him and Walker down to the cells.

Savundra soon recovered enough to launch an appeal against his conviction. It was doomed to fail, and he was sentenced to eight years' imprisonment and a fine of £50,000, in default of which he would serve a further two years.

Walker got five years and a £3,000 fine. Savundra then appealed against the judgment to the Master of the Rolls and then to the House of Lords. Both rejected the appeal, so Savundra launched another appeal against the length of his sentence, on the ground that his trial had been prejudiced by the Frost interview. Lord Justice Salmon quashed the appeal, but not before he had condemned the television programme as 'deplorable', and concluded, 'Trial by television will not be tolerated in a civilised country. This court hopes that no interview of this kind will ever again be televised.'

His Lordship then found it necessary to define more clearly the balance between fair trial and free comment. The resulting dictum about the perils to those who went on air or into print 'having good reason to suspect that proceedings were imminent' has since given many a journalist a sleepless night.

Savundra was refused permission to appeal again to the House of Lords. Inexplicably, his entire court battle was legally aided, while at the same time he was turning up every day in a Rolls-Royce. He was to exchange that for a Black Maria on his way to Wormwood Scrubs. Meanwhile, he had been declared bankrupt, but at his public examination by the Registrar, refused to answer any questions.

Partly as a result, nobody ever found out what really happened to 'the missing millions' that were milked from FAM, and Savundra himself showed no contrition and admitted no responsibility for what had happened.

Prisoner number 9630 was released from jail on 4 October 1974, having served just over six and a half years of his ten-year sentence. He announced his intention to take his case to the European Court of Human Rights, but nothing came of it.

The next big earner was to be the sale of Pushpam's family estates in North Ceylon. It seems the Americans wanted this territory, near the old British airbase at Trincomalee, for the establishment of a strategic nuclear base. However, the $200,000,000 deal was predicated on Pushpam's becoming Queen of North Ceylon, something that was never going to happen.

White Walls had long gone, so Savundra and Pushpam now lived almost reclusive lives in a relatively small house at Old Windsor. Two years after leaving prison, and four days before Christmas 1976, Savundra's heart gave out, genuinely and for good. He was fifty-three.

Perhaps the best summary of Savundra the man came in the form of a revealing, if backhanded, compliment at his trial: 'He is no ordinary mortal,' said Rudolf Lyons QC, 'and, if he is a crook, he is no ordinary crook. He is a man with a tremendous and fantastic personality, something of a genius with an uncanny knowledge of the law relating to companies in England, America and the Continent.'

Like so many of those featured in this book, one wonders if such genius might have produced as much, if not more, profit if deployed honestly.

5

MICHAEL JEFFERY: THE GREAT ROCK'N'ROLL RIP-OFF

At 11.45 a.m. on Sunday, 18 January 1970, James Marshall Hendrix was pronounced dead on arrival at St Mary Abbot's Hospital, Kensington, West London. He had apparently overdosed on sleeping pills and red wine, and had asphyxiated on his own vomit.

In just four short years Jimi Hendrix had rocketed from utter obscurity to international stardom. He revolutionised and redefined the electric guitar, songwriting and performing. Together with drummer Mitch Mitchell and bass player Noel Redding, Hendrix synthesised blues, jazz and rock into a new and visceral musical force.

The Jimi Hendrix Experience (as the band were called) had an enormous influence on musicians all over the world (Eric Clapton, then in his pomp as an official rock deity, was an early and awestruck fan). And the Hendrix musical legacy has permeated even the very vocabulary of modern music:

the term 'heavy metal' was coined in an attempt to describe the furious combination of his pounding rhythms, feedback and sheer volume.

But Hendrix bequeathed something even more potent and long-lasting than his musical legacy: a labyrinthine international financial mystery bound up in a web of court cases that dwarf even Dickens's infamous *Jarndyce v. Jarndyce* law suit from *Bleak House*.

At the heart of the mystery are two simple questions. Since Hendrix recorded only four albums prior to his death, how is it that there are now more six hundred releases bearing his name? And how could it be that a man who bestrode the world like a true rock god – commanding huge audiences, vast adulation and massive record sales – died with just a few thousand dollars to his name?

The answer to both questions is the same: Michael Jeffery.

You *really* had to want to find Noel Redding. It had taken us several hours already, navigating roads that bordered occasionally on the suicidal: potholes, sheep and people seemed equally uninterested in our safety or (where appropriate) theirs. In 1986 taking the road from Dublin to Clonakilty was definitely an adventure.

We could, in theory, have got a bit closer by flying into the nearest airport. But, in those pre-budget-airline days, Cork Airport was not exactly overburdened with flight options, and the seemingly ever-present fog tended to make travel plans utterly unreliable. And so we drove.

Even today Clonakilty is not a big town. It may have been named (in an EU-sponsored competition) Best Emerging Rural Tourism Destination 2007, and its website may hold out the enticing – if altogether unlikely – promise, '50 Ways to Enjoy Clonakilty', but it is, in truth, still a small market town in deepest West Cork. Back in 1986 it was smaller still and determinedly sleepy. Which at least made it easy to abandon the car in the middle of the main street and ask directions from someone who looked like an extra from *Ryan's Daughter*.

Noel Redding really, really wanted a quiet life. He didn't even live in Clonakilty itself, but in a tiny hamlet several miles further on. But, once we were there, his ramshackle, tumbledown farmhouse – all loose gutterings, damp walls and missing roof tiles – wasn't difficult to locate. It's not every house that's called Dun Owin.

Redding had first met Jimi Hendrix in September 1966. He'd gone to audition as a new guitarist for the (then) top British band the Animals in a basement nightclub off Jermyn Street in London's Soho. But the Animals' bass player, Chas Chandler, had other ideas. He'd just become the co-manager of a slightly wild-looking American guitarist, so he steered Redding over to a corner and introduced them. Within an hour Noel Redding was officially Hendrix's bass player: Hendrix was twenty-three, Redding just twenty.

The following month they had a drummer, Mitch Mitchell, and on 11 October the three musicians signed the first of what would become a welter of confusing and often contradictory contracts. And then they set off to conquer the world.

For the next four years the Jimi Hendrix Experience rehearsed, recorded and toured almost continuously. The gigs were high-profile and increasingly rapturously received. From the earliest crowds of a few hundred, they were very soon playing to thousands. TV shows all over Europe quickly followed. Singles shot up the charts, gig followed gig, and adoring fans flocked to follow the Experience. As Redding recalled, 'It began to get crazy. We'd get ambushed and mauled going to gigs. Girls in the audience would scream our names louder than we could play our songs.'

The Jimi Hendrix Experience had done the musical equivalent of accelerating from zero to full speed without time to stop and think. Had they done so, they might have spotted the clues that, by start of 1967, they were on course not just for international stardom but for lead roles in the Greatest Rock'n'Roll Rip-off ever.

For a start they were all being paid wages of just £15 a week. Given that their very first short tour to Paris in the autumn of 1966 had earned thousands – and that short tour was followed by a grinding but highly lucrative schedule of concerts all over Britain and Germany – a combined weekly wage of just £45 was a little bit on the low side.

Redding kept a diary of the band's appearances: page after page of gigs, TV shows, radio sessions and personal appearances. The money was pouring in – but the three band members were habitually skint and frequently reduced to scrounging strings, plectrums, spare guitars and replacement amplifiers.

Where on earth was the money going?

Nassau is the capital, largest city, and commercial centre of the Commonwealth of the Bahamas, an archipelago of two thousand cays and seven hundred islands set in the Atlantic roughly 200 miles south of Florida. Situated on New Providence Island, it is a sleepy sort of town where the loudest thing around is probably the clothing sported by the tens of thousands of American tourists who flock there each year.

Nevertheless, it is a Mecca for offshore companies seeking secrecy and favourable tax status. And it was here, in 1966, that Mike Jeffery decided to establish a new company called Yameta Ltd.

Jeffery was – possibly still is – a deliberately enigmatic figure. Born in South London in 1933, the only child of two post office workers, Michael Frank Jeffery left school in 1949 and got a job as a clerk for Mobil, one of the dominant oil companies of the day.

But these were Britain's immediate postwar years. National Service was still very much in force and in 1951, at the statutory age of eighteen, Jeffery was called up to give his compulsory year and a half to Queen and country. He was, by the few accounts anyone has managed to scrape together, a noticeably bright young man. Although men drafted into National Service were pressed into combat in Britain's post-colonial wars in Kenya, Malaya and Cyprus, postwar conscription placed some value on education – and in developing likely minds. After all, so the military brass reasoned, you never know when you might need a bright young man.

Mike Jeffery scored particularly well in science tests and seems to have been assigned not to front line fighting but to the Army Educational Corps. And he apparently liked the service life. At the end of his eighteen months – and just as rock and roll was being born – he signed on as a regular professional soldier. Once again he seems to have avoided any kind of duty involving rifles and ammunition. Instead he joined the Intelligence Corps. And at this point information about his army career simply evaporates.

Diligent digging by a pair of Jimi Hendrix's subsequent

biographers – Harry Shapiro and Caesar Glebbeek – reveals a tantalising glimpse of what the man may have been up to. They report that Jeffery often boasted of:

> Undercover work against the Russians, of murder, mayhem and torture in foreign cities... His father says Mike rarely spoke about what he did – itself perhaps indicative of the sensitive nature of his work – but confirms that much of Mike's military career was spent in 'civvies,' that he was stationed in Egypt and that he could speak Russian. [Harry Shapiro and Caesar Glebbeek, Electric Gypsy, William Heinemann, 1990.]

Whatever the truth, in the early 1960s, Mike Jeffery finally abandoned army life and embraced rock and roll. He had somehow acquired a nightclub in Newcastle on Tyne – the Club A-Go-Go – and became the manager of a promising local rhythm-and-blues outfit called the Animals.

This was the time of the boom in British pop: Liverpool had a thriving beat scene, Birmingham was nurturing the extraordinary talent that would yield up bands as diverse as the Moody Blues, Electric Light Orchestra and Led Zeppelin. But Newcastle on Tyne was out on something of a limb, so Mike Jeffery approached a London agent, seeking help to get his newly acquired band noticed.

There are many stories about Don Arden, the man Jeffery hooked up with. None of them are favourable. He was then one of Britain's leading pop impresarios, but his rapacious contracts and negotiating methods with acts who had the temerity to ask for their money were frequently less than subtle.

He repeatedly threatened to throw both rivals and clients from his second-floor office windows and had a nasty reputation for attempting to strangle those who disagreed with him. One lead guitarist had his hand crushed in a vice until he 'saw sense'. Not for nothing did he enjoy the sobriquet of 'the Al Capone of Pop'.

His own daughter, the recent queen of television talent shows, Sharon Osbourne, was estranged from Arden for twenty years after he set his dogs on her during a dispute over who would manage her subsequent husband, the heavy-metal star Ozzy Osbourne. He also volubly (and, it has to be said, entertainingly) threatened – on air – truly unpleasant repercussions during one of the early radio investigations for our BBC series *Checkpoint*. Such was the man from whom Mike Jeffery chose to learn.

Arden agreed a deal with Jeffery: in return for bringing the Animals to London and putting them on at the influential Scene Club, he became co-manager and assumed sole ownership of all rights to promote the band throughout the world.

Given that the very next year the Animals had a Number 1 hit in Britain, America and several other countries with 'House of the Rising Sun', Jeffery could feel well pleased with his investment. Unfortunately, the Animals were rather less impressed. Within a year the band were in turmoil. They complained bitterly that Jeffery was flogging the creativity out of them in pursuit of ever more numerous gigs and a punishing recording schedule. Keyboard player and founder member Alan Price left and, by 1966, even the amiable Chas Chandler had had enough. He decided to quit and move into managing acts on his own. Jimi Hendrix was his first signing.

In theory, Chandler was rich. The Animals had been a

chart-topping band for more than two years and money had flowed into the band's coffers. The problem was they had no control over those coffers and no idea where they had been hidden.

'Frankly,' Chandler was later to recall for us, 'the whole thing was a complete bloody mess. And only Mike Jeffery knew what was going on. The problem was that he was a devious bugger at the best of times.'

Jeffery's version of events – as given to the Animals – was that he had invested their income in an offshore tax haven and thus saved them from the predations of Harold Wilson's Labour government. And, since the government was then starting to run into the choppy seas of economic disaster, the explanation seemed plausible. But it didn't make it any easier for the band members to get their hands on what they'd earned.

It should have been a warning sign for what would happen to the Jimi Hendrix Experience; yet somehow Chandler was persuaded to let Jeffery co-manage the band.

On 12 May 1967, the Experience released their first album. *Are You Experienced* contained none of the three Top Ten singles the Experience had already racked up. Despite this, it shot to Number 2 in the album charts: only the Beatles' seminal *Sgt Pepper's Lonely Hearts Club Band* kept it off the top spot, but it stayed in the charts for more than a hundred weeks. It was the same story in America: *Are You Experienced* shot to Number 5 in the US album charts and resolutely kept on selling for month after month after month.

At the end of a triumphant British tour, Jeffery booked the Experience in for an extraordinary European blitz: the band were to play seventeen gigs in fifteen days in countries right across Western Europe. And, in between, they had to fit in TV shows.

Noel Redding, always the canniest of the three band members, began wondering what was happening to all the money. He, Mitch Mitchell and Hendrix himself were still receiving wages of only £25 a week: yet they were playing sell-out concerts and had a massive international album hit; and Jeffery was busy signing contracts with European record labels and television stations, each netting tens of thousands of dollars a time.

The stimulus for Redding was finding himself stony broke at London airport *en route* to that seventeen-date European tour. He had to borrow a pound from one of the band's entourage just to buy a pack of cigarettes.

'It brought on a serious discussion within the group,' he would recall twenty years later. 'We discovered we were clearing more than £300 a night profit from each gig – a fortune in those days when flights were as cheap as the hotel rooms we had to share – and yet we were getting these pitiful wages.'

A confrontation with Jeffery led to a pay rise: weekly wages were to be £45, plus a £500 advance each for expenses on the forthcoming American tour.

'We were naïve I suppose. We were musicians, not breadheads, and, when Jeffery made the right noises and smoothed some of our feathers, we went away happy. Until the next time.'

The American tour was short, but culminated in what was widely expected to be the biggest musical event of the decade: the Monterey Pop Festival. The festival, held on the Californian town's county fairground, was billed as the ultimate expression of the Summer of Love. The roll call of performers was extraordinary and, as a result, almost a quarter of a million people flocked to Monterey.

The Experience had been booked on the express recommendation of Paul McCartney and the gig was to be the tipping point for the band in America. Although *Are You Experienced* had cracked the US album chart the band didn't receive much in the way of mainstream airplay or attention. The forty-five-minute set at Monterey changed all that.

At the end of the performance Hendrix squatted down on the stage and set fire to his guitar. As the flames flared up the audience went wild. From that moment on, the Jimi Hendrix Experience officially joined the ranks of rock superstars. Years later, Jimi was acclaimed by *Rolling Stone* magazine as number one on their list of the hundred best guitarists of all time.

Back then, backstage, a wild and adrenaline-fuelled party began. The three band members were offered a smorgasbord of drink, drugs and adoring women. It took Chas Chandler more than half an hour to fight his way through the throng, but, when he did, he was astonished to find the Experience meekly lined up before a livid Mike Jeffery. The manager of the newly crowned rock gods was delivering a vicious tongue-lashing: how, he wanted to know, could they have contrived to damage a microphone stand? Didn't they know how much these things cost? The answer was $150.

In the heady, dope-laden atmosphere of the late 1960s, Jeffery cut a very odd figure. Photographs – such few as there are – show a man given to Roger Moore-style safari suits and distinctly unfashionable spectacles. And he seemed to have little understanding of the sort of music the

Experience were pioneering. A month after Monterey, he breathlessly told the band of his latest managerial coup: they were to support the squeaky-clean and utterly synthetic Monkees on a short US tour.

Given that the Monkees' fan base was at best indifferent (and generally downright hostile) to the sort of wild, drug-influenced musical experimentation favoured by Hendrix, the plan could end only one way. And so it proved. It was a miserable experience for all concerned – save Jeffery. For him, the financial rewards were all that mattered.

1967 was the Experience's *annus mirabilis*. The next two years – while extraordinarily lucrative – saw the band begin to fall apart. Two more chart-topping albums and a brutal touring schedule raked in millions of dollars, but drugs, drink and – above all – worries over money were beginning to sap their strength.

True to form, Noel Redding at least tried to get a handle on where the band's earnings were going. Not that it did him much good.

'Whenever I asked I was told, "All the money is being sent down to Nassau – and you won't have to pay any tax." And I'd say, "Great: when do we get it?" To which the response would be, "Er... look, just don't worry . . ." '

Jeffery persuaded Redding and Mitchell to fly to the Bahamas to see for themselves the magical place that was preserving all their hand-earned cash and keeping it from the voracious clutches of the tax man.

'Jeffery acted like someone from the Nassau tourist board. Everything was great there – fantastic business opportunities: why not buy some land? I thought to myself, "I'm a muso: what do I want with a bit of some island in the

Atlantic?" But Jeffery made it sound like Heaven on earth and so we went.

'I realised one thing straight away: this place was about as far from Heaven as it gets. The people were hostile and the luxury hotel ($100 a night – to be deducted from our earnings, naturally) took one look at our hair and clothes and promptly lost our reservations.'

Redding and Mitchell returned home to England and resumed the soul-destroying, grinding schedule of gigs, recording and TV shows. They didn't know it but they had, in truth, had a lucky escape. Their co-manager, Chas Chandler, would later have a much more frightening experience when he flew down to inspect Mike Jeffery's favourite financial bolthole.

'I first went to the bank where Yameta Ltd was meant to keep its accounts,' Chandler told us in 1986. 'They didn't seem very helpful, so after a bit of furtling around I located what was supposed to be some kind of office where I could draw out some of my share of the money from the Experience. Except that, when I asked to do so, the bloke behind the desk drew and gun and suggested I might like to leave quite quickly – for the good of my health, sort of thing.'

As the sixties drew to an end so did the Jimi Hendrix Experience. Redding was fed up with the atmosphere surrounding the band, and particularly displeased to discover that his share of the enormous proceeds from playing New York's Madison Square Garden was approximately $40. Ticket sales alone had exceeded $100,000.

On 30 June 1969, he officially walked out of the Experience and began casting around to form his own band. He assumed that he must be a rich man – after all, the band's earnings were, in theory, safely tucked away for them in the Bahamas.

Hendrix carried on in various concert and recording incarnations. But he too was finally beginning to worry about money. He had decided to build his own recording studio and by early 1970 the project was more than halfway completed. Suddenly, he discovered that he didn't have enough cash to finish the job.

According to his biographer, Curtis Knight, Hendrix announced, 'I know I have been spending a lot of money lately but I have also been making a lot of money and I was shocked to learn what my financial situation is. I had a lot of faith in the people that were handling my affairs – I trusted them. But there are definitely going to be some changes made. The vultures have lived off me long enough.'[8]

Away from the limelight, Noel Redding set about investigating where all the Experience's money had gone. He began with Yameta Ltd, the supposed safe-haven company keeping the band's revenue safe from the British taxman.

Perhaps if Redding had known at the outset that his investigations would take seventeen years, all of his remaining (and subsequent) money and still get him absolutely nowhere, he might have thought twice. As it was, he plunged headlong into the labyrinth of front companies and corporate brass plates that Mike Jeffery had created.

In 1986, perched on an old stool behind a mountain of files and paper, Redding tried to talk us through the maze. Scarecrow thin, but with big hair and NHS wire-rimmed glasses, he had a look of perpetual puzzlement as he leafed through page after closely typed page.

'I'm just a muso, man. I was never going to work this lot

out. While the Experience was on the road or in the studio, we didn't have time to be businessmen, even if we'd been up to it. We were turned over, man, by a bunch of faceless bastards.

'The money was meant to have been sent to Yameta Ltd in Nassau. But, when I investigated, I discovered that Yameta Ltd seemed to be a front company. It was owned by the Caicos Trust, which had an address of care of the Bank of Nova Scotia. In turn that had an address of care of the Bank of New Providence. I spent years following the paper trail round all these little islands. And I still haven't found where my money went.'

What he did unearth was an extraordinary treasure trove of documents: contracts between Hendrix, the various band members and Jeffery that in some cases Redding had never seen, much less agreed to. Some contradicted or conflicted with the others, but the unifying factor of each was, inevitably, the generous portions of their earnings the Experience were apparently signing over to their managers.

Redding, though, wasn't the only one surprised by the contracts: Chas Chandler was equally nonplussed when we showed him some of the contracts – especially the ones that bore what purported to be his signature.

'I've looked at these now and I can tell you that they're really poor forgeries by Mike Jeffery. In fact, on two of them, Jeffery even signed his own name under the space for my name, as well as in the bit he was supposed to sign.

'He was always trying to get the boys to sign one piece of paper after another. I think he worked on the basis that the more pieces of paper there were the more confusing it would be.

'He really had a very convoluted mind. He was like an

idiot genius. In all the time I knew him I came to realise that he got more thrill out of stealing a pound than earning one honestly.'

When Hendrix died, Chandler joined Redding, Mitchell and a host of others who had worked with the band to mourn his loss. But not Mike Jeffery. Biographers John McDermott and Eddie Kramer spoke to Jim Marron, a nightclub owner from Manhattan, who was on holiday with Jeffery in Spain when news of Hendrix's death reached him.

'We were supposed to have dinner that night in Majorca,' Marron recalled. 'Jeffery called me from his club in Palma saying that we would have to cancel... I've just got word from London. Jimi's dead.'

Apparently, far from being devastated, the manager of the Jimi Hendrix Experience took the news completely in stride. 'I always knew that son of a bitch would pull a quickie,' Jeffery told Marron.

Marron could barely believe Jeffery's reaction. 'Basically, he had lost a major property. You had the feeling that he had just lost a couple of million dollars – and was the first to realise it.'[9]

At the time of Hendrix's death, Jeffery had a worldwide empire of nightclubs, properties and mysterious companies on off-shore tax havens, from Nassau to Curaçao. He also had Noel Redding on his trail.

By 1973 one of several complex legal actions that Redding had filed against his managers was steadily steaming towards a court hearing.

In March his lawyers were gearing up take a deposition from Jeffery – an American legal procedure by which Jeffery would be forced to answer a series of questions, in person and recorded by a stenographer. This testimony would then be used – perhaps against him – in the court hearings. But the deposition never took place.

That March, French air traffic controllers had gone on strike. Military controllers were called in as emergency replacements for the civilian staff, but, because they were much less familiar with the systems, all air traffic was reduced, delayed and subject to stringent rules about when and in which 'channels' planes could fly.

On the morning of Monday, 5 March, Mike Jeffery was booked on an Iberian Airlines DC-9 from Majorca to London. He was supposed to be attending court in one of the preliminary hearings over Jimi Hendrix's estate.

But the DC-9 had been accidentally assigned to the same flight path or channel over the French city of Nantes as another aircraft. In what an inquiry would later determine was an accident caused by 'imprecise navigation, lack of complete radar coverage and imperfect radio communications', the two planes collided. The DC-9 crashed, killing all sixty-one passengers and seven crew.

But none of their remains were ever located and Noel Redding was not entirely convinced that Mike Jefferies had been on board.

'I must admit that I have got doubts. Jeffery had a real thing about flying. He would regularly book on a flight, deliberately miss it and catch the next – almost like some superstition about getting better odds on a safe flight.

'I really wouldn't put it past him to have done that on March 5 and, when he heard about the crash, to have seized the opportunity to disappear with all the loot. He was a quick thinker and it would have been completely in character for him to do this.

egor MacGregor.

Dr Emil Savundra making his feelings clear as he leaves a Board of Trade meeting in January 1967.

Frank Abagnale Jr and, *bottom*, with Leonardo DiCaprio, who played him in the movie of his life, *Catch Me If You Can*, and Tom Hanks, who played his nemesis agent Carl Hanratty, not based on a real person.

Top: Barry Edward Gray.

Bottom: Victor Lustig.

Top: Peter Foster outside Carole Caplin's house at the height of the media interest in his connection with Cherie Blair in 2002.

Bottom: Foster at Suva hospital in Fiji in November 2006. To his left is his mother.

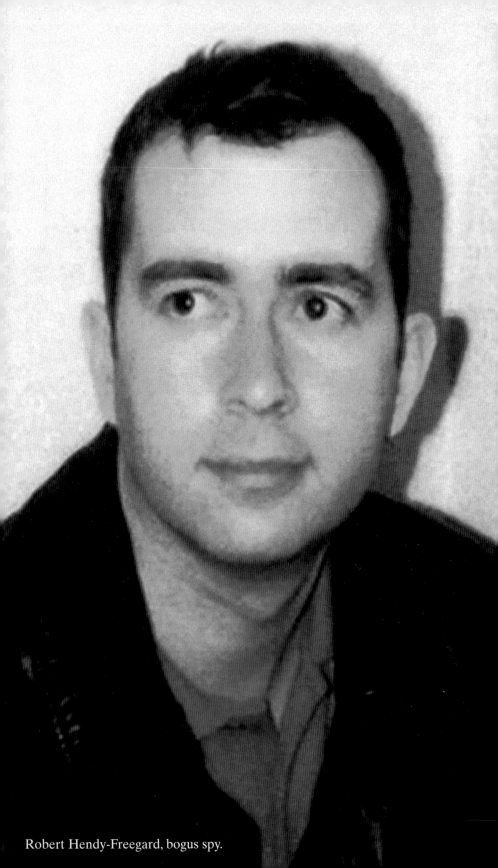

Robert Hendy-Freegard, bogus spy.

FBI Special Agent Jaclyn Zappacosta assisted in the Freegard case.

cent victims of Hardy-Freegard's cruel and prolonged deception: *right*: Caroline Cowper, solicitor.

om right: Maria Hendy.

John Palmer leaves the Old Bailey in April 2001.

'And no one knew how much he stashed away of the Experience's money, and the Animals' money, too, for that matter. We just knew it was a hell of a lot.[10] But the net was closing in on him: his main earner was dead and he was about to be put through the deposition [process] in my suit against him. What better time to slip away and live happily ever after with all his ill-gotten gains?'

In the end, none of Noel Redding's lawsuits yielded very much in the way of financial recompense. By 1986 he had spent around $80,000 chasing the spiral of Jeffery's companies around the world. In desperation, he signed a once-and-for-all settlement giving him barely more than he had already spent. At that stage, he estimated his losses – conservatively – at £6 million.

We left him in a bar in Clonakilty. The man who had played Monterey Pop Festival in the Summer of Love and helped to sell out Madison Square Garden in New York was reduced to playing pub gigs in a remote corner of southwest Ireland. Still, the £10 he took home in his pocket was his to keep.

The only real money he ever made from the Experience was, initially, reluctantly earned. The second time we visited him in Clonakilty, part of the farmhouse roof was falling in and he couldn't afford to have it fixed. We suggested that the Fender jazz bass that he'd played with Hendrix was probably a very valuable collector's item (one of Jimi's Fender Stratocasters had recently sold for over $100,000) and that now might be the time to sell it. Noel shook his head vigorously.

'I could never do that,' he said dolefully. 'It's part of me, man.'

We stayed in touch and, the next time we met, he was

smartly turned out and altogether more chipper. He'd had the roof fixed and bought a newer car – but how?

'Remember that jazz bass I wouldn't sell?' he asked with an impish grin, 'Well I've sold four of 'em now!'

And there, in 1986, the story might have ended. Except that somebody, somewhere, was still making a lot of money out of Jimi Hendrix and the Experience.

The band had released just three studio albums, with a fourth live recording issued almost immediately after Hendrix's death. Yet by 1986 Noel Redding had been able to show us a stack of eighty-four separate Hendrix albums. The proceeds from some of these appeared still to funnelling to Yameta Ltd, down in Nassau.

Twenty years on and that pile of eighty-four albums has grown exponentially. By the time Redding died in 2003 there were hundreds more. Today, no one is quite sure how many separate CDs of Jimi Hendrix and/or the Experience are on the market.

In theory the proceeds from the sales of these are sent to Experience Hendrix, an American company owned and managed by the Hendrix family. But in 2006 a name from the past came back to haunt them: Yameta Ltd. The company, which had been thought to have been quietly dissolved after Mike Jeffery's apparent death, surfaced again and claimed the rights to Hendrix's recordings.

The claimant, though, was not Mike Jeffery. Instead it was his former lawyer, John Hillman. Hillman, who had nothing to do with Jeffery's scams, claimed throughout a series of yet more court hearings, that he had set up Yameta Ltd on behalf of Jeffery and that a 1966 contract assigned to Yameta Ltd all rights in Jimi Hendrix's performances. Hillman also claimed that Jeffery had turned Yameta Ltd over to him before his death.

It would take almost two years of litigation before, in spring 2007, Hillman's claims were dismissed by the High Court in London. More than twenty-seven years after Hendrix's death, the final chapter in one of the most extraordinary stories in rock'n'roll had finally been closed.

Perhaps.

6

FRANK ABAGNALE JR: CATCH ME IF YOU CAN!

As the British Viscount VC1-10 made its final approach t Runway 13 at New York's JFK airport, Frank Abagnale Jr calmly unlatched his seat belt and strolled to one of the onboard toilets.

After carefully locking the door he reached behind the lavatory bowl and searched for the two small pull-bolts that secured it to the floor. A swift tug and turn on each, and the entire toilet – lid, bowl and self-contained plumbing system – came free in his hands.

Beneath it was a square hatch, two-feet by two feet, and beneath that a large pipe used by ground crews to service the lavatory. The pipe and the hatch were all that stood between him and the outside air.

As soon as he felt the aircraft wheels make contact with the tarmac, Abagnale pulled open the hatch, squeezed his lanky frame through the hole and – as VC-10 slowed to a crawl on the taxiway – dropped down to the tarmac below. It was pitch black and he was airside at one of the world's busiest airports. There were FBI agents waiting for him in the terminal and a prison cell with his name on it somewhere across the city.

But Frank Abagnale wasn't about to come quietly. In fact, if he could help it he wasn't about to come at all. He sprinted through the darkness, climbed a perimeter fence and dropped down on the side of the Van Wyck Expressway. Five minutes later he was sitting in a New York taxicab, heading for Grand Central Station – and freedom.

Abagnale's flight from JFK took place nearly forty years ago. Fast-forward to February 2006 and a tall, elegant, silver-haired man is standing behind a podium in Orlando, Florida. He adjusts a pair of fashionable horn-rimmed glasses and begins the keynote address at the National Automobile Dealers Association Convention.

Over the next sixty minutes he will present the résumé of one of the world's most daring, inventive and persistent conmen. The career he outlines involves thefts, frauds, forgeries and impersonations – not to mention sexual adventures – across more than a score of separate countries. The total value of the scams runs into many millions. So huge and so colourful was this life of crime, explains the man at the podium, that Hollywood's finest film director recently made a high-profile movie about it.

The reason for this remarkable account of a remarkable criminal record – and the reason the tall and elegant man is addressing the assembled car dealers in the first place – is to highlight the ridiculous ease with which dedicated con artists can exploit loopholes in the modern electronic world.

Few men on the planet know more about these loopholes – and about the men and women who profit from them – than the speaker at the podium. For thirty-five years he has been the FBI's most respected expert consultant on frauds, scams and cons the world over. He teaches the subject at the FBI's internationally renowned academy in Quantico, Virginia, and has been responsible for developing fraud prevention technology used by 78 per cent of banks and more than 91 per cent of governments worldwide.

These highly innovative inventions are used to protect passports, car records, birth certificates, personal identification – social security systems and the like – as well as stocks, shares, bonds and countless other financial instruments. He also runs his own vastly successful anti-scam consulting business.

No one on Earth knows more than this man about conmen and their chosen line of business. Because this man is Frank Abagnale Jr – and for five extraordinary years he was the undisputed international (and seemingly uncatchable) reigning King Con.

'I was a millionaire twice over and a half again before I was 21. I stole every nickel of it and blew the bulk of the bundle on fine threads, gourmet foods, luxurious lodgings, fantastic foxes, fine wheels and other sensual goodies.'[11]

Thus begins Frank Abagnale's first-hand account of his five-year life as an international criminal.

I partied in every capital in Europe, basked on all the famous beaches and good-timed it in South America, the South Seas, the Orient and the more palatable parts of Africa...

I've been described... as one of this century's cleverest bum-cheque passers, flimflam artists and crooks, a conman of Academy Award calibre. I was a swindler and poseur of astonishing ability...

Oddly enough, I never felt like a criminal.[12]

He was a criminal, though – and a remarkably assiduous one at that. In his five-year career he passed bad cheques worth (then) $2.5 million, spreading them across twenty-six separate countries. He used eight aliases, impersonated a lawyer, a doctor and a pilot; he conned airlines into providing him with more than 1 million miles' worth of free travel; and, when he was finally caught, governments across the planet queued up to extradite and arrest him. And it all began with a set of tyres.

In 1963 Frank William Abagnale was living with his father in Bronxville, a small town in Westchester County, just north of New York City. He was born in April 1948, the third of four middle-class children. His mother was a glamorous woman of French-Algerian decent who met his father while he was in army service during World War Two.

When Frank Jr was fifteen his parents divorced and he chose to live with his father – the owner of a highly successful stationery store on the junction of Madison Avenue and 40th Avenue in Manhattan. He had, by this time, acquired a car – a Ford saloon of advanced years – which was to be the spur for his life of crime. Like countless teenagers before him, Frank Abagnale learned the most important equation ever devised: cars = girls.

'When Henry Ford invented the Model-T women shed their bloomers and put sex on the road: [my] Ford fractured every moral fibre in my body. It introduced me to girls. I didn't come to my senses for six years.'[13]

But there is a third part of that equation, which, equally typically, the young Abagnale failed to spot until he was thoroughly hooked by the first two sides. Cars may equal girls, but car + girls = money (need for).

As a sixteen-year-old schoolboy, Frank wasn't able to earn nearly enough money to support his motorised obsession with the female sex. Not legitimately, anyway. Years later, interviewed by American radio, he would recall how his ability to solve this seemingly impossible new equation led him directly to a career in crime.

I was very creative, and I remember that I asked my father if I could have a gas credit card to use, and that I would pay the gas bill. And so he and I having the same name, me being a junior, he gave me one of his cards for Mobil gas, and he said, 'Go ahead and just use this, and then you be responsible for the bill.'

But I would go into a gas station and I would say to the attendant that I'd like to buy four brand-new tyres, and he'd pull them down off the rack and I'd give him the credit card, and he'd get an authorisation and then he'd say, 'OK, you want me to put them on?' and I'd say 'No, but I'll sell them back to you for 50% of what they're worth, and if you give me the money, that way you'll get the money from Mobil, plus you get to keep the tyres.

And they always said Yes. So I was always able to get spending money that way.

Unfortunately, this 'creative' response was as guaranteed to backfire as was Frank's elderly Ford (or 'fox trap' as he liked to think of it). Within three months he had clocked up almost $3,500 on the card – but failed to make a single payment.

Inevitably, an investigator for the petrol company turned up at the stationery store and politely asked his father whether, since young Master Abagnale's car had in the past twelve weeks required fourteen sets of tyres, twenty-two new batteries and tankers full of petrol, it might be more cost-effective to buy a brand-new vehicle.

Frank Abagnale Sr was evidently a remarkably forgiving sort of man. When he confronted his son and was met with the admission that every penny of the $3,500 had been spent on the pursuit of girls, he was sufficiently sympathetic to pay off the debt himself.

But Paula Abagnale was a great deal less tolerant. Concerned that her former husband was allowing their son to run riot, she packed Frank off to a private boarding school for problem boys, run by monks in upstate New York.

He spent a year here – a year which he would later liken to a serious jail sentence – before returning to his father's house. But by the time he got home, the stationery business had collapsed and the Abagnales were distinctly down on their luck. Within weeks he had packed his bags and left without a word to anyone.

He headed straight for New York City, but, at the age of just sixteen and with only $200 in his bank account, knew that staying in a hotel or renting an apartment was out of the question.

He got round the problem by striking up a conversation with a boy of his own age and telling him a sob story: he was, he said, an orphan who had come to the Big Apple to make his fortune. Within an hour, he had been invited to the young man's home, where his parents generously allowed him to stay – free of charge – until his fortunes improved.

But at minimum wage of $1.50 an hour this wasn't about to happen any time soon. Even some judicious doctoring of his driving licence to make himself instantly ten years older yielded only a meagre rise to $2.75. And so, untroubled by anything as petty as the law, Frank Abagnale began writing bad cheques. In this he was no different from any other small-time hustler or petty crook struggling to keep afloat in New York City.

It was a short-term strategy and bound to end – sooner or later – in arrest. Nor was his little scam yielding him much more than spending money – all of it inevitably lavished on a succession of women. But then, quite out of the blue, Frank found his road to Damascus. It was 42nd Street.

As he trudged down the sidewalk, a vision in blue uniform stepped out of the revolving doors of the Commodore Hotel. On his neatly tailored jacket there was gold braid. On either arm a pretty young woman in matching uniforms. He was looking at an airline pilot and two stewardesses. Frank stood and watched as the aircrew climbed into a service van, bound – he presumed – for the airport.

'As they loaded the van, I thought to myself, "That's it. If I could pose as a pilot, I could travel all over the world for free. I could probably get just about anybody, anywhere to cash a cheque for me."'

Many young men dream of being airline pilots. Many dream not only of the attractions of flying but also the possibility of serially dating attractive flight attendants.

Many go on to fulfil at least one part of this dream. Frank Abagnale differed from them in one vital regard: he determined there and then to do both, but without putting himself through the tiresome and expensive business of actually learning to fly a plane.

First he picked a suitable airline for which he was (notionally at least) going to work. Pan American World Airways was then the most glamorous carrier in the country and Frank quite definitely liked the idea of glamour. He located their New York phone number and called up posing as an entirely fictitious first officer or copilot. His name, he told someone in its purchasing department, was Robert Black and he had just flown in from California. Unfortunately his uniform had somehow gone missing from his hotel – where could he urgently get a spare?

Pan Am helpfully sent him to its uniform supplier across town. The uniform supplier helpfully fitted him out with a copilot's outfit and, even more helpfully still, offered to send the bill directly to Pan Am on his behalf.

Next stop for Pan Am's newest first officer was an airport. The New York region has three – JFK, Newark and La Guardia. Abagnale/Black picked the last on the simple grounds that it was the closest. He arrived in his new uniform with the single-minded intention of getting himself on a plane. It didn't much matter what plane or where it was bound – he figured the bad-cheque scam was likely to catch up with him before much longer and, anyway, he fancied a change.

But after a morning of wandering around the airport, checking out the routines of air crew and ground staff, it became depressingly clear that he had a major problem. As he recalled to the convention of automobile dealers more than forty years later, 'Everybody had an airline ID card, plastic laminated card much like a driver's licence today. Without the ID card, my uniform was worthless. I went back to Manhattan pretty discouraged thinking, "Where would I come up with a Pan American Airline Corporate ID?"

Happily, help was at hand.

'I noticed the big thick Manhattan Yellow Pages on the dresser, so I flipped them open and came to the word "Identification". There were three or four pages of companies who made convention badges, metal badges, police badges.

'I started to call around and finally one company said, "Listen, most of those airline IDs are manufactured by Polaroid 3M Company; [you] need to call one of them."

'I finally got the 3M Company on the phone in Manhattan. And they said, "Yeah we manufacture Pan Am's identification system along with a number of other carriers." So I said, "I'm a purchasing officer for a major US carrier. I'm in New York just for the day. We're getting ready to expand our routes, hire a lot of new employees, go to a formal ID [system]. We're very impressed with this Pan Am format – wondered if I came by your office this afternoon briefly, we could discuss quantity and price.'[14]

Yes, said 3M, come on down. By the end of his meeting with their sales representative, Abagnale (now calling himself Frank Williams) had a sample ID card made out in his name complete with colour photograph and in a format that exactly matched that of Pan Am. All it lacked was Pan Am's distinctive crest – an omission rectified for the price of a $2.75 model-aircraft kit, complete with the company's logo in the form of a stick-on decal.

Next a phone call to Pan Am, posing as a high school student doing a project on airlines and pilots, revealed an exotic-sounding procedure call 'deadheading'. It was to be the final key to the skies for Frank Williams, alias Frank Abagnale.

'Deadheading' is the industry's jargon for its system of getting off-duty pilots between airports in time to fly their next plane. It's essentially a form of organised hitchhiking in which each carrier will happily accommodate an in-transit pilot from any other airline in a small jump-seat at the back of the cockpit.

All that was required was a plastic airline ID card and the nerve to fill in the pink self-authorisation slip. Armed with both, 'First Officer Frank Williams' was ready to report for his in-transit co-pilot's seat. It was as easy as that – just so long as no one asked him to actually fly the plane.

For the next two years he 'deadheaded' his way across and around the world. Pan Am would eventually estimate that he flew well over a million miles free of charge; and in doing so he boarded more than 250 aircraft and visited more than 26 countries. But although he posed as one of its senior pilots – generally claiming to be based in San Francisco – he was careful never to deadhead on a Pan Am plane.

'I never flew on Pan Am because I was afraid someone might say to me, "You know, I'm based in San Francisco. I've been out there twenty-eight years. I don't recall ever meeting you before." Or someone might say, "You know, your ID card is not exactly like my ID card." '[16]

But he had no qualms about charging all his hotel and room service bills back to Pam Am. That was a simple matter of finding out which luxury hotel chain accommodated the company's aircrews in whichever exotic location he found himself, and then presenting his bogus ID card to reception. It was a wonderful life – free travel, food, drink and hotel suites, not mention the inevitable succession of dalliances with attractive female flight attendants.

What's more, his smart uniform and international travelling breathed new life into the old Abagnale bad-cheque scams. He found very quickly that, such was the respect in which pilots were held, hotels were very happy to cash personal cheques without asking for any form of security. Of course, these cheques would bounce – but by the time they did the dashing First Officer would be long gone. Once again, the money rolled in.

It was while spending it on the latest of his conquests that Abagnale discovered an even more profitable wrinkle. Airline counter staff at check-in desks had instructions to cash any personal cheque presented by any pilot no matter which company he apparently worked for. Out came the rubber cheque book again. And again. And again.

'I'd go out to JFK or LAX [Los Angles International Airport] and I'd go to every desk – Northeast, National, KLM, Air France. It would take me a good eight hours stopping at every counter and every building. By the time I got all the way around the other end of the airport at least eight hours had gone by.

'What do you have in eight hours? Shift change, new people. So I'd go all the way back around the other way again. I made a great deal of money.'[17]

It was very easy money. Because the sad truth, as Abagnale would later recall, is that pursuing the writers of bad cheques has universally low priority for police forces across the globe.

Very few police departments, if any, have a hot cheque division... that is adequately staffed – not even metropolitan forces. Fraudulent cheque swindles are the most common of crimes and the professional paperhanger [bad cheque writer] is the wiliest of criminals, the hardest to nab. That's true today and it was true then...

So what do the detectives do? They make the routine gestures... and pigeonhole the complaint for future reference.'[18]

And so, in his guise as First Officer Frank Williams, Abagnale greedily lived the high life in exotic locations all over the world. His love life was equally fruitful and now expanding beyond the airline industry. A handsome man in uniform, armed with wads of cash and enjoying the hospitality of the best hotels in town, attracted women like moths to a flame. Mostly they were passing fancies; sometimes he allowed his liaisons to last longer but never to the point where wedding bells might have sounded the alarm. After all, he reasoned, his mother wouldn't approve of her son getting married when he was still just seventeen.

It couldn't last, of course. So extensive were his 'deadheading' wanderings and bad-cheque frauds that he knew even the most trusting of airlines would have to spot something, sometime – and, when they did, surely even most overstretched of police forces would get round to asking awkward questions.

In the end, it wasn't left to an overworked local force to start an investigation. At the tender age of eighteen, Frank Abagnale attracted the attention of the FBI – a far more worrying proposition – and a warrant for the distinctly serious federal charge of interstate transportation of fraudulent cheques. Not that the FBI knew exactly who it was looking for: since he'd used a false and untraceable name, the warrant was issued in the name of 'John Doe', US law enforcement's version of 'A N Other'.

Nonetheless it was still a little to close for comfort. It was time to retire – at least for the time being – First Officer Frank Williams and his hyperactive chequebooks.

Using the stash of ill-gotten cash he had acquired over the previous two years, he moved into an exclusive apartment complex in River Bend, just outside Atlanta, Georgia. The lease agreement form contained a list of questions, one of which was 'occupation'. Abagnale was about to write down 'airline pilot' when he noticed the next three questions: 'Employed by', 'Supervisor's Name' and 'Telephone Contact'. He decided – very quickly – to change professions. On a whim he wrote down the word 'doctor'. Pressed by the apartment manager for specifics, he refined that choice further: his chosen branch of medicine was paediatrics.

It was – depending on how you look at it – either fortunate or very unfortunate that the chief resident paediatrician for the county hospital happened to live in the same block. And that he sought out his newly arrived fellow medic for late-night conversations. True to his form as a very professional conman, Abagnale successfully bluffed his way through these conversations.

So successfully, in fact, that when the resident paediatrician had to go out of town – first for a few weeks, then indefinitely – he advised the county hospital to ask Abagnale to cover for him. And, for the price of a consultant's very generous salary, Abagnale was happy to oblige. The fact that his only medical knowledge came from skim-reading enough medical journals to maintain his cover didn't seem to worry him.

According to his autobiography, he stayed at the hospital for ten months. He survived by passing on the responsibility for each and every medical decision to his 'junior' colleagues.

Only a near-fatal incident in which he was asked to save the life of a 'blue baby' (one starved of oxygen at birth) gave him pause for thought; otherwise, he was as shameless as a doctor as he had been in every other aspect of his life.

The end of his medical career came not through exposure, but because the hospital finally got round to appointing a permanent replacement for the absent resident paediatrician. Pausing just long enough to collect his final paycheque, Frank Abagnale changed professions once again.

This time he became a lawyer. It began, once again with a liaison with a new and 'foxy' female friend. She happened to be based in Louisiana, and so he surrendered the lease on his River Bend apartment and headed for the Bayou State.

Though he didn't know it, the move was an astute choice. For some months the FBI had been sniffing ever closer to his trail and had recently appointed a very experienced and determined agent to investigate his case on an exclusive, full-time basis. Louisiana would prove to be both a safe bolthole and a profitable career change.

He led his new love to believe that he was an airline pilot taking time out from flying. But he simultaneously managed to burnish his credentials with an invented law degree from Harvard. And, when she mentioned that the state's Attorney General was looking for talented staff, the challenge was just too tempting. An afternoon at the library, followed by a session with scissors, glue, instant lettering and a sheaf of legal paper produced a remarkably accurate-looking Harvard degree certificate.

A job interview swiftly followed, as did a job offer – the only condition was that he pass the Louisiana State Bar exam. Since his only knowledge of the law came from a very practical education in breaking it, this might have posed a problem. But, in Louisiana, there was no bar to a candidate's taking the exam as many times as he or she wanted. Abagnale took it three times, treating the first two attempts as an effective exercise in working out what he had to learn in order to pass the third. Pass it he did, and a man on the FBI's Most Wanted List went on to spend eight months on the legal staff of a state Attorney General.

In the end, it was the Harvard business that made him decide to quit. Bluffing his way through the law was easy; it was being hounded with questions about his experiences at America's most prestigious university that proved troublesome – particularly since one of his colleagues had genuinely been there.

Time, then, for another change of direction. He discovered the key to his next scam in a bank in California. He had gone into the bank with the intention (unusual for him) of depositing rather than withdrawing money. But his chequebook didn't have any pay-in slips and so he was forced to ask the counter staff for assistance. The bank teller helpfully pointed him to the piles of blank pay-in slips neatly stacked on a table in the lobby. And a new con came to the fertile imagination of Frank Abagnale. He left the bank with a bundle of the useful little slips.

For an accomplished forger, it was absurdly easy to print his own account number in the relevant box on each form. And a simple matter to leave them casually lying around on the bank table for unwary depositors to use, thereby putting their money into his account.

Four days later he returned to the bank and checked his balance. It was $42,876.45. He swiftly asked for a baker's draft for $40,000 and flew to Honolulu.

For the next two years Frank Abagnale became a 'paperhanger' (*see also* Chapter 3, 'Philip Morrel Wilson: The Bogus Bank of Sark'), developing, perfecting and deploying a succession of fraudulent cheque scams. By 1969, his creative cons had netted him more than $2.5 million, involved a dozen aliases, stints as a doctor, a lawyer and a teacher, and enabled him to live the high life in almost any country he chose.

When the end came, he was in France, posing as 'Robert Monjo' – a successful author and screenwriter. He invested some of his stash in a pretty cottage just outside Montpelier, a stone's throw from the Mediterranean and all the glamour of the Riviera.

Ironically, he was enjoying his sojourn in the South of France so much that he was even contemplating going straight. Montpelier boasted an outstanding university – perhaps he might actually study for a degree rather than forge the certificate for one. Or maybe he could start a legitimate business – a vineyard or even a stationery store like the one his father had owned in New York. But, as contemplated these radical options and drank in the drowsy heat of that French summer, five very busy years of international crime were about to catch up with him.

Twice a week, regular as clockwork, he shopped at a small grocery store on the outskirts of Montpelier. But one afternoon, as he queued at the checkout, four burly and unsmiling men walked up behind him. They wore the unmistakable uniform of the *gendarmerie* – and they were armed. One had a machine pistol, one a shotgun and the remaining two carried pistols. Worse still, they knew his real name. The game was undoubtedly up.

It turned out that the *gendarmes* wanted to arrest him on behalf of the Swedish police. A warrant, issued via Interpol, sought a Mr Frank Abagnale on charges of forgery and fraud. In vain he protested that he was Robert Monjo. The *gendarmes* were unmoved and conducted him swiftly to the nearest jail. He was twenty-one years old.

It could have been worse, he told himself. Sweden's prisons were internationally renowned as being civilised places to do time, very different from jails in the other twenty-five countries in which he had worked his scams, France included.

And then it did get worse. While Montpelier's finest processed the Interpol paperwork, their colleagues in Paris were discovering what the energetic Mr Abagnale had been up to all over France. They put the Swedish request on hold and worked up a charge sheet of their own: Abagnale was transferred to the unwelcoming confines of La Maison D'arrêt in Perpignan. And it was a far cry from the comforts of a Scandinavian lockup.

For six months he endured a prison regime that tolerated violence and encouraged brutal punishments; the cells were squalid and his body – once clothed in the finest fashions – crawled with lice.

'Bread and water for breakfast, bread and soup for lunch,

bread and coffee for dinner. No electricity, no plumbing, no furniture – just a blanket on a floor with a hole in the floor to go to the bathroom. I entered the prison weighing 198 pounds, left the prison at 109 pounds.'[19]

And when the French system was through with him, it spat him out and sent him to Sweden. His trial there began with the heavyweight charge of forging financial instruments, but clever legal footwork reduced it to the lesser offence of fraud. Although Frank Abagnale had indeed forged cheques, his lawyer managed to argue that the very fact that they were counterfeit prevented them from being financial instruments. And if they weren't financial instruments, then Mr Abagnale couldn't be charged with forging them.

The prosecutor refiled the case as fraud, the court duly found him guilty as charged, and Frank Abagnale, now aged twenty-two, was whisked off for a second six-month sojourn, this time in Malmö Prison. This, at least, lived up to Sweden's reputation for enlightened punishment. It was a mixed-sex prison with barely any sign of bars or barbed wire; and, if he wished to study, the Swedish government would happily pay the costs of his tuition. For a man who had effectively lived a life on the run for five busy years – and then endured the misery of La Maison d'Arrêt in Perpignan – it was a very welcome respite.

'Escape never entered my mind: I loved it at Malmö Prison... and the six months passed swiftly, too swiftly...'

As the end of his sentence approached, he was disturbed to discover he was not about to be allowed to go free. The Swedish government had received extradition requests from their counterparts in Italy, Spain, Turkey, Germany, Britain, Switzerland, Greece, Denmark, Norway, Egypt, Lebanon and Cyprus – and all of them wanted to charge him with a succession of serious frauds. Italy – which had a penal system that made Perpignan's Maison d'Arrêt seem like a rest home – was first in line. And the charges there carried a likely twenty-year sentence.

Frank Abagnale didn't want to go to Italy. He didn't want to go to Spain, Turkey, Germany, Britain, Switzerland, Greece, Denmark, Norway, Egypt, Lebanon or Cyprus, either. But he really, really didn't want to go to Italy. As the clock ran out on his stay in the civilised atmosphere of Malmö Prison, he filed attempt after attempt to persuade Swedish courts not to extradite him to Rome. Each and every one was turned down.

'The Devil looks after his own' is one of those phrases that are repeated so often they become truisms. But the point that tends to be overlooked about truisms is that they have a habit of being true.

On the night before he was due to be forcibly put on a plane to Italy, Frank Abagnale was asked – politely, of course – to take tea with the latest judge to reject his appeal against extradition. The judge, apparently, was a civilised and caring man and he was concerned at the likely impact of twenty years in an Italian prison on a man who – for all his criminal globetrotting – was barely twenty-three years old.

But, as there was nothing wrong with the Italian extradition warrant, he could not legally refuse it. And so, reluctantly, he had decided that the only way to save the young man from the hell of a Roman cell was to violate his civil rights, as defined by the ever-liberal Swedish law. He had called a friend of his in the American Embassy and asked him to revoke Frank Abagnale's passport.

His friend had agreed and, as a result, Mr Abagnale was an unwelcome alien in Sweden; and with no valid passport he could – would – be deported to his own country. Within the hour he would be escorted to the airport and put on a plane to New York City.

It wasn't all wine and roses, of course. When the plane landed at JFK, Abagnale would not be joining the other passengers at the baggage reclaim carousel and heading off to enjoy the cosmopolitan delights of Manhattan. The FBI had been advised that one of their most wanted criminals was on board and would be meeting him at the gate.

Doubtless, they would want to discuss a large number of very serious offences with him and would detain him in a Federal lockup while they did so. But at least it was better than Italy.

And so it was that Abagnale, one of the most prolific and most talented conmen of the age, was sent home, unescorted and unshackled, on a British Viscount VC-10. Which, of course, is where we came in.

As Frank Abagnale settled back in the cab whisking him down the Van Wyck Expressway, he knew he wouldn't have long. FBI agents were waiting to grab him the moment the plane arrived at the gate and, the instant the doors swung open, they were going to be seriously irritated by his absence.

Thanks to his isolation in the respective penal systems of France and Sweden he didn't know which of his boltholes they had discovered and who among his friends, acquaintances and – most pertinently – his conquests might have turned against him.

He directed the cab to the Bronx and the address of a

girlfriend in whose loyalty he felt reasonably confident. He hadn't had sex for well over a year but, even so, he stopped long enough only to change his clothes and pick up a fistful of dollars. Then he hopped on a train bound for Montreal.

He had $20,000 stashed in a Canadian safety deposit box – more than enough to pay for a flight to Brazil and a comfortable life in the anonymity of São Paolo. Best of all, America had no extradition treaty with Brazil. He could almost smell freedom.

He got off the train; he went to the bank; he picked up his money and headed for the airport. He even bought the ticket for São Paolo. As he did so, he felt a heavy hand on his shoulder, and turned to face Constable James Hastings of the Royal Canadian Mounted Police. Frank Abagnale had forgotten one crucial fact: the legendary Mounties always get their man.

Technically, he wasn't their man at all. But it didn't seem to matter to Constable Hastings. A night in the cells was followed by a drive to the border and a formal handover to officers of the US Border Patrol. After a distinctly abrupt hearing before a local magistrate, Frank Abagnale found himself in a Federal lockup. Two months later, he was driven to the State Penitentiary in Georgia and consigned to its sweaty cells to await trial.

Frank Abagnale was now twenty-four. He was an accomplished – talented, even – conman and forger. He had conned his way quite literally across the world; he had evaded capture in twenty-eight separate countries – not to mention a good proportion of the contiguous United States. He had served prison sentences in two countries and escaped while being returned home to face another. He had even been given his own nickname in the press – 'The Skywayman'. So you might have thought someone would keep a careful eye on him.

Wrong!

While waiting for a trial he knew would go badly, Abagnale was transferred to Atlanta's Federal Detention Center. These were difficult years in America: the assassinations of Martin Luther and Bobby Kennedy had shaken the country less than three years before; the Vietnam War was dividing young and old, rich and poor, black and white. and the prison system had – rightly – been exposed again and again for gross breaches of human or civil rights.

The Atlanta facility had been on the receiving end of a great deal of criticism from the prison inspectorate. It had even sent undercover investigators inside the system, posing as prisoners to discover the truth about life behind bars.

And so, when a harassed US marshal delivered Frank Abagnale to the Federal Detention Center without all the correct paperwork – just one of those routine bureaucratic cockups – the guard made a crucial assumption: this well-spoken young man was another damn undercover inspector.

The regime surrounding Abagnale was – unsurprisingly – less than severe. And so, with the aid of one of his string of local girlfriends, he concocted a plan. First she arranged to meet a local FBI officer called Sean O'Reilly; then – posing as a freelance journalist – to meet with the chief inspector of prisons in Washington, DC. Both willingly gave her their business cards.

A quick visit to a stationery print shop yielded five hundred almost exact replicas of the FBI agent's card; only the phone number was changed – to that of Abagnale's girlfriend. She easily slipped this new version, together with the prison inspector's card, to Frank on a routine prison visit.

The following evening, Abagnale 'confessed' to the guard who had booked him in: he confirmed that the guard's suspicion had been correct – he was an undercover prison inspector. His mission was now through – and, by the way, the jail had passed with flying colours. So could he be let out, please?

As evidence, he showed the card from the DC-based chief inspector. But – ever the consummate conman – he clinched the trick by asking the guard to make a call to the FBI agent with whom he, Abagnale, was working. He handed over the doctored card.

When the phone rang at the other end, an accomplice enlisted by Abagnale's girlfriend picked it up. Yes, he was Agent O'Reilly; yes, he confirmed Abagnale's story. Within minutes a meeting had been sanctioned outside the detention centre. Frank Abagnale was even escorted to the prison gates by uniformed guards, and as he climbed into his girlfriend's car, he grinned and kissed her with sheer pleasure.

That same evening, he slipped on board a Greyhound bus, bound for New York. His escape plan was the same as before: Brazil, São Paolo, freedom. But he knew he needed to lie low – his ingenious jail break had been splashed all over the press and television. One New York newspaper summed up the fantastical nature of his escape in big bold type:

Frank Abagnale, known to the police the world over as the Skywayman and who once flushed himself down an airline toilet to elude officers, is at large again...

After two weeks holed up in the New York suburb of Queens, he took the train to Washington, DC, rented a car and checked into an anonymous motel on the outskirts of the nation's capital. He had chosen DC as the final stopping-off point before his flight to São Paolo for two reasons. First, he had several large caches of money stashed in banks in neighbouring Virginia; and, second, the very nature of the city – with its huge suburban population and ever-shifting tourist traffic – held out the promise of complete camouflage.

Frank Abagnale made only one mistake. He chose the wrong motel.

The clerk at the check-in desk happened to be a former airline stewardess. She had instantly recognised the world's most infamous conman and 'deadheader', and, as Abagnale settled into his room, she called the police. They quickly surrounded the motel.

The news that Frank Abagnale was cornered inside his room was swiftly passed to the unfortunate Agent O'Reilly. Not unreasonably, the FBI agent was determined to handle this arrest personally. The police surrounding the motel were ordered to wait.

Up in his room Abagnale happened to glance out of the window and spotted uniformed officers scuttling around the perimeter. He quickly weighed up his options, and there was only one that stood a chance – albeit remote – of working.

He pulled a raincoat over his clothes, slipped out of the door and strolled nonchalantly round the back of the building. Before he could take more than a few steps two police officers walked towards him. They pointed handguns at him and told him to stay right where he was.

Five years of deadheading, scams and consummate con

artistry kicked in: Frank Abagnale walked towards them, a picture of relaxation. He pulled his wallet from his pocket and casually announced himself as 'Agent Davis – FBI'. And as the pistols were lowered he pulled his masterstroke: 'Is Agent O'Reilly here yet? Tell you what: you guys keep this area covered and I'll go check.' And then he walked off into the night.

It couldn't last, of course. Less than a month later two New York City detectives spotted him as he walked through Manhattan. He was turned over within the hour to a thoroughly relieved FBI.

What followed was an American version of the earlier international legal scrum. All fifty states in the union wanted to get their hands on Frank Abagnale and were rapidly filing an enormous stack of charges: forgery, passing dud cheques, mail fraud, counterfeiting and plain old swindling. Each state vied to be the first to bring the Skywayman to trial.

It didn't take much in the way of brains to realise he needed to cut a deal. And Abagnale was never short in that department. In 1971, he agreed a plea bargain with federal authorities by which all his crimes 'known and unknown' were wrapped up in seven sample counts of fraud and one count of unlawful escape. He got ten years for the former and two years for the latter – all sentences to run concurrently.

This meant he faced spending the next twelve years in the Federal Correctional Institute in Petersburg, Virginia. It was hardly the lap of luxury, but infinitely preferable to the local state prisons; and, compared with the Maison D'arrêt in Perpignan, the place seemed like a country club.

He served only four of those years. In 1975 US government officials arrived at Petersburg and made him an offer: if he agreed to work with the FBI on fraud-prevention strategies for the duration of his sentence, he would be freed on parole straightaway.

More than thirty-three years later, Frank Abagnale is still working with the FBI. In the interim, he founded and still runs a highly successful international consultancy advising companies on fraud prevention. The business has made him a multimillionaire and he proudly claims to have paid back every penny that he scammed, conned, swindled or stole.

All of which makes his story unique in the annals of conmen and their crimes: a happy ending from which everyone benefits. The world's most notorious poacher is transformed into one of its most successful gamekeepers.

Except that, when it comes to scams, it's never quite as cosy as that.

The world has become a much smaller place since Frank Abagnale flew around it as a deadheading con artist. It is infinitely better and constantly connected: nations speak instantly unto nations and law enforcement has access to international intelligence at the touch of a button. Which should make fraud much more difficult. Shouldn't it?

'The truth is that what I did thirty years ago is two hundred times easier to do today than it was then,' he told ABC radio in an interview, 'and five years from now will be seven hundred times easier than it is today, and that's because of one word: technology.

'Technology breeds crime, and it always has. When I did these things thirty years ago, if I had to make a cheque, I literally had to print the cheque, so I had to be a skilled printer. I had to know how to do colour separations, make negatives, make plates, and it was very time-consuming and tedious. Today, sitting at home in an apartment with a PC, a scanner, a colour printer, an inkjet printer or a colour copier, you can reproduce just about any type of document, including currency and paper.

'Thirty years ago, bank tellers were professional employees with hours and months of training. Today banks don't want to pay benefits, so they don't hire full-time employees: they hire part-time help, and there's very little training. So, if a bank teller can't tell me the difference between a good bill and a bad bill, then what can they tell me in the hotel lobby, or in the retail store?

'We have to alert consumers today: we have to tell them that you need to be a very smart consumer. Because, in the end, the police can't protect you; the government can't protect you; your bank can't protect you. Only you can protect yourself.'[20]

7

BARRY GRAY AND JOE FLYNN: THE KINGS OF STING

If asked, 'What papers do you take?' Barry Gray might well have answered, 'Nearly all of them, and for quite a lot of money too.'

However, money doesn't seem to have been his prime motivation. The man they dubbed 'the King of Sting' relished the challenge of bettering those who should have known better – public figures, senior executives in major companies and, above all, senior reporters on national newspapers. His stock in trade was selling information – bogus information, but beautifully crafted.

Barry Edward Gray, also known as Joe Flynn – and who knows how many other aliases? – took some spectacular scalps in a career spanning more than forty years and encircling the globe. Notable victims included Guinness, Citibank, Royal Life Assurance, Virgin Atlantic, The *Sunday Times* and *Daily Mirror*, TNT Express, the CIA and the

KGB. In the eighties and nineties, Gray's roll call of victims was most impressive. However, details are hard to come by, since few people are willing to admit they've been taken for a ride. Here is an outline of a few of Gray's 'successes'.

The *Sunday Times* was persuaded to run an erroneous front-page story alleging Gray had been hired by the Australian entrepreneur Alan Bond to spy on commercial rivals.

Derbyshire County Council leader David Bookbinder was led to believe he was under surveillance during a long-running dispute over council spending with the then Conservative government.

False information sold by Gray led to the collapse of major takeover negotiations between the sportswear specialists Pentland Group and the French firm Adidas.

When Rosemary Aberdour was convicted of stealing £2.7 million from the charity she worked for, Gray contacted her employer and suggested Aberdour had hidden her ill-gotten gains. This led the judge to threaten her with a longer sentence.

He also convinced the brewers Guinness that its one-time takeover competitor Argyll was conducting a secret surveillance operation against the company and its senior executives. Guinness was so concerned it ordered its headquarters to be electronically swept.

He duped a *Daily Express* reporter by claiming to be a defecting IRA man who would take the reporter on an IRA arms run.

He conned Asil Nadir, chairman of Polly Peck, into believing that his enemies had hired Gray to bug his offices and steal company secrets.

Gray deceived the *Guardian*'s Westminster correspondent and the Department of the Environment's Property Services

Agency (PSA), claiming that a dismissed PSA employee had siphoned £200,000 into a Liberian bank account.

In 1991, after a hostile £126 million bid had been launched by the brewing company Boddingtons for the West Country brewer Devenish, Gray approached Devenish claiming to be a private investigator who had been hired by Boddingtons to spy against the company. As an adviser to Devenish, Jeff Katz, now the boss of the corporate investigations specialists Bishop International, told me that he helped them keep Gray at arm's length.

'I later found out that, as I expected, Gray had also approached Boddingtons and told them the same story from the other side. In other words, he said that Devenish had hired him to spy on Boddingtons. He could play both sides of a situation in the full knowledge that neither was going to check with the other.'

Katz believes that Gray's efforts had a direct effect on the bid. 'Devenish was controlled by a family shareholding. The family was reluctant to sell, but were trying to decide whether or not the bid signalled the appropriate moment to get out. It required a gentle approach.

'But I suspect that Denis Cassidy, the chairman of Boddingtons, was unsettled by Gray's alleged spying activities. As a result, it appears that he tried to push the deal through quickly. In my opinion, this was quite the wrong way to deal with the family. They reacted against the pressure and refused to sell. The bid failed.'

Shortly afterwards, Jeff Katz – then heading Kroll Associates' London operation – was invited to lunch by a senior security manager at BP.

'During lunch I asked him if he had heard about Gray. He

had not. I explained how Gray operated and the hallmarks of his scams. About two weeks later the security manager phoned me and said he suspected BP had received a call from Gray.

'At the time the chairman of BP, Bob Horton, was fighting an internal battle, news of which had reached the press. Gray had obviously read about the controversy and put in a call with his usual patter about having been hired to spy on Horton. The security manager sent me a tape of the phone call. I was a managing director of Kroll in London at the time and on the tape Gray alleged that he had been hired to spy on Horton by Kroll.'

Perhaps Gray's cheekiest con was the extraction of a small fortune from Rupert Murdoch for a pair of scuffed, brown shoes that Flynn had claimed were worn by the controversial leader of the US Teamsters' Union, Jimmy Hoffa, when he was murdered. Hoffa had an unhealthily close relationship with the Mafia, and the Mob was alleged variously to have dumped his body in the sea or buried it beneath concrete pillars holding up an expressway.

Reporters at Murdoch's *National Star* had received a letter from someone claiming to know the full details of Hoffa's mysterious disappearance. The writer instructed the newspaper to take out an ad in the *Herald Tribune* under the heading OLD FRENCH SHEET MUSIC REQUIRED if they were interested in the story. They did so and were subsequently contacted (by letter) by a man calling himself 'Mr Josephs'. He claimed to have been asked to murder Hoffa, but had refused. As a result (and given Hoffa's disappearance) he was now terrified that the Mob were going to come after him and dispose of him because he could identify them.

The reporters took the Josephs letter to Murdoch. He authorised them to fly Josephs from London to Las Vegas. The plan was then for a reporter to meet Josephs outside the Roxy Theater on Sunset Boulevard and hand over a wad of cash as a down payment.

The *Star* reporters then had a series of meetings with Josephs in which he outlined a lurid tale of the torture and subsequent murder of Hoffa in the back of a van. His body had been buried somewhere in New Jersey.

Josephs also offered hard evidence to back up his story: the actual shoes that Jimmy Hoffa had been wearing when he was killed. Not, of course, that he had them with him: they were safely under lock and key in a luggage locker at Cologne airport. But, if the reporters would care to stump up a further $20,000, Mr Josephs promised they could have the shoes – and he, Mr Josephs, would feel rather less threatened by the Mafia killers who he felt sure were hot on his trail.

The reporters duly reported back to their boss, and Murdoch happily paid up for what he believed would be a major scoop. He even sent his secretary to deliver personally the envelope of cash to the reporters holed up in Vegas. One reporter, Piers Ackerman, then flew to Cologne. On Mr Josephs's explicit instructions he was to hand over the cash to an associate known only as 'the Dutchman'. The Dutchman would, in return, tell him how to get his hands on Hoffa's footwear.

In a hotel lobby, Ackerman duly parted with Murdoch's money and the Dutchman then directed him to the Lufthansa office at the airport, where he could pick up a key and the location of the locker it opened.

All went to plan. Ackerman collected the key and found

the locker, and when he opened it he found himself staring at a pair of old and really rather scuffed, two-tone, brown-leather shoes. These were rushed, excitedly, to a forensics lab for spectrographic analysis.

A battery of tests sadly revealed no evidence of any link between the shoes and the missing Teamsters leader. Undeterred, the reporters proudly took the shoes to Hoffa's son to see if he could shed any light. He could – he could confirm unequivocally that the shoes were nothing like anything his father had ever worn. In fact, Gray had bought them for $3.50 in a Las Vegas pawnshop. For his efforts – in one of the first of many stings on journalists in a long and profitable career – he trousered $30,000 of Rupert Murdoch's money.

Born in London, Gray went as a young man to Australia, where, in 1958, he served his first prison sentence (five months) for 'long-firming' – filling a shop in Adelaide with photographic equipment, taking orders, and then disappearing before the goods were paid for. Later, he developed substantial holdings in property and hotels, claiming that money for their expansion came from Mike Hand, the American boss of the notorious CIA-linked Nugan Hand Bank, which then financed heroin trafficking in the Far East. While flying around the Pacific selling property, Gray says he occasionally also ran errands for Hand, such as dropping radio equipment for use by anticommunist rebels in Indonesia.

In 1975, his business empire collapsed in the worldwide property crash. He had to flee Australia using the alias Joe Flynn, which stuck. Believing that the CIA had pulled the rug from him, he nursed a grievance against the intelligence agency – leading to one of his most celebrated stings, when he claimed to have information about Nicholas Shadrin, a Soviet defector who disappeared while on an assignment for the CIA in Vienna in 1975.

Taking the name, he swears, from a packet of Benson & Hedges cigarettes, he called himself Benson in dealings with Richard Copaken, a top Washington lawyer who worked for Shadrin's wife, Eva. By amazing coincidence, Benson was the codename of the man who had debriefed Shadrin when he fled Russia in 1959. The CIA, FBI and Mrs Shadrin were convinced by Gray's story and parted with more than $3,500 for bogus leads.

Much of Gray's success came from his plausibility. He was always immaculately turned out in blazer and tie, carrying a briefcase full of what seemed to be relevant documentation. He credits his mother, who worked in the music hall as a wardrobe mistress, for teaching him well.

'I study my targets, I find out what makes them tick. She stressed the importance of dressing well and making a good impression.'

Gray's technique was simple but effective. He would scan the British newspapers – the *Daily Telegraph* and, much later, the *Independent on Sunday* were his favourites – for stories of business disputes, particularly contested takeovers. Then, telephoning from 'somewhere in Europe', he would tell one of the squabbling parties that he had information of 'great value' that might interest them (he always primed them with just enough detail from his meticulous newspaper research).

If they cared to meet him, usually at Schiphol airport in Amsterdam, he would tell them more. No, he wasn't interested in being paid: he would be quite happy with a few hundred pounds for his expenses. Then he would go to the other party in the dispute and regale them with a variation on the same theme. A follow-up sting then swung into operation, often involving a new identity and a different accent. 'Not bad for a day's work,' Gray would say.

Guinness was conned into thinking that its business rival Argyll had bugged its boardroom, and vice versa. The Hanson Group handed over money to learn more of a nonexistent undercover operation by ICI. Gray swindled £600 from the managing director of Peter de Savary's holding company for a cock-and-bull story that he had been hired by rival Manpower to dig up the dirt on the British entrepreneur's controversial deal with recruitment consultants Blue Arrow. And there were many others.

Gray enjoyed showing up media gullibility as much as corporate paranoia.

'Without people like them, there wouldn't be people like me. I just told them what they wanted to hear,' he said.

The persuasive conman could usually make extra money selling the story of some latest exploit to the media. Sometimes his cheek was breathtaking. In January 1990, Jeff Randall, then the City editor of the *Sunday Times*, was lured to Madrid to hear 'private investigator' Barry Gray's claims that he had been hired by the Australian entrepreneur Alan Bond to bug his rival Robert Holmes à Court. Not only did he use his real name, but his photograph appeared in the paper, alongside a completely fictitious story, on the front page.

The conman had a useful sideline, immersing himself in the details of political intrigues and conspiracy theories.

In the early eighties he could always earn a crust tipping off Middle Eastern embassies about nonexistent terrorist arms caches. In September 1981, posing as Edward Christian, an Athens-based arms dealer, he tricked nearly £3,000 out of the *News of the World* with his story that the Libyan leader Colonel Gadaffi was 'masterminding a secret plot to arm black revolutionary murder squads in Britain'.

In February 1983, he hoodwinked a leading firm of London solicitors that he had information about the death of the Italian banker Roberto Calvi. In November 1991, Matthew Evans, chairman of the publishers Faber & Faber, took the Schiphol route after Flynn had convinced him and the American investigative journalist Seymour Hersh that he had evidence of Robert Maxwell's involvement in arms deals and espionage.

The police were seldom interested in Gray's heists, largely because his victims were reluctant to come forward and reveal their gullibility. But by the early nineties he became an unlikely victim of the recession. Newspapers no longer provided the source material on contested takeovers. Who was interested when Flynn tried his tricks on bidders for the privatisation of the Tees and Hartlepool Ports Authority?

Looking for new targets in March 1992, he alighted on Paul Meyer, director of the National Hospital Development Fund, a charity that had been swindled out of £2.7 million by the bogus aristocrat 'Lady' Rosemary Aberdour. Gray told Meyer that, contrary to her testimony in court, Aberdour had stashed money away in secret offshore bank accounts. Meyer travelled to Antwerp and handed over 700 Swiss francs, hoping for more information. Subsequently realising he had been duped, Meyer went to the police, who showed him a file picture of Gray. This was to land him in court – of which more later.

Gray had mastered a range of convincing accents. In his 1990s sting on the *Sunday Times*, he was described as 'a mysterious man with an Anglo-Australian accent'. Two years before, when he was interviewed by the *Guardian* in Nice, he was using an East End accent.

One of his favourite roles was that of an international financier, who had suddenly found himself being used by thieves and fraudsters. He would also pretend to be a private investigator, employed by 'the other side', who now nursed a grievance against them and was prepared to tell all. Either way, he was offering what looked like a major scoop. As a result, journalists had been persuaded to fly all over the world to rendezvous with him.

The Cook Report was once targeted by Gray, then using the name Barry Walters. In the spring of 1995, he cold-called our offices in Birmingham with a story that sounded very promising. It was a new and surprising angle on a story that was then making headlines.

If we were interested, he could send us a few sample documents as a 'taster.' When they arrived, they looked good and certainly seemed to prove what he was saying, though of course he hadn't given us the full story. He rang again and suggested a face-to-face meeting in Bilbao, northern Spain.

This seemed a little strange, since both the documents and the phone calls had originated within the UK. However, on the basis of 'nothing ventured, nothing gained', the director and I flew out to Bilbao a few days later and met our new source in the elegant lounge of the Carlton Hotel.

Barry Walters turned out to be pretty well turned out himself: grey-haired, smartly suited and sporting an expensive attaché case and a conspiratorial look. He sat between us and began by explaining that he admired and trusted *The Cook Report*. He said he'd come across the story in his role as an international financial consultant – and wanted us to help him blow the whistle. Money was not mentioned.

Carefully, he laid out the new documents on the coffee table, and, in a voice barely above a whisper, he talked us through them, explaining the true significance of each as he went. Truth to tell, we were beginning to get quite excited, but tried not to show it. As an indication of his trust, he said that he would leave us alone with the documents for an hour or so, in order that we could read and digest them properly, while he transacted some important business elsewhere.

The convoluted paperwork purported to show how a British company was flouting a United Nations arms embargo. Many cups of coffee later, he was back – keen to know what we thought.

We told him that, impressive though his documents looked, we couldn't make a television programme from pictures of pieces of paper. We needed interviewees through whom we could tell the tale, with his documents in support. Walters paused for thought. Yes, he probably could come up with some people to talk to us, but that would take more time and cost real money. How much he didn't say, but he did make it clear that the money should come from our pockets rather than his.

It was obvious to all that a deal was not going to be concluded then and there, as he'd clearly hoped, so it was agreed that he'd call us again, back in the UK, in about a week. He didn't want to part with any of his new documents yet, but as a 'gesture of good faith', he gave us what he said was his second passport (he probably had dozens), which he said he would retrieve later in return for all the extra documents, a list of interviewees and their contact numbers – and a fee to be negotiated.

We thought this was a bit peculiar, too, but agreed. Back at base we examined the passport. It was either genuine or the best forgery anyone had ever seen, but there was something not quite right about it. We stared at it until the penny dropped. The stated date of birth meant that the man we'd met must have aged prematurely. Walters looked to be in his mid-fifties, but the passport said he was forty-three.

We made some phone calls on the basis of the documents we had originally been given, together with what we had gleaned in Bilbao. It didn't add up properly. So when Mr Walters rang as arranged and told us that finding witnesses was going to take still more time and that he'd need a substantial cash advance, we put our growing suspicions to him.

The documents had turned out to be dubious and didn't connect in the way he'd suggested, and the second passport looked as if it might have been the result of Walters assuming the identity of someone long dead and getting duplicate paperwork as if the departed were still alive – just as the hit man had done in Frederick Forsyth's book, *The Day of the Jackal*.

There was a pregnant pause – followed by a guffaw of laughter. Walters told us he was actually Joe Flynn, and that, although he'd made a pretty good living out of misleading the media, he clearly wasn't going to make much out of us. But that's life, he said, before wishing us well, hanging up, and setting off in search of his next victim. We'd had a lucky escape.

As the 'King of the Sting', Gray was a great escapee himself, and was rarely prosecuted. Ironically, one of his few appearances in court involved offences that had netted him very little.

Jeff Katz, annoyed that Gray had more than once posed as a Kroll employee, joined forces with Scotland Yard.

'We tracked him down in France, where he was arrested and thrown into jail in Marseilles. He fought extradition for nearly two years on the grounds that the British request was politically motivated because the British government believed he was the source of the so-called "Squidgy-gate" tapes, recordings of private conversations of Diana, Princess of Wales, which had been made public by the media. Not surprisingly, his story was a complete fabrication, but it delayed his day in court for a while.'

At the age of sixty-one, in June 1995, he found himself in Southwark Crown Court in south London in the very week he had published his autobiography – entitled *Gentleman Swindler* – in France.

At some stage in his career, it seems that every conman likes to be recognised for his finesse and his consummate professionalism. The court was told that Gray had revelled in his reputation as an international conman. The book had apparently sold ten thousand copies within days of its release. Here's a sample of his deathless prose – perhaps best taken with a pinch of salt:

My revelations, for the most part imaginary, have proved on more than one occasion to be true. For example: Robert Maxwell. When I pulled one over on him I was living in Lisbon, where he sent his valet to me, carrying a suitcase intended to pay for my information about hidden microphones in his offices. In the course of our conversation he cited a number of names, people in his entourage whom he distrusted. I contacted them and sold them the same sort of revelation: Maxwell was bugging them.

Without knowing it, I told them the truth. After Maxwell's death, an international agency of private detectives... became a witness that that he (Maxwell) had given them a list of names of people to spy on. I am often amazed by these coincidences, asking myself if by chance my granny gave me her gift of divination.

Unfortunately for him, he didn't see his arrest coming. In court, the judge, Geoffrey Rivlin QC, told him, 'You virtually dedicated the whole of your life to committing offences of this nature, a matter of which I am sure you hoped and still hope to trade on by the sale of picture, television and film rights.'

Brendan Finucane, for the prosecution, said that Gray, aged sixty-one, spun tales of industrial espionage, telephone bugging, secret surveillance and blackmail.

'It really is his life. He would regard it as his profession.'

Gray pleaded guilty to nine charges of deception and one of attempted deception between 1991 and 1993 for having duped the director of the National Hospital Development Fund with false stories about Rosemary Abelour siphoning the charity's funds into secret offshore bank accounts. Gray was sentenced to two years' imprisonment.

But Gray had the last laugh. Confusion over the judge's sentencing remarks meant that 'the King of the Sting' walked free the same day.

His last words before disappearing must have sent a chill down the spines of those who plotted to entrap him: 'I won't exactly be going back to my old tricks, but I have got a few old scores to settle, more than a few.'

Among those most fearful of reprisals must have been the cadre of ex-Flying Squad officers now working for big private companies and security firms hit by Flynn, who put pressure on senior commanders at New Scotland Yard to put him behind bars.

The ten sample charges of deception, amounting to a meagre £3,250, that brought Flynn to book were never going to do justice to the quite breathtaking list of dupes among the great, the good and the not so good who have fallen foul of him. It is a roll call of which Flynn clearly remains proud, but hearing this from the horse's mouth was unusual. Understandably, Gray didn't usually do interviews.

'Any fool can go along and forge a cheque, but to set up a sting, to set up a scene where you have a lot of intelligent people believing it and parting with their money, is a different thing entirely,' Flynn says.

'To do it successfully, you've got to be one jump ahead, you've got to think what their lawyer's thinking, got to watch every movement. Do they trust me? Are they aware? Have they tuned in? You're living on your wits. To me, the con game isn't criminal, it's a profession.

'When I end up pulling a sting, I actually believe it. In one, when I was posing as an Irishman, I spoke like a Paddy for ten hours to myself beforehand in the hotel room. I forget everything. As far as I am concerned, I am what I am at that moment.'

So what motivated him during his forty-year career? It

couldn't only have been the money – most of his stings netted him a few thousand each, though he claims to have pulled off thousands.

'I'm like Marks & Spencer. I sell it cheap, but I sell it often.'

But, above all, he did like the challenge – pitting his wits against those who should have known better. And perhaps there was a sense of rejection over past business failure, tinged with a desire still to run with the big boys.

'It's really a pleasure, a real sense of achievement that I can still do it. As for the banks, the finance companies, the institutions, the politicians... they're all a bunch of legalised conmen, every one of them. They feather their own nests. I know who I am. They honestly believe they are honest. I know I am a crook. Whatever way you flower it up, I'm a crook – but I don't pretend to myself that I am anything else.'[21]

Nothing has been heard of Gray for some years now, but the trouble for those unlucky enough to cross the path of this latter-day Iago is that they stand every chance of not realising who he is – until it's too late.

8

PETER FOSTER: 'TRUST ME – I CAN MAKE YOU SLIM!'

It is – to misquote Miss Austen – a truth universally acknowledged that a single woman in possession of an overweight body must be in want of a diet, or at least a man selling one. Unfortunately, the sort of man she generally turns to is Peter Foster.

Of all the scams in the history of con tricks, the single most consistently profitable is the miracle slimming cure. From early Victorian times newspapers – and not just of the tabloid or penny-dreadful variety – were positively stuffed with advertisements promising instant weight loss via pills, potions or creams.

Nor did the reader necessarily need to ingest or absorb the answer to their dietary prayers: the advertisement pages also boasted an eye-watering display of nineteenth-century mechanical ingenuity.

And even a cursory examination of these guaranteed and

patented 'cures' reveals a remarkable similarity to some of today's widely advertised slimming machines. The 'galvanic electrical chair' (invented 1899) and the 'obesity belt' (1892), for example, both promised to send fat-busting electrical impulses through the skin and are surely the precursors of the electric stimulus pads and 'toning' body wraps sold to today's desperate slimmers.

Without exception, all of the turn-of-the-century dieting devices held out the prospect of finally and painlessly parting the readers from their unwanted extra pounds. And – in one way at least – they did exactly that: sales were universally healthy, even in a world that had yet to discover rampant consumerism.

Today, only two things have changed: (1) the size of the market – twenty-first-century consumers spend between $33 billion and $55 billion every year on weight-loss products and services – and (2) the gulf between the overweight and the underfed.

Despite the fact that significant numbers of men, women and children throughout Africa and parts of Asia are starving to death, the population of the developed world is generally overweight, and, since much of this is due to laziness (in one form or another), there is a substantial market for products that promise to make weight loss easier, quicker, cheaper or less painful.

Only the very stupid or terminally incompetent ever go bust while attempting to tap into this 'fix me quick' market. Peter Foster was neither. He may have been sentenced by a dozen courts, jailed on three continents and hold the world record for launching the greatest number of slimming scams ever, but he has also made millions and enjoyed an extraordinarily lavish lifestyle, all from duping the gullible and the desperate.

Turning forty is a milestone in our lives – and most of us like to mark the occasion with a party. It is, particularly for men, a sort of modern rite of passage – the moment we leave behind the careless irresponsibility of youth and enter (with varying degrees of sobriety) the choppy waters of middle age.

On the evening of Thursday, 26 September 2002, Peter Foster celebrated his fortieth birthday with friends. What distinguished Foster's party from countless others taking place that same night in London was the location. And the hosts.

It's no longer possible to stroll into Downing Street without an invitation, a government pass or recognised accreditation as member of the press. Solidly built, wrought-iron gates block the turn from Whitehall. These are guarded by armed policemen of a similar build.

That evening, behind the shiny black door of Number 10, Prime Minister Tony Blair and his wife Cherie were hosting a party. Strictly speaking, it wasn't a birthday party for Peter Foster, but both he and his girlfriend Carole Caplin had been invited on the strength of Caplin's close friendship with Cherie Blair.

As he surveyed the elegant interior of the most powerful address in Britain, Foster was undoubtedly a happy man. And a lucky man, too: not many habitual criminals with a record as long as his had found themselves quaffing the Prime Ministerial champagne.

Peter Clarence Foster was born in Queensland, on Australia's Gold Coast. By all accounts, in those days it had something of the feel of California during the gold rush,

populated by the sort of get-rich-quick merchants who flock
to boom towns in search of a fortune.

Chris Nyst, one of his former lawyers, painted a vivid
portrait of the young Foster. 'He's very much a child of the
Gold Coast,' he said. 'It's a boom-town type place. It's gaudy
and it's flash, maybe it's crass. Foster grew up in that
environment and the people of the Gold Coast see him as one
of their own. He's a spiv and he's a rat, but, you know, he's
our spiv and he's our rat; he's part of what we are.'[22]

Foster first ventured into business as a schoolboy. At the
age of fourteen he began renting pinball machines to the
high-rise apartment buildings that lined the beaches of
Surfers Paradise. By the time he reached fifteen, he was
earning several times more money than his teachers, so he
decided to leave school and become a full-time entrepreneur.

Within two years he hit the headlines: the international
and local press descended on Queensland to write glowing
features about 'the world's youngest boxing promoter'.

Foster had somehow talked his way into staging a world
elimination title fight featuring British and European light-
heavyweight champion Bunny Johnson and Australia's Tony
Mundine. The fight was an impressive financial success and
more headlines followed, singing the praises of 'the
milkshake tycoon' (a reference to his tender years and baby-
faced looks).

Unfortunately, these were destined to be both the first and
last positive news stories about Peter Foster. A rematch
between Johnson and Mundine turned into an organisational
and financial disaster. And, at the tender of twenty, Peter
Forster acquired the first of his many criminal convictions –
and a $40,000 fine – for an insurance fraud.

Undeterred, he reinvented himself as a television producer and set out to court Muhammad Ali as the subject of a proposed documentary. Somewhere along the line he claimed to have persuaded Ali – then in the declining years of his glorious boxing career – to undertake a fight in Australia.

The 'Milk-Shake Tycoon' sold tickets by the barrowload. As James Small, one of his subsequent colleagues and confidants would later recall, money rolled in like breakers on the beaches of Foster's native Gold Coast.

'It was Peter's first real introduction to real wealth. But unfortunately some negative publicity came up about Ali going back into another fight somewhere else. The negative publicity caused Peter's fight not to go on. Peter retained a lot of the monies from the ringside sales and that was his first real kick into making himself an entrepreneur.'[23]

Less robust people might have felt a little embarrassed by the turn of events. But Peter Foster had a strong stomach and a definite case of brass neck.

By 1983 he was still (or so he boasted) close friends with Ali and was apparently a regular visitor at the boxer's home on Los Angeles' Wilshire Boulevard. And it was in the United States that he discovered the 'slimming cure' that would shortly bring him considerable wealth, an impressive stable of women – and the next in his collection of court appearances.

Bai Lin Tea was, Foster claimed, an ancient Chinese mystical drink with the miraculous ability to transform overweight bodies into slim and healthy shape – all in a convenient and easily digested tea-like drink.

He returned to Australia with the rights to distribute this revolutionary product, formed a company and set about marketing his sure-fire dieting wonder.

There were, as the Australian Competition and Consumer Commission (ACCC) would subsequently note, two distinct types of victim of Foster's diet tea scam. First, there were the consumers – men and (most typically) women desperate to lose weight but somehow unable to do so by the conventional approaches of eating less and taking more exercise.

The second category included people who invested in local distributorship operations for Bai Lin Tea: Foster sold around fifty such franchises across Australia at $10,000 a go. But somehow Australia was proving slower on the uptake than Peter Foster wanted. Bai Lin Tea and the franchises to distribute it were a nice little earner but not as profitable as someone of his undoubted talents surely deserved.

That this was due, as the ACCC reported, to the fact that Bai Lin Tea had absolutely no slimming properties (for the very simple reason that it was no different from ordinary tea) was, naturally, a completely irrelevant detail as far as Foster was concerned. It was time to set sail in search of new and more lucrative markets: South Africa and then Britain beckoned.

By the mid-1980s Britain's population – or at least those portions of it not reduced to poverty by Margaret Thatcher's economic revolution – was gripped by rampant consumerism and the ambition to acquire for itself the trappings of a good life. These were the Yuppie Years – the decade of Filofaxes and red braces, expense-account lunches and the deification of greed.

Greed's traditional partner, gluttony, was also having an effect. As a result, the 1980s were also the decade of Jane Fonda workouts and the Green Goddess exercises on breakfast television. Britain was, in short, a country ripe for Peter Foster and his miraculous slimming tea.

Foster was now in his mid-twenties and sufficiently advanced in his chosen career to have come up with a master plan – effectively a carefully constructed script to which all his subsequent slimming scams would conform.

And, as he later explained to convicted bank robber and prison escapee Bernie Matthews across the comfort of a shared jail cell, he wasn't remotely ashamed.

'To be a great salesman is to be a great conman. Selling is an art. You are an actor and acting is all about conning people and making them believe what you want them to believe.

'I am not being unethical – in fact being a conman is one of the most prestigious professions you can pursue.'[24]

And Foster had carefully worked out exactly whom he needed to pursue in the furtherance of this 'prestigious' profession.

'In the diet industry, our normal target market is women 25–55. We understand that, while men make up 49% of the population, and they are equally as overweight as women, it is the woman who will purchase the product.

'She will buy it for her husband, boyfriend, son. He is normally too self-conscious to buy a weight-loss product. So we must direct our message to the woman as she controls the purse strings'.

But the relatively slow uptake of Bai Lin in Australia had also taught him that grandiose claims on their own would not be enough to sell his bogus slimming cures. To reach his goal of becoming a diet millionaire he needed major celebrity endorsement, targeted at his core market. And in 1980s Britain there was only one name big enough to do the job.

When historians write definitive accounts of the 1980s

they tend to overlook the extraordinary and revealing story of Samantha Karen Fox. And yet few figures in popular British culture so effectively sum up the decade.

Sam Fox was born in London's Mile End, the unremarkable daughter of unremarkable market traders. But on Tuesday, 22 February 1983, she became very – if unaccountably – very famous indeed.

It was, as its editor was often given to claiming, the *Sun* 'wot dun it'. Under the utterly shameless headline SAM, 16, QUITS A-LEVELS FOR OOH-LEVELS, the tabloid's popular Page 3 photograph featured Fox's cheerful smile and naked 36D breasts.

By the time she retired from Page 3 modelling in 1986, Sam Fox was the nation's pin-up. Feminism was forgotten: Fox's 5 foot 1 inch nude body was plastered across workplaces up and down the country. She became a staple of popular television and a byword for cheery (if undressed) cockney charm.

Peter Foster wanted Sam Fox. In this he was probably far from alone, but he wanted her not just for her body, but also for her marketing value. And, true to form, he got both.

Foster has been designated (by qualified psychologists) a 'charming psychopath' – someone who makes his way through life by deluding others, but in reality is incapable of empathising with anyone other than himself.

Perhaps that explains his success with glamorous women. Certainly Sam Fox fell under his spell and soon became the public face of Bai Lin Tea in Britain. According to Foster's sister Jill, who had joined him in England, Britain's favourite topless model never stood a chance.

'We had a field day in England. They were heady days

indeed. True salad days. We had a ball. We had more money than sense, and I don't know which one we spent first. There were three major influential women in Britain at the time. There was the Queen, Sam Fox and Margaret Thatcher.

'Peter said [of Sam Fox], "That's going to be my Bai Lin tea girl." And we just howled him down like, right, yeah. But it appealed to her. I mean she was in the snare before she knew it.'[25]

And the outcome astonished even Peter Foster. By the end of 1987 he had sold British slimmers $7 million worth of the utterly ineffective 'weight-loss' tea.

He had also expanded his promotional network, roping in jockey Lester Piggott and Sarah Ferguson, Duchess of York, to endorse the slimming sensation that was Bai Lin. Both were unaware of Foster's dishonesty and, like Sam Fox, were innocent victims of Foster.

He then became a major sponsor of Chelsea Football Club – and that season the team trooped out onto the turf at Stamford Bridge proudly bearing the Bai Lin Tea logo on their shirts, with nobody at the club having any idea of Foster's true character.

According to investigators with the California Department of Health Services (who would soon take very close interest in Peter Foster and Bai Lin tea) all this success enabled him to acquire a $2.5 million Spanish villa, a Rolls-Royce, eight racehorses and a luxury London townhouse.

Unfortunately for Foster, Bai Lin tea had one unpleasant side effect. It tended to attract complaints from dissatisfied customers who had unaccountably failed to shed their excess weight.

As 1988 dawned, many thousands of consumer

complaints had come to the attention of trading-standards officers. The officers repeated some of the same tests as had their Australian counterparts, came to exactly the same conclusion, and arrested Foster on the perfectly reasonable charge that his miraculous slimming tea did no such thing.

Fraud, however, is not traditionally viewed by the courts as a terribly threatening sort of crime. At an initial procedural hearing, bail was set at £50,000 pounds and Peter Foster was politely asked to come back in a few weeks.

Instead, he jumped bail and fled (briefly) back to Australia. From there, in February 1988, he flew to America with a fellow Australian scammer, Trevor Brine.

In 1989 a new and even more miraculous-sounding diet product was proudly announced in newspapers across the United States. Cho Low Tea would, so the adverts ran, reduce blood cholesterol levels while still allowing users to eat whatever they pleased. The adverts appeared in more than a hundred major newspapers, from the *Washington Post* on the east coast to the *Los Angeles Times* on the west.

They also featured the photograph and testimonial of a prominent young television actor, endorsements from seven medical sources, and the logo of the Better Business Bureau (BBB). Peter Foster was back in business.

Foster and Trevor Brine made only one really big mistake: they cheekily asked the newspapers to extend them credit. It was – and still is – standard operating practice for the American Newspaper Publishers Association (ANPA) to assign one of its credit bureau staff to check out companies who wanted to place their adverts on tick. And it didn't take long to discover that Foster's and Brine's credit references were phoney.

The ANPA got on the phone to the police. Four days after the ad appeared, the BBB's national office notified newspapers that the marketer was not a Bureau member and lacked permission to use its logo. Meanwhile, the US postal service used its powers to block orders through the mail.

Then the Food and Drug Branch of the California Department of Health Services persuaded the mail-order company that Foster had duped into agreeing to distribute the tea on his behalf to freeze any payments pending further investigation. Within a few short weeks, Los Angeles police arrested both Foster and Brine.

They quickly discovered no Cho Low Tea actually existed. Foster and Brine said they had planned to repackage another company's tea but hadn't quite got round to it. The testimonials and endorsements in the adverts turned out to be equally bogus and Foster and Brine pleaded 'no contest' to false and misleading advertising as well as falsely representing a substance to have medicinal properties.

Foster was ordered to spend four months in the Los Angeles county jail, followed by three months cleaning up freeways with a California Department of Transportation crew. In addition, he was ordered to pay $228,000 still owed to newspapers that had carried the adverts. Brine was given a three-month sentence. Finally, the court also banned both men from selling tea or any product purported to have a health benefit.

Coupled with his difficulties in Australia and skipping bail while facing charges in England, the sentence would have broken a lesser conman. But throughout his career Peter Foster has repeatedly demonstrated a steely determination not to be cowed by the petty demands of obeying the law.

And he usually made much more money than he lost. So, within months, he was at it again.

Soon after Foster was released from jail, newspapers across the country were contacted by a new business calling itself 'World Stage Advertising & Publishing Group'. From an address in North Hollywood, California, the company asked the papers to extend it credit for a series of adverts.

This time the product was a royal-jelly concoction bearing the enticing brand name Ageless Aging.

The breathless advertising copy claimed that smearing this amazing unguent over salient portions of the anatomy would magically increase the body's energy and counter the toxins that – as everyone surely knew – 'contribute greatly to the aging process'.

Only quick work by eagle-eyed investigators spotted a remarkable similarity of approach between the adverts for Ageless Aging and Cho Low Tea. Subsequent enquiries revealed that the brains behind World Stage Advertising & Publishing Group belonged to none other than Peter Foster. Newspapers across the United States were warned against publishing the adverts. Clearly the game was up in America – it was time to go home.

Australia had been remarkably lenient with Peter Foster in the past. Despite the strong evidence that Bai Lin was nothing but a scam, the Australian Competition and Consumer Commission hadn't prosecuted, leaving the way clear for him to run the same con in Britain. But almost ten years later, when he flew from Los Angeles to Queensland, the ACCC was to prove much less tolerant.

It didn't take Foster long to get a new con off the ground: a franchising scheme for a new 'thigh-reducing' cream bearing the impressively scientific-sounding name of 'Biometrics'. It was, in effect, the same scam as Ageless Ageing – and ran on the same lines as Bai Lin. Only the product was different, though it was equally bogus.

As the early 1990s wore on, the list of Foster's franchised victims mounted. According to James Small, his former sales manager, most were people on the rebound from losing their jobs and hoping to find a new way to make a living.

'The type of people that we would involve in these distribution managements were people with redundancy payouts. Middle-income earners. People that might go and get a mortgage on their property to buy the business.'

The fact that his victims might – and sometimes did – lose their homes as well as their savings didn't seem to worry Peter Foster in the slightest. He invented yet more bogus testimonials to ensnare them, and told Small to promise huge central promotional campaigns to support the franchises.

'That was one of my key selling points. There's going to be two million dollars' worth of advertising over the next two years to promote this product. The money never was there at the end of the day. It was utilised in other areas, for personal gains and other investments.

'The funds that were supposed to be put into the business at the end of the day just didn't happen.'[26]

Many of the victims of this con complained to the ACCC. Its investigators painstakingly accumulated large bundles of evidence, all pointing the finger at one man: Peter Foster. ACCC chairman Professor Allan Fels decided that enough was enough. Foster and several of his associates were issued with injunctions banning them from making false claims about Biometrics.

'These people preyed on those wanting to become independent and earn their own way. Many people became involved and lost large sums of money.'

Foster, though, wasn't about to come quietly. He refused to accept the injunctions – then, when the ACCC took the case to court, he followed his own standard operating procedure and fled the country.

Unfortunately, he made two cardinal errors. The first was choice of destination: England. The second was his decision to start a new scam almost as soon as he landed.

In February 1995 a new British business was entered on the ledgers of Companies House. These ledgers reveal that Foremost Bodycare Corporation Ltd was established and run by one Peter Clarence Foster.

The main business of Foremost Bodycare Corporation Ltd was to be the manufacture and marketing of a new slimming pill. Conscious of the need for a famous face to promote the product, Foster approached Pamela Anderson's agent, seeking to use the pneumatic US actress's image to endorse the new pills.

Whether the former *Baywatch* beauty would have given her consent remains a tantalising mystery, because Foster ran into a little difficulty with his potential suppliers before a single tablet could be produced.

In the middle of 1995 Foster approached Inter Health, a reputable supplier of raw materials to the 'nutritional food' industry. One of its product lines was a natural appetite suppressant used in various brands of slimming pill.

In typically ostentatious Foster style, he invited Inter Health's representatives to negotiations at the Ritz Hotel in London. These talks were apparently satisfactory and in late

June Foster told Inter Health that he was ready to place an order worth nearly half a million US dollars.

Inter Health was happy to help. There was just the small matter paying for the order upfront. This was because Foremost Bodycare Corporation Ltd was a new, unproven company and so no credit could be given. Foster was furious – how dare Inter Health question his credit-worthiness? Angrily, he announced that the deal was off.

Inter Health was surprised by the vehemence of Foster's reaction and asked him to reconsider. Foster's response was to send out a letter proclaiming Foremost's credit-worthiness. Among other claims, the letter stated that the company had in the region of $4.5 million in cash, sitting in the bank.

In July 1995 Inter Health wrote back. It offered Foremost a discount on the order price, but regretfully restated the condition that it could go into production only if the appetite suppressant was paid for in advance. And, to make matters easier for Foremost, it attached a pro forma invoice for the half-million dollars.

Pro forma invoices, as the name suggests, are simply a convenient, easy-to-use way for a purchaser to pay his supplier for goods in advance. But Foster had a novel use for Inter Health's invoice – he boldly altered it in such a way as to suggest that Inter Health was extending him credit. And, since the company had spent the past two months politely but firmly refusing that credit, Foster was deliberately committing a serious fraud.

Next he tried to use the forged document as a way of persuading another supplier of the same product – Gee Lawson Chemicals – to give him credit. After all, Foster suggested, if Inter Health was prepared to hand over the goods on thirty days' free credit, Gee Lawson should surely be willing to match these terms.

But one of Gee Lawson's directors spotted something odd: close examination revealed that the words 'Terms: 30 days' were in a slightly different typeface from that used in the rest of the document. As a result, neither Inter Health nor Gee Lawson was willing to do business with Foremost Bodycare Corporation or its irritable young director.

Undeterred, Foster started casting around for a company to manufacture his brand-new miracle slimming pills – despite the small problem of not actually having any ingredients to put in them. He settled on Custom Pharmaceuticals Ltd, a well-established manufacturer of tablets and capsules for the legitimate health and pharmaceutical industries.

He knew by now that he had a credit-rating problem and that, with no track record in Britain, Foremost wasn't about to be given goods on tick. But, ever-resourceful, he worked out a solution. The fact that this was even more fraudulent than the rest of the scheme put together was just a minor detail.

Dunn & Bradstreet is one of the biggest and most influential companies providing credit-reference information. Foster held a series of meetings with its representatives, telling them that he was unhappy with the information D&B held on Foremost and arguing that this did not reflect the true financial position of the company.

He proudly announced that Foremost had £2.5 million in the bank and a turnover of £22 million; what's more, he claimed, it had seven thousand retail outlets and expected to have another five thousand by Christmas. Finally he handed over a number of documents on the basis of which he expected D&B to revise its credit assessment.

Over the ensuing weeks he maintained a regular correspondence with the people from Dunn & Bradstreet. In answer to his letters – and at his request – the company sent Foster a number of documents relating to Foremost Bodycare Corporation's credit rating. Foster knew exactly what to do with them. Out came the scissors, the glue and the correction fluid and, as if by magic, Foremost suddenly had a much more favourable rating. He then took the newly doctored documents along to Custom Pharmaceuticals.

In fact, by the time he forged its apparent blessing on him, Dunn & Bradstreet had smelled a rat and withdrawn any credit rating at all for Foremost Bodycare Corporation. But Custom Pharmaceuticals saw only the bogus report and was therefore ready to extend credit. Fortunately, senior management at Gee Lawson heard about the proposed deal and told Custom the story of its unsettling dealings with Foremost.

By the end of 1995, Foster was in serous trouble. He had already been fined the— for him— piffling sum of £21,000 over the original British Bai Lin scheme and had also just been convicted of breaching trading-standards regulations over a relatively minor sideline scam in which he had promoted similarly bogus 'slimming granules'. These were routine risks he usually shrugged off. However, it was the elaborate machinations surrounding Custom Pharmaceuticals that had him really worried.

The details of the scam had landed on the desk of investigators at the Serious Fraud Office. The SFO had been set up seven years earlier specifically to handle cases of complex frauds involving more than £1 million. Its staff were specialists and its bite could be fatal. By the start of 1996, Foster had been arrested and was staring a prison sentence in the face. There was only one logical option – true to form, he did a runner.

Once again, he sought out the comfort of his birthplace. But when he landed at Brisbane Airport he found himself in the less than welcoming embrace of the police. The warrant they held for his arrest concerned his withholding information from the Australian federal authorities over the Biometrics scam – then they discovered that the passport on which Foster was travelling was a forgery. This time he did not pass go. They took him directly to jail.

For the next five months he was held behind bars at the Queensland's Arthur Gorrie Correctional Centre. It was here that he met and struck up a friendship with the convicted armed robber Bernie Matthews. According to the career criminal, Foster asked his help in using one of the prison computers to write a 200-page manuscript about his life as a conman.

Matthews would, in later years, reinvent himself as a journalist, and, as luck would have it, he happened at that point to have retained a copy of the Foster memoirs.

Reading them is a faintly surreal experience. They are a cross between a self-justifying instruction manual for would-be con artists and a bizarre narrative in which Foster claims to have been an undercover agent for police forces on both sides of the world.

> I went undercover for the [Australian] Federal Police as an operative to infiltrate and crush a major international drug trafficking syndicate. Working with the field name

'Mr Clarence', I wore listening devises and covertly recorded meetings with the Mr Bigs of the proposed largest importation of heroin in Australia's history.

What sounds inconceivable considering the public perception of me is a hard fact. It is for ever acknowledged in a letter from the Australian Federal Police, held on file by the Supreme Court, confirming that I had on several occasions risked my life to bring our operation to a successful conclusion.

My drug busting crusade also extended to England, where I became a registered undercover informer for the British police. My task in the operation codenamed 'Outreach' was exposing corruption within a prison-run charity. Established to educate our children about the perils of drug use, the fund was being plundered by putrescent prison officers, placing at risk the lives of innocent children.

Inevitably, there is not a scrap of evidence to support any of these claims. But the memoir wasn't the only published work of Peter Foster during his months spent in Correctional Centre.

Back in London, the Serious Fraud Office was determined to get its hands on the runaway conman.

By the middle of 1997, he had been convicted for his part in the Biometrics scam, had been fined $15,000 and forced to give an undertaking to stop making further statements about the supposed physiological or therapeutic effects of the treatment.

But, although this now freed him from his Australian travails, the SFO had begun extradition proceedings over the

Foremost Bodycare fraud. The Federal Police arrested him and then, rather foolishly, let him out on bail. Inevitably, Foster once again took to his toes.

His time on the run was cut short in February 1998 and he was returned to a secure cell at the Arthur Gorrie Correctional Centre, pending the resolution of the extradition process. Somehow, he persuaded the prison authorities to allow him access to a video camera. And, with the panache and chutzpah of a seasoned con artist, Foster filmed an emotional and heartfelt plea for protection from the British authorities.

If his written memoirs were surreal, this video was straight out of *Alice in Wonderland*: staring straight at the camera Foster put a truly inventive spin on the truth.

'I haven't been convicted of fraud. I've never been charged with stealing a cent in my life. I've been accused of being an overzealous promoter... but I'm not a thief.

'Look I'm no angel. I'm far from it. I've made a lot of mistakes in my life. So many, you know, I keep wishing I could turn the clock back and turn the clock back. And I keep going back and back and back and before you know it I'm in the womb again. Where do you go from there?'

Next he made an ill-founded bid for sympathy from the court: 'They've all but broken me. They've ruined me financially. My reputation is trashed for ever. I'm a social and business leper. All I have left in this world is my mother and my sister and my niece. And, if they don't ease up, they'll take my mother off me also. She's not well, and this is killing us.'

And then he added what he believed to be the icing the cake: a warning that, should the Australian courts return him to Britain, they could be signing his death warrant.

'The reason I won't go back to England without fighting is

because I know I won't survive. I don't have any doubt about that. I don't... You can't be a police informer against corrupt prison officers and be returned to prison.'

Strangely, the Australian court was entirely unmoved by the self-justification, the plea for sympathy and the dire predictions of a death in prison. On 30 March 1999 the extradition warrant was signed.

It would take another fifteen months of legal wrangling before Peter Clarence Foster was forcibly put on a plane bound for London Heathrow. He was met there by the police and SFO and charged with using forged documents in the Foremost Bodycare scam.

On 18 September 2000 he pleaded guilty to three counts of using what the law calls 'forged instruments' contrary to the Forgery and Counterfeiting Act. Ten days later, St Albans Crown Court sentenced him to thirty-three months' imprisonment and disqualified him from acting as a company director for the next five years.

Yet he never served a day of that sentence. Because he had spent so long in Australian custody while fighting the extradition proceedings, he was deemed to have worked off the British sentence. He walked out into the early-autumn air a free man once again. But Britain had – temporarily at least – lost its lustre and within a few weeks Foster was to be found on the other side of the world.

It's one of those mysteries that seem to surround Peter Foster that, less than a year after committing to videotape an impassioned plea for leniency on the grounds of financial hardship, he was able to afford the luxury of sunning himself on the cruise liner *Mystique Princess* as it lazily sailed around the Yasawa Islands near Fiji in the south Pacific.

Foster was the last thing that Fiji needed at the time. The dawn of the millennium had seen the democratically elected Fijian government fall to a military coup. In November 2000, guns started blazing in the streets of the capital, Suva, as mutinous soldiers tried to kill the man who had led the coup, Commodore Frank Bainimarama. Fiji became very unstable, very quickly.

To Foster's mind the troubles were a heaven-sent opportunity. The Fijian government was in a state of flux. It needed all the friends it could get. International businessmen who answered its call for help in these troubled times would surely be blessed with some reward once peace and tranquillity returned to Suva. And so, in the general election that ensued, the 'financially ruined' Foster gave $1 million to one of the political parties.

Oddly, perhaps, no one seemed to question how a man who had spent so much of his recent time in prison could dole out such largesse at such short notice. There was, of course, only one answer: Peter Foster had another scam running.

Two years earlier, the formation of a new company calling itself the Chaste Corporation had gone unnoticed in Australia. Although it was set up both to market miracle slimming pills and to franchise the right to distribute them – in other words, a classic Foster scam – none of the Australian authorities had managed to join the dots.

In fairness, Foster wasn't listed as a director and, given that he was then an enforced guest at the Arthur Gorrie Correctional Centre, he might have seemed unlikely to be the brains behind it. But, unfortunately, he was.

The new wonder drug (non-prescription of course) that Chaste was to market and franchise was to be promoted under the promising name 'TRIMit'. And the advertising copy was equally alluring:

> TRIMit contains an extract from a rare Asian tamarind fruit, often referred to as 'the fat fighting fruit', along with a combination of natural ingredients.
>
> By combining the compound from the fat fighting fruit with Levocarnitine and three forms of natural chromium, together with an important manufacturing process, it is believed that a breakthrough resulting in a very effective diet pill has been achieved.
>
> Combined in easily dispensed tablet form and taken daily, TRIMit is a potent blend of carefully researched natural ingredients that work together in perfect harmony to promote weight loss.
>
> It is a completely safe and natural product, but as with any weight loss product, there are certain people who are advised against taking TRIMit.
>
> TRIMit normalises the neurotransmitters in your brain which control eating behaviour. Now, the desire to binge or eat too much has been removed and you are free to follow the other simple steps in the TRIMit plan.

There was just one tiny little snag with all of this: not a single word of it was true.

Chaste also claimed that that TRIMit had been successfully launched in the United States. What's more, it had been scientifically tested at eleven universities. Given that these impressive-sounding claims were actually published before Foster had decided on the actual ingredients for the pills, it was hardly a surprise that not a single word of these claims was true either.

But that didn't stop Foster franchising his miracle slimming cure. Chaste Corporation recruited seventy 'area managers', charging each one $39,900 for the right to distribute TRIMit. These fees were immediately split between Foster and the frontman he had hired to run Chaste Corporation.

As with all his previous slimming scams, the money flowed in. Foster alone received more than $1 million between December 1999 and November 2001, when the Chaste Corporation suddenly went into liquidation.

Foster was now thirty-nine. He had knocked around the world of dodgy diet pills for nearly two decades and he had learned one lesson above all: if you're going to scam, scam big.

And so, untroubled by any basis in fact, TRIMit was marketed and franchised around the world. In addition to the Chaste Corporation in Australia, he set up separate companies in the UK and the Republic of Ireland – though, perhaps with his recent disqualification from being a company director in mind, he installed his seventy-year-old mother at the official helm.

In Ireland, he based the business in a splendid Georgian mansion overlooking Dublin Bay. From here, he targeted rich Irish investors with a series of adverts in the local Sunday newspapers. Without even the slightest hint of irony, these promised huge profits to anyone with the 'honesty and integrity' to put up £120,000. Foster also told his would-be franchisees that they would recoup their investment within three months and would be millionaires within a year

But rewarding though Australia had been for TRIMit – and

however promising the Irish market was looking – Foster had his heart set on a much bigger and more lucrative opportunity.

British consumers had proved time and time again that they would buy any old rubbish if someone told them it would painlessly strip unwanted pounds from their burgeoning waists. But, by the time TRIMit was fully up and running in 2001, less than a year had passed since the unpleasantness surrounding Foremost Bodycare. So, in order to get away with another slimming scam so soon, Foster would need some seriously impressive connections.

Cherie Blair had known and liked Carole Caplin since 1989. At the time she was no more famous than any other leading barrister, married to an ambitious opposition MP. Caplin, then twenty-seven, was a former professional dancer and model whose chief claim on the public's attention was that she had posed topless for *Men Only* magazine. The pair met in a gym and became firm friends.

Caplin went on to form a lifestyle consultation company – influenced by both her passion for fitness and a debilitating bout of ME. By the time Cherie Blair was a national figure, living in the media spotlight as the Prime Minister's wife, Carole Caplin had become her style adviser. There was no secret about any of this – the press and television regularly referred to Caplin's alleged influence over Blair. So, when Peter Foster discovered the friendship, he knew that a mouthwatering opportunity had opened up for him.

According to Michael Carroll, one of his closest associates in the TRIMit scheme, Foster deliberately targeted Caplin and somehow managed to become her boyfriend purely to gain entrance to the Blairs' inner circle. With Caplin's help, he hoped to use the Blairs in a publicity campaign intended to boost sales of TRIMit.

'It was a game plan that the Blairs were targeted from the start in June,' he said. 'Cherie was targeted from the very first day as his overall aim. He used Carole Caplin to get to Cherie Blair. Then he would use her to get to Tony Blair.'[27]

Bizarre as this sounded, by September 2002 Foster and Caplin were able to toast the conman's birthday inside Number 10 Downing Street.

And emails sent by Foster to a former leading footballer a few weeks later seem to support the claims that – as Michael Carroll put it – 'he was doing a £6 million scam with the Blairs all around him'.

From a rented office in a Surrey stately home, Foster had repositioned his (still nonexistent) diet pill as a solution to childhood obesity, and conned former England footballer Paul Walsh into investing £75,000 in the company. Walsh was also encouraged to mobilise his football contacts to promote a healthy-living campaign planned by TRIMit. This, the unwitting Walsh was told, was to bear the impressive title of 'the Children's Education Programme' and would be backed by a national tour of schools.

On 17 October 2002 Foster sent an email to Walsh updating him on progress:

Carole spoke to Cherie Blair on Wednesday and told her exactly what we want Tony to do with you and the children education programme. She thinks it's great. (Cherie has a lot of influence over him.) I am 100 per cent confident we will make this move forward. Carole is certain.

At the time the Blairs' eldest son, Euan, was just starting an undergraduate degree at the University of Bristol.

Cherie Blair decided that it would be a sensible idea to buy a flat there – both as an investment and as somewhere for her son to live. She asked Caplin to have a look round the city and identify possible locations. It was just the open door Peter Foster needed.

Within a matter of days, Foster had inserted himself into the process, had emailed Cherie Blair to tell her about a pair of promising-sounding flats, and begun to boast publicly of his close association with Britain's First Family.

As it happened, Foster had a rather more pressing need to create the impression of friendship with the Blairs than simple monetary gain. The Australian government had applied to extradite him back to Queensland so that he could face criminal prosecution for his role in the Chaste Corporation's version of the TRIMit scam. Foster, unsurprisingly, was contesting the extradition and hoped a connection with the Prime Minister and his wife might tilt the scales in his favour.

Instead, his scheming merely created a minor political scandal for the Blairs. As 'Cheriegate' (as the press quickly dubbed it) reverberated around Fleet Street that December, Peter Foster was deported to Australia.

Despite the fact that he would shortly be charged with serious criminal offences, Foster gave every impression of being happy to be home. He was soon living the high life back on the Gold Coast, driving a smart new red sports car and enjoying the companionship of an attractive new girlfriend.

It took until September 2005 for the Chaste Corporation

scam to reach court. To no one's great surprise Foster and his associates were found guilty. The court ruled that Foster had been the driving force behind the con, banned him from participating in any weight-loss, cosmetic or health-industry-related business for the next five years and fined him AUD$150,000.

Given that the court also ruled that Foster's personal share of the scam had been $1 million, the fine looked a little derisory. And with no prison sentence imposed, the world was once again his oyster.

Within a month, he was back in Fiji. As a convicted criminal he was, in theory, not allowed to enter the country, but he overcame that little problem by the simple expedient of producing false documents. And it wasn't long before he announced his next business venture.

He obtained a lease on 45 hectares of waterfront land on the unspoilt Champagne Beach. He claimed to have gathered $1.5 million from Australian investors to develop a number of world-class luxury condominiums there. In an interview with the *Sydney Morning Herald*, he announced, 'I'm going to build homes for 50 of the world's most successful and interesting people... that's my dream. For me, that would be as good as it gets.'

That was, indeed, as good as it got. Faced by a rival developer also seeking permission to develop Champagne Beach, Foster began a campaign of misinformation, creating false websites that suggested that his rival's resort was being created as a haven for paedophiles.

These were claims that the Fijian police were duty-bound to investigate. They did so, and, with a weary inevitability, discovered Foster's elaborate and unpleasant tissue of lies.

However, in the course of their enquiries, the police also discovered the false documents Foster had used to get into the country – yet another prosecution and deportation seemed on the cards.

It was time for Foster to call in the favours owed as a result of his generosity to politicians six years earlier. First, instead of being dragged off to jail, he was allowed to live in some luxury in an attractive beachside residence in Deuba, a popular watering hole on Fiji's Coral Coast.

But the real return on his investment came in December 2006. By then Fijian police had finally mustered enough political support to get permission to arrest him and a full Tactical Support Group unit duly headed out to Deuba.

What happened next borders on the farcical. As the police approached, Foster was seen to leap from a moving vehicle and dive into the nearby lagoon. The Tactical Support Group quickly commandeered a powerboat and gave chase, but, as they closed in on the floundering conman, he somehow struck his head on the boat's propeller and received a deep head wound. Television pictures show an undignified Foster, clad only in black underpants, being hauled semiconscious onto the deck.

To the existing crimes of entering Fiji illegally and carrying forged papers, Foster could now be charged with resisting arrest. The police also wanted to question him about an alleged fraud against a bank in Micronesia. All in all, the future wasn't looking rosy.

And yet, as soon as he was released from hospital, a court ordered that he should be given bail. The only condition was that he stay in a luxury hotel in Suva. And, while he recuperated in some style from his injuries, another political coup put paid to any prospect of a prosecution. It may have cost him $1 million, but Peter Foster appeared to have acquired a very powerful Get Out of Jail Free card.

As 2007 dawned, Foster had every reason to feel well satisfied with the way things had panned out. He had made a fortune from running and rerunning the same slimming scams in countries across the world; he had lived the high-life of beautiful women, powerful friends and extravagant luxury – and by and large he'd got away with it.

There was also the money he'd managed to extract from that bank in Micronesia: $300,000 loaned on the strength of forged documents and intended for a luxury development that could now never be built. As he boarded the plane and headed home to Queensland, life must have seemed particularly good.

For his victims, of course – and they have been legion over the decades – there was precious little cheer. But just before Christmas 2007 they finally received news of something to celebrate.

On Sunday, 9 December (Australian courts seem not to worry about sitting on the Sabbath), Foster pleaded guilty in Brisbane's Supreme Court to defrauding the Bank of the Federated States of Micronesia of that $300,000. He was sentenced to four-and-a half-years in prison. As we write, he is still there.

9

ROBERT HENDY-FREEGARD: THE SPY WHO CONNED ME

At the trial of Robert Hendy-Freegard at Blackfriars Crown Court in June 2005, Andrew West, the senior prosecutor, had this to say of the thirty-four-year old in the dock:

'Although the jury has had to grapple with what seemed like a paperback plot, the public should be in no doubt that Robert Hendy-Freegard's deceptions were often so slick as to beggar belief. He is an arrogant and cruel man who has scarred the lives of many of his victims and who tricked them out of tens of thousands of pounds, years of their lives, and their dignity.'

Over a period of ten years, Hendy-Freegard, a semi-literate former car salesman, had managed to con a million pounds out of at least a dozen people, all of whom had been convinced that he was an either an MI5 secret agent or a Special Branch undercover officer.

The fortune that he stole from his various victims disappeared without trace, used to fund a James Bond lifestyle. The eventual twenty-four-count indictment was made up of numerous counts of financial fraud, but most unusual were the kidnap charges.

His victims had been entrapped 'unlawfully and by fraud' rather than by force. They had become his willing accomplices and he 'had exerted complete control over their minds and their movements'.

'The traditional idea of kidnap is one where people are physically restrained,' said Andrew West. 'On the surface, all of the victims could have walked away but such was his hold on them they feared for their lives if they did. In the end they had made such an investment in his fictions that there was no going back. Most would simply not believe the police were not impostors at the end.'

These remarks came at the conclusion of a tangled tale that started at a Shropshire agricultural college in 1993, moved from Somerset to Scotland, Leeds to London and the French Alps, and finally ended with a joint Metropolitan Police and FBI sting at Heathrow airport.

Hendy-Freegard certainly lived up to his nickname: 'the Puppetmaster'. 'The most accomplished liar the police had ever come across' had serially seduced and ruthlessly exploited his victims, despite the fact that they were all intelligent and respectable people.

Using a blend of deceitful but magnetic charm, claims that he was a secret agent, and fear engendered by hair-raising tales of shadowy IRA killers, he systematically destroyed his victims' self-respect, turned most into virtual slaves and swindled others out of huge sums of money.

At least seven of his victims were women – and he got engaged to most of them. They included a solicitor, a psychologist, a company director and a recently married PA, who left her husband for the swindler and ended up sleeping on park benches, living on a portion of Mars Bar a day and foraging for fresh water in public lavatories.

A twenty-one-year-old student, one of two men to fall prey to Hendy-Freegard's Svengali-like powers of persuasion, in turn persuaded his parents to hand over hundreds of thousands of pounds. Because he thought he was being recruited to the fight against terrorism, he abandoned his university finals for a three-year life on the run, fleeing from imaginary Republican hit men. With him went two other students who endured what must have seemed like a lifetime of poverty and degradation, while under orders from Hendy-Freegard to carry out bizarre 'missions' and 'loyalty tests' up and down the country.

While they suffered, their tormentor – whose motto might have been 'lies have to be big to be convincing' – used the cash he ordered them to earn, beg and borrow to fund a life of unstinting personal luxury.

His ever-changing fleet of exclusive cars included no fewer than seven top-of the-range BMWs and a £100,000 Aston Martin Volante. He wore bespoke designer suits, handmade shoes and a gold Rolex, ate expensive meals and took five-star holidays to exotic destinations such as Brazil.

Judge Deva Pillay said the conman's victims had fallen prey to his 'devious charm'. Witnesses spoke of Stockholm syndrome, a psychological phenomenon whereby victims come to identify so closely with their captor that they will do his every bidding without question and even resist attempts to rescue them.

Hendy-Freegard lounged impassively in one of the dock chairs as the judge told him, 'In my judgment, the several guilty verdicts of the jury in this case represent a vindication of your victims and a telling testament to their courage, tenacity and spirit to survive and overcome adversity, despite the depths of despair to which they were driven by you. It was plain to me as I listened to the evidence for many months that you are an egotistical and opinionated confidence trickster who has shown not a shred of remorse nor compassion for the degradation and suffering to which your victims were subjected.'

Robert David Hendy-Freegard was born just plain Robert Freegard at Kilton in Nottinghamshire in 1971. He left school at fifteen and trained as a carpenter and joiner, but, in the firm belief that he would one day be famous, he soon invented an alternative life and used his consummate charm to turn his fantasy into a rather warped reality.

His first non-student victim was Simon Young, who ran the watch department of a large jewellery shop in Sheffield. Here was an added challenge. Could Hendy-Freegard 'master' someone from scratch, away from the contained atmosphere of an educational establishment? Over the course of several carefully orchestrated social outings, he gradually won Simon's trust. When he was sure of his ground, he then regaled the young man with stories of his 'top-secret' espionage work, and concluded by suggesting that Simon was wasting his talents selling timepieces.

'He tried to enrol me into an organisation and offered me a job as well as certain training,' said Young. 'Of course I was interested in doing government work like this. It was every schoolboy's fantasy.'

Young was then sent on several seemingly pointless missions. One involved travelling to a particular shop in Manchester, where he had been told to spend £1.25 on a specified model of can opener. He was given detailed instructions about the route he should take and the various means of transport he should use, and warned he would be under constant surveillance. He thought he'd carried it all off with flying colours, but Hendy-Freegard told him he had failed, and ordered him on another mission.

He was told to buy a copy of the *Gay Times* and make a show of reading it on the train to London. The kiosk at Sheffield coach station didn't have the magazine, but Young headed for the capital anyway, carrying the can opener. Following his orders to the letter, he found his way to a designated West End pub and asked the barman for a particular person by name. He was told nobody answering to that name ever patronised the pub, but, thinking it was yet another test and all part of his MI5 recruitment process, he desperately tried to figure out what a superspy would do. Then it came to him. Handing the can opener to the baffled barman, he said, 'Well, when you see him, give him this.'

Proud of his quick thinking, he returned to Sheffield and told Hendy-Freegard how he had managed this very tricky situation. His suspicions were aroused only when Hendy-Freegard – having asked Simon for a full account of his mission – failed to keep a straight face as he listened to it. The jeweller demanded to see Hendy-Freegard's spymaster bosses. A meeting was arranged – but, unsurprisingly, Mr Young was the only one there. By that time he had ceased to believe anything Hendy-Freegard said and would have nothing more to do with him. Hendy-Freegard was probably having a practice run. Simon Young certainly had a lucky escape.

In 1993, while Hendy-Freegard was working as a part-time barman at the Swan pub near Harper Adams Agricultural College in Newport, Shropshire, he befriended three final-year students: wealthy farmer's offspring John Atkinson and his then girlfriend Sarah Smith, and Maria Hendy, who was soon to become Hendy-Freegard's girlfriend.

He impressed them all with his claim to be the brother of Duran Duran bass player John Taylor and to have a master's degree in psychology from Oxford. When John Atkinson asked why someone with such connections and qualifications was working as a humble barman, Hendy-Freegard took him aside and explained, confidentially, that he was actually a Special Branch officer planted as a sleeper to monitor an IRA cell preparing to attack the Parachute Regiment barracks at nearby Ternhill.

The barracks had been bombed four years previously and one of those allegedly responsible was a Harper student, though this was never proved. But it was enough of a connection to convince John Atkinson. The IRA bombings in Manchester that week put the seal on it. Hendy-Freegard chose his moment. He said that John was ideally placed to carry out additional undercover surveillance that would help break up the IRA cell, which he claimed was based at the college. Didn't John feel a sense of duty to his country? He did, and Hendy-Freegard had him hooked.

Almost before he knew it, he was being 'trained' for his new role. He allowed himself to be beaten black and blue and repeatedly punched in the stomach in order to toughen him up. Not long afterwards, Hendy-Freegard abruptly announced that his cover had been blown and that they must flee immediately.

He then told the two girls that Atkinson was dying of liver cancer and persuaded them to come on a farewell journey around the UK. The 'dying man' had played along with this charade, believing that it would keep the girls out of danger.

Though it was only a month before finals, the distraught friends set off, heading south. They had got as far as Bournemouth when Hendy-Freegard told the women the IRA story, warning them that contracts had been taken out on their lives, and that of John Atkinson, because of their association with him. A massive IRA bombing in Warrington, which killed two and injured fifty people, gave further credence to Hendy-Freegard's claims.

Day by disorienting day, they moved from town to town as Hendy-Freegard increased his control over them, forbidding all contact with friends and family, dictating what they did, what they ate and even when they were allowed to go to the lavatory. Eventually they reached Sheffield, where Hendy-Freegard rented what he called a safe house.

While waiting to be called up for duty, Young was ordered to get a cover job as a barman. Smith was forced to work sixteen-hour shifts in a chip shop. They gave most of their wages directly to their tormentor, leaving them virtually nothing to live on. Sarah Smith became so hungry she even resorted to eating leftover chip batter.

He manipulated all three of them like puppets, subjecting them to bizarre and degrading tests supposedly set by their spymasters, and making them hand over all their earnings. Like many of his victims, the college friends were also forced to obtain money for him from their families, money Hendy-Freegard spent on living out his James Bond fantasy.

As he became more confident, the would-be superspy controlled up to five victims at a time, keeping them in various 'safe houses' around the country and using a mixture of charm, menace and relentless pressure to keep them under his spell.

In order to eliminate their ability to support each other, he decided to split the three friends up. He now exerted so much control over them that he no longer had to be physically present to maintain it. He even allowed Atkinson to visit his parents to explain his extraordinary behaviour and sudden disappearance from College.

So convincing was he that his parents believed him. So convinced was Atkinson by Hendy-Freegard that in a telephone call he roundly abused Sarah's parents and accused them of putting her life in jeopardy by trying to trace her. Hendy-Freegard moved out of the safe house to live elsewhere in Sheffield with Maria Hendy, who had given birth to their first child.

After leaving Shropshire, Hendy-Freegard had become a very successful car salesman whose customers were usually well-heeled females, whom he often dated as well.

At first, he was the perfect boyfriend – handsome, attentive, generous and a good listener. But then life with him would become increasingly weird. He would disappear for weeks, and then start to drop hints that he wasn't just a car salesman and that his real job was something much more exciting. He would eventually confide that he was, in fact, an MI5 spy or a Special Branch officer being hunted by IRA killers, and this was the reason for his obsessive secrecy and for keeping almost constantly on the move.

Sarah Smith crisscrossed Britain for ten years, camping in shabby flats and bedsits in an effort to evade her mythical would-be assassins. She once wore a bucket on her head while being moved from one 'safe' location to another, unwittingly stayed with another of Hendy-Freegard's victims while pretending not to speak any English, and on another occasion spent three weeks hiding in a tiny bathroom because he said the IRA were closing in on her.

She took a series of short-term, low-paid jobs in order to live, but, even then, Hendy-Freegard took most of her earnings. John Atkinson endured similar bizarre treatment for three years, and his family were conned out of almost half a million pounds 'to buy protection'.

Smith's family were persuaded to part with nearly £200,000 in loans and from the proceeds of a trust fund he had persuaded them to cash.

Hendy spent nine years in his thrall, mostly living in a cramped and squalid flat in Sheffield and giving birth to their two daughters. In contrast, Hendy-Freegard treated himself to a life of unalloyed luxury.

According to the BMW salesman who supplied many of his expensive cars, 'When he bought a luxury car, he wanted every extra that money could buy. If he could have had a diamond-encrusted cigarette lighter, he would have.'

Maria Hendy, trapped in Hendy-Freegard's frightening but imaginary world of spies and assassins, became a virtual prisoner. He told her the phones were tapped and she was not allowed out without his express permission. She lived on the pitiful deposits he made into her bank account – unaware that they were actually the major part of Sarah Smith's wages.

Living in fear of assassination and of Hendy-Freegard's explosively violent temper, she struggled in silence to bring up her two daughters single-handed. Eventually, she plucked up the courage to leave.

None of the women knew about his relationships with the others. He often used one woman's money to woo another with gifts and expensive dinners as he juggled several of them at the same time. He ruled by fear. His rages were violent and unpredictable.

On more than one occasion he stopped his car on the motorway and threatened to throw one or other of his victims out of the car. After Hendy complained that he was a poor father to their children, because at that stage she had barely seen him for two years, she was punched in the face, had her eyes blackened and one of her front teeth knocked out. Hendy-Freegard later forced her to lie to the dentist and say she had fallen downstairs. He promised his lovers he would marry them. But, in the end, all he left were huge holes in their bank accounts and a trail of broken hearts.

Leslie Gardner was twenty-eight when she met Hendy-Freegard in a Newcastle nightclub in 1996. She was ensnared within weeks, and in the ensuing six years she gave him close to £30,000. She even sold her car because he said he urgently needed cash to 'buy off some killers', who he said were paramilitary bombers released under the Good Friday Agreement.

Hendy-Freegard also told the civil servant he had to pay off IRA blackmailers and buy himself out of the police, and needed money to start a new life and, later, to help his gravely ill mother.

Three months after he gave her a shiny new Volkswagen

Golf to replace the car she'd sold, Gardner discovered that it wasn't a gift at all. She received a letter from a finance company demanding three overdue monthly payments of £260 each. Unbeknown to her, Hendy-Freegard had signed her up for a hire-purchase agreement and pocketed his salesman's commission. Long after he had gone, Gardner was still paying for the car.

Elizabeth Bartholemew, who worked as a personal assistant and sales administrator at a car dealership in Sheffield, was twenty-two, and her marriage just six-months-old when she met Hendy-Freegard. She became a regular customer, and would even look after his two daughters while he test-drove a string of exclusive-range vehicles.

He bought her expensive perfume, gave her the attention and affection she was not getting at home and 'was very good in bed'.

But, as she later recalled, the 'horrifying eight-year nightmare' that followed cost her marriage, her health, her self-respect and £14,500.

'When he was in a good mood he was charming and couldn't do enough for you. But everything had to be precise with him. For example, if his shirt was even slightly creased, he would tear it off and throw a temper tantrum.

'It was like he had a trigger switch and it got to the stage where his anger really scared me. He was like a Jekyll and Hyde, a freak of nature.'

Hendy-Freegard had revealed to her his 'other life as a secret service spy'. He told her she was in danger from IRA terrorists and ordered her to sever all contact with family and friends, change her name from Bartholemew to Richardson and tell the deed poll officer it was because she had been molested as a child. Hendy-Freegard also got her drunk, took photographs of her naked and then threatened her that if she ever disobeyed him he would show them to her jealous husband.

She loved him desperately, but was told she would have to endure 'loyalty tests' to satisfy MI5 they could marry. They included becoming a blonde, going without make-up and sanitary towels, sleeping in Heathrow airport for several nights at a time, and living on park benches in Peterborough for weeks during winter.

She was in a constant state of terror and when she could not sleep – which was often – she would walk endlessly around in an effort to keep warm and out of danger. Hendy-Freegard confiscated her jacket, leaving her shivering in just a T-shirt and jeans. She celebrated her thirty-first birthday waiting fourteen hours for him at a bitterly cold rendezvous at Kettering railway station. He never turned up.

It was just another example of the kind of mind games he relished playing. Allowed only £1 a week to live on, Elizabeth Richardson often survived on nothing more than a cheap loaf of bread. Because it had to last, it was often mouldy by the time it was finished.

'Then there was the time when I was living on a Mars bar a week. I cut them in slices and rationed myself to a piece a day.'

Emaciated and encrusted with eczema, her feet covered in bleeding, oozing sores, Richardson spent most days in libraries to keep from freezing. Then, one day, a Good Samaritan spotted her wandering among the books and offered her lodgings in Dunton Bassett, Leicestershire.

To the police who eventually found her there – months

after Hendy-Freegard's arrest – it was 'a hovel'. To Richardson it was a heaven-sent, if short-lived, refuge. Hendy-Freegard had found her and told her that she was being targeted by a sniper, so, in order to keep out of sight, she crawled from room to room below window level and spent every evening in the dark.

She finally tried to escape his clutches, but could never shake him off. Despite her moving to Leeds, getting a new job and changing her phone number, he tracked her down, warning she could never get away.

As he had done with his other female victims, Hendy-Freegard ordered her to take out loans for him – in this case for £6,500 and then £8,000. Each time he pocketed the cash, said his 'MI5 superiors' wanted to see him urgently, and drove off without another word. It seems that Hendy-Freegard's motives were not purely financial. He clearly enjoyed exercising control and inflicting suffering. She, too, was being kept perpetually on the move, forced to live in sub-slum conditions, and reduced to near starvation.

She never talked to anyone about her plight, because she had been told that 'dangerous people would be watching her every movement'. To keep her compliant Hendy-Freegard raised her hopes by telling Richardson that MI5 had given them a choice of three towns to live in and that she had to tour them, visiting shops, pubs, doctors' surgeries and hospitals, and then write an extensive report. She had been led to believe that Hendy-Freegard was waiting for official permission for them to live together.

'This has all been so traumatically painful for me for so long now I can't even remember what normal life is actually like,' Smith said. 'He has totally ruined me, broken me. My confidence is nil and I still have nightmares. I keep seeing his face every time I fall asleep.'

Elizabeth Richardson also initially refused to cooperate with police officers investigating Hendy-Freegard, suspecting another MI5 'loyalty test'.

Cleaning company director Renata Kister was seven months pregnant and had recently split from her partner when she met Hendy-Freegard at Normand Continental, the West London VW dealership where he then worked. Still in emotional turmoil, she quickly fell under his spell.

'He was extremely well mannered, a true gentleman, and he was so funny.'

She signed up for a new VW Golf.

Their relationship blossomed, he moved into her flat, and, during holiday in Spain, he proposed to her on a beach in Marbella. She readily accepted, and they planned a wedding in a picture-book church in Wales. He told Kister about his double life as a spy and that his MI5 bosses had ordered him to 'watch someone' using the dealership as a cover for large-scale illegal activity. He said that after they were married they would adopt new identities. He would become Harry Sinclair and she would change her first name to Monica – after which his department 'would erase all record of their previous lives'.

He said he'd arranged to rent a house at Sunninghill in Berkshire and Renata Kister was looking forward to moving in with him, together with her baby daughter Ola. Hendy-Freegard gave her a set of keys so she could have a look around and move in some furniture, but the keys didn't fit.

Not surprising, really, because Sarah Smith was concealed inside. Fortunately for Hendy-Freegard, Kister changed her mind about making the house her marital home.

He persuaded her to buy a better car, but kept the £10,000 he made on her old one, and then persuaded her to take out a £15,000 loan for him. Whenever she asked him for the money, he said he had not yet been paid for his secret assignment. Eventually, she paid out more than £60,000 for cars he persuaded her to buy. Some of them she never actually saw.

Hendy-Freegard inveigled Kister into providing temporary accommodation for Sarah Smith, saying she was on a witness-protection scheme, having fled her violent husband. Kister, who is Polish, said that she was also persuaded to let Smith stay on and let her work as a cleaner.

But to prevent them from comparing notes he said her guest was Spanish and could not speak a word of English. And he warned the former student to pretend she could not understand anything said to her for security reasons. As a result they never exchanged a single word in three months.

Kister had not seen hide nor hair of Hendy-Freegard for several weeks when she heard that he'd been sacked from Normand's.

The manager told her that it was because his former star salesman had been hassling female customers – and gave her a forwarding address. Kister confronted Hendy-Freegard and demanded her money back, failing which she would call the police. Hendy-Freegard threatened to kill her and little Ola if she did, and then calmly said he'd fallen in love with someone else.

After his eventual arrest, police found Kister's telephone number among Hendy-Freegard's papers. But, as usual, he had so thoroughly brainwashed her that she initially thought the officers were part of an MI5 'loyalty test' and refused to have anything to do with them. According to case officer Detective Sergeant Bob Brandon, 'It took us a long time to convince her to come to the police station. And when she did and we showed her a picture of Sarah Smith she at first said she didn't know her. It was only later she called us back to say she did – and handed over her address.'

Caroline Cowper was a high-flying solicitor of thirty-four who met Hendy-Freegard in 2001 when she traded in her £16,000 Mercedes against a top-of-the-line, £20,000 Volkswagen Golf – at the same dealership where he had met Renata Kister. She decided that the smiling salesman was both charming and good-looking. So, having done the deal, she gave Hendy-Freegard her phone number.

Unaware he had several other 'fiancées', she soon fell in love with the handsome salesman, who seduced her with promises of love, happiness and marriage – by now a well-tried cocktail of deceit designed to con her out of every penny she had.

She was not only swept off her feet, but so captivated by his bedroom prowess that, when asked in a VW customer-satisfaction form to describe the salesman's performance, she added 'in bed' and gave him '11 out of 10' for technique. Soon afterwards he proposed and she accepted. They went shopping for an engagement ring in Hatton Garden, central London. The diamond-encrusted creation cost £6,500 and she was impressed when Hendy-Freegard paid without batting an eyelid. She was unaware that he had secretly pocketed half the trade-in value of her old car.

Blissfully ignorant that she was just one of several women – including several other 'fiancées' – he was sleeping with at the time, she regarded the ring as a glittering expression of true love. Not long afterwards he borrowed £1,500 from her. To pay her back he offered her an antique desk, which he said was of equivalent value. But he had doctored a receipt to add a further £1,700 to its value and then made her pay the balance.

And, when she later discovered he had pocketed £8,000 of her Mercedes trade-in money, he repeatedly promised to pay her back – once he had received a six-figure salary cheque from his MI5 bosses. Of course, the cheque was perpetually in the post, but, still infatuated, she clung to those promises nevertheless.

They took holidays in some of the world's most exclusive resorts and, although she was unaware of it, her money paid for those as well. He also persuaded her to give him cash for another car that was to kick-start a leasing business she had agreed to run with him. When the vehicle did not appear and she asked for the money back, he said that was not possible and the car was not available because it was being used by the 'Polish Mafia'.

Then, a year after their 'engagement', she discovered he had secretly plundered her Internet bank account of nearly £14,000. It was the last straw. Furious, she told him their relationship was over. By now £41,000 the poorer, she first took him to the Small Claims Court and won. The judgment produced nothing, so she made him bankrupt. But she had not finished yet.

She turned detective and tracked down Maria Hendy, the mother of Hendy-Freegard's two children, who dumped the conman after discovering his affair with Cowper. She also learned how he had targeted others, and, after 'piecing together bits of the jigsaw', finally went to the police. Their subsequent investigation put them on the trail of John Atkinson and Sarah Smith. But it was his involvement with thirty-two-year-old American child psychologist Dr Kimberley ('Kim') Adams that eventually led to his arrest.

Hendy-Freegard must have thought he had struck gold when he met Adams in August 2002, and discovered that her stepfather had recently had a multimillion-dollar lottery win. Adams, a single parent with a young son from a previous marriage, had not long moved to the UK. She was lonely and being treated for depression at the time so was an easy target. She fell for Hendy-Freegard within days, and found his stories so exciting that she was completely carried away. He then phoned her parents and told them that he had recruited her as a spy and they must send thousands of pounds pay for her training.

'He said he was working undercover, infiltrating a very dangerous criminal network,' Adams later recalled. 'I had no doubt he was telling the truth. He said that his job required him to be violent and boasted about murdering a man who had discovered that he was working undercover and had threatened to expose him. So the man was shot in the head. He said he was also present at a kneecapping, and when others held another person down and drilled into his skull.'

She was horrified, but mesmerised and completely hooked.

Just weeks into the fourteen-month relationship came the now very familiar marriage proposal. She was thirty-one, in love, said yes, and spent £405 on a wedding dress. He told her life with him would mean she, too, would have to be a spy.

She barely hesitated, even though it was made clear she would have to resign from her job in Reading and be forbidden all contact with her family and friends without his permission. He phoned her employers, telling them she was terminally ill and would not be returning to work, and told her they would live in a Hebridean lighthouse, monitoring the movements of Russian submarines in the North Sea. However, she would first have to undergo various 'tests' and adopt a new identity.

He also told her MI5 and Scotland Yard would examine and evaluate everything she had ever done and she must tell him about all her sexual encounters in detail. When she confessed she had kissed someone else – a man called Paul Heffner – shortly after taking up with Hendy-Freegard, he flew into a rage.

She was stunned by the sudden, chameleon-like change in her fiancé's mood. 'He said he was going to kill Paul and that I would have to cut off his balls.' Hendy-Freegard then tightened the screw still further. He said that the marriage was off and threatened her son.

It was an example of Hendy-Freegard's increasing desire for total control and the pleasure he got from creating a climate of fear.

'He said I was such an awful woman it would be much better for my son to die than for me to be a mother,' said Dr Adams, 'and that, if I refused to kill my son, he would have to bury him alive.'

Hendy-Freegard later said he had taken out a contract on her and her son, who attended school in America.

'I had sacrificed my son's life with my lies, and by the end of the night I would be glad to be dead,' she was told. 'I was completely terrified, physically shaking,'

And, of course, she was unable to tell any outsider of her

ordeal – an ordeal about which she still has nightmares. Later that day, an apparently remorseful Hendy-Freegard said he'd no intention of harming her, but that he couldn't bear to think of her with anyone else, and professed undying love.

Kim, still shaken, believed him. But later, when she told Hendy-Freegard that she'd had second thoughts and did not want to spend twenty-five years in a lighthouse, he told her they would have to repay the state £80,000 because all the arrangements had already been made.

However, if she could raise £20,00 for training, he would fund the balance. She phoned her father, film producer John Adams, in Omaha, Nebraska, and asked for £20,000 to pay for 'spy school', as she put it.

Not having the cash readily available, he turned to his ex-wife and his daughter's stepfather, who had recently won more than US $20 million on the lottery in Phoenix, Arizona. The money was swiftly paid over, but actually funded a luxury twelve-week European tour for Hendy-Freegard and his fifth 'fiancée'. To help cover his tracks, the conman travelled on a Polish passport.

But by that time Caroline Cowper had involved the police and Adams's name had come to light. After hearing of her stepfather's new wealth, they knew Hendy-Freegard would never willingly let her go. And when local Met officers telephoned her stepfather and her parents they refused to cooperate. The conman had warned them such contacts would be either double agents or MI5 agents testing their reliability.

So Scotland Yard was called in and the FBI contacted. Special Agent Jaclyn Zappacosta, with twenty years' experience with fraud and other white-collar crime, was assigned to the US Embassy in London to help hunt the conman and his latest victim. The case officer, Detective Sergeant Bob Brandon, briefed her: 'He told me a story that was so extraordinary I had no option but to believe it,' she recalled.

With Dr Adams's parents and stepfather finally on side, bank account withdrawals were examined and the couple's phone calls from Europe taped for weeks. But neither yielded any clue as to where the pair might be.

'He was such an accomplished fraudster, those avenues were dead-ended,' said Zappacosta. 'This Hendy-Freegard provided quite the challenge. During all these recordings Kimberley was crying, but she would not say where she was.'

The first breakthrough came when she rang to say Hendy-Freegard had told her she had failed spy school and needed £10,000 to resit exams. The FBI and Scotland Yard came up with a game plan in which they would provide the money as bait and Adams's mother would hand it over in London on condition she could see that her daughter was safe and well. A few days later, in May 2003, she flew into Heathrow and spent the next twenty-four hours being briefed and equipped with a hidden tape recorder and transmitter.

The next day Hendy-Freegard drove to Terminal 4, thinking the mother had just arrived, and took her to his car, where Kimberley Adams was waiting. Hendy-Freegard was promptly arrested and Adams was rescued.

'But for hours she refused to accept we were police officers,' said Metropolitan Police Family Liaison Officer PC Cathy Harrison.

'She was immensely traumatised, as were all the victims, and when she opened up it was unbelievable to hear how such a bright, intelligent woman had been so duped by this man. She found it very difficult to accept her relationship with Hendy-Freegard had been based on a complete fraud.'

Meanwhile, Hendy-Freegard refused to tell police the whereabouts of Sarah Smith and Elizabeth Richardson. Fortunately, Adams, who only then realised how thoroughly she had been duped, remembered that her tormentor had left a briefcase in the Hotel Buffalo at Chambery in France, and that it contained papers that could be crucial.

There was a real danger that the hotel would discard items from the room once it became apparent that the occupants were not coming back. Detectives hightailed it across the Channel and, with the assistance of the French Regional Crime Squad, they seized the briefcase. Fortunately, it contained documents relating to Sarah Smith, Renata Kister, Elizabeth Richardson and Lesley Gardner.

This provided police – who feared for the safety of the other victims – with a much-needed second breakthrough. Initially it led them to Renata Kister's west London home, and eventually to Sarah Smith, who had not been in contact with her family for over a year. Both women initially refused to believe what the officers were telling them.

Finally, five months after Hendy-Freegard's arrest, the briefcase paperwork helped police trace Richardson. At first she, too, believed the officers were part of an MI5 loyalty test. It took them a long time to convince her she had been comprehensively conned.

Finding her meant that charges against Hendy-Freegard could be finalised at last. He had consistently refused to answer any questions, but after he was charged, he changed his mind and said he wanted to talk. However, when police switched on the tape recorder, he spoke 'utter nonsense' for two and a half hours, claiming the case against him was a massive conspiracy invented by his accusers.

Nevertheless, his ten-year reign of terror now over, he was charged with kidnapping Sarah Smith and John Atkinson, and a number of other fraud and deception offences involving Elizabeth Richardson and Maria Hendy.

The stage was set for the trial, which was to prove far from straightforward. After three false starts while Hendy-Freegard changed his legal team, it dragged on for eight months and cost £2.5 million.

Eventually, Hendy-Freegard was convicted on eighteen charges of theft and deception, for which he was sentenced to nine years' imprisonment; and for the kidnapping of Sarah Smith and John Atkinson the sentence was life.

Then – to the shock, outrage and utter dismay of his victims – three years after his trial, the kidnapping convictions were overturned on a legal technicality.

The Lord Chief Justice, Lord Phillips, ruled that the convictions were unsafe because the victims were not physically deprived of their liberty and that it was not enough for the victims just to be ensnared psychologically.

The victims and their relatives lambasted the Court of Appeal's decision and spoke of their terror that he might pursue them again. They also insisted that the unassuming thirty-six-year-old – whose ten-year con was described as 'an unbelievable odyssey of deceit'– would continue to be a danger to the public on his release.

One of his victims, Sarah Smith, told the *Daily Mail*, 'I am absolutely stunned and devastated by the decision. I thought justice had been done – now my faith in the courts is completely shaken. I am also concerned that if he is let out it would be so easy for other people to be at risk. I am sure he will do it again. Whichever way you look at it, I was deprived of my liberty for ten years. What happened to me could have happened to anybody – and that is proved by the fact that so many people were taken in by him.'

Another of Hendy-Freegard's victims – who remained so frightened of him that she did not want to be named – simply said, 'He was a complete and utter control freak. He has ruined mine and other people's lives. And it is not just the people he has already damaged – what about the future damage this man is going to cause when he gets out?'

As we write, Robert Hendy-Freegard, is still serving the remainder of a nine-year sentence for theft and deception. But nobody can tell – and even now the police are not sure – whether all his past victims have been discovered.

10

JOHN PALMER – GOLDFINGER!

What, we wondered in the summer of 2007, do you call a man whose estimated wealth exceeded that of the Queen; who lived in a £3 million house, had a string of properties abroad and owned his own luxury yacht?

The answer – apparently – was 'bankrupt'. Or at least it was if you were John Palmer.

We were then preparing a film about Palmer – one the nastiest and most Teflon-coated villains *The Cook Report* ever crossed swords with. He was the brains behind the world's biggest-ever timeshare fraud – a scam worth more than £30 million and with at least 17,000 victims. The sheer scale and cruelty of the operation made Palmer the poster boy of international con-artistry.

But he was much more than simply a conman: over a thirty-year career he was the recipient of huge quantities of stolen gold; a self-confessed launderer of dirty money; and the boss of a vast and violent organised-crime network based in the Canary Islands.

He had tended to be portrayed in the media as little more than a street-smart thug who left school hardly able to read and write. But this public image is very far from the truth: John Palmer is, in fact, a highly sophisticated criminal – and one who seems to have had an uncanny knack for avoiding almost every attempt to bring him to justice.

John Palmer was born in 1950, one of seven children growing up in poverty on a council estate in Olton in the West Midlands. A self-confessed failure at school, he emerged barely literate and more reliant on low cunning than high intelligence.

After an initial spell working as a roof tiler and market trader, he moved into second-hand car dealing, with a sideline selling paraffin out of the back of a van. At the age of twenty-three he clocked up the first of what would turn out to be a lifetime of run-ins with the police: he was charged, convicted and fined for handling a stolen car.

By 1976 he had moved down the M5 to the West Country. Here he developed a new string to his bow – doing the rounds of pubs across Wiltshire and Somerset, selling 'moody' watches.

He was a very persistent salesman, but more notable than his tenacity was his reputation for having a very short fuse. Word quickly spread that it could be bad for the health to complain when John Palmer's 'bargain' timepieces mysteriously stopped working.

From dodgy wristwatches he branched out into coin dealing. And within a few short years he had transformed himself from being a thuggish Arthur Daley[28] figure to an outwardly respectable dealer in jewellery and gold.

Business was, apparently, good: Palmer's empire soon encompassed a chain of shops across the southwest of England and a sumptuous Georgian manor house in the hills outside Bath.

Beneath the surface, though, Palmer was mixing with – and benefiting from – some of the most notorious and heavyweight criminals in Britain. Kenneth Noye, then an up-and-coming 'face' (now a convicted murderer), introduced him to armed robbers Mickey MacEvoy and Tony White, career criminal Brian Robinson and several members of the Adams and Richardson crime families, to name but a few. The upwardly mobile young jewellery dealer was rising inexorably into the criminal Premiership.

By 1983 the gang he had fallen in with was planning an audacious robbery. They had found themselves a tasty target – the Brinks Mat bullion depot at Heathrow Airport – and a security guard called Anthony Black passed them inside information about the amount of cash and gold stored there. According to the police, he also told them that a huge new consignment of gold and cash would soon be arriving, and that it was to be stored at the depot for one night only prior to being flown out to Hong Kong.

Crucially, Black, who was living with Brian Robinson's sister at the time, also passed on details that would enable potential robbers to disable the depot's complex alarm system.

And so, at just after 6.40 a.m. on 26 November 1983, six men – all armed and wearing balaclavas – broke into the Brinks Mat depot. After neutralising the alarm, the gang bound and gagged the security guards. For good measure they also doused them with petrol and threatened to set them alight unless they revealed the combinations to the final locks on the vault doors.

The sheer volume of gold inside took them by surprise. They had expected far more cash and far fewer ingots. By the time they had finished, three tons of gold – 6,800 ingots – had been packed into 76 boxes. The total value of the haul was £26,369,778.

The robbery was Britain's biggest-ever heist and it changed the face of organised crime overnight. Prior to Brinks Mat, robbery was a strictly cash business and none of the robbers – or their immediate circle of contacts – had any experience of handling such huge quantities of bullion.

Some of it was passed to Kenneth Noye with instructions to turn the gold, somehow, into something much more portable. But so huge was the quantity of bullion that Noye realised that it would need smelting down on an almost industrial scale. Fortunately, he knew just the man to turn to.

John Palmer was by then used to dealing in precious metals and so was not unduly phased by Noye's request for help to smelt down what he claimed were legitimately acquired gold ingots. But Palmer's company, Scadlynn Ltd, did not have the facilities to do the job.

Ever resourceful, John Palmer built a makeshift – but thoroughly serviceable – private smelting furnace in the backyard of his lavish Bath mansion. Large quantities of the Brinks Mat gold ingots, with highly incriminating serial numbers etched or stamped into them, disappeared into its maw to be mixed with other old gold jewellery and old pieces of silver. When it emerged the gold was completely unrecognisable and untraceable; it has since been estimated that anyone who has bought gold jewellery since 1983 is likely to be wearing a bit of Brinks Mat.

The end product was sold back into the legitimate gold market through Scadlynn Ltd, and the majority of the proceeds were deposited in a Bristol branch of Barclay's Bank – where the usual processes of high street banking effectively concealed any connection between the recipient accounts and the Brinks Mat bullion.

But the money was no use sitting in Bristol: the gang needed it back where they could get their hands on it. And so, over a period of five months, it slowly found its way out of the Barclays accounts and into other banks dotted across the map.

It was a clever plan and might have succeeded but for one thing: so much money was withdrawn from the Bristol branch – nearly £10 million – and over such a relatively short period from such a small number of accounts, that suspicions were aroused and the Bank of England was notified.

The word then went out from Threadneedle Street to Scotland Yard. The Metropolitan Police Serious and Organised Crime Squad was in charge of the Brinks Mat investigation, and it added John Palmer to its ever-growing list of 'interesting' names.

The net was already beginning to close on the Brinks Mat robbers themselves. In February 1984, Anthony Black – the security guard 'mole' who had given the gang inside information – was sentenced to six years at the Old Bailey.

Ten months later, in December, two of the robbers themselves were convicted and given twenty-five-year terms. But of the £26 million haul there was – frustratingly – no sign. Detectives began to switch their focus to the men suspected of enabling its disappearance; high on the list was Kenneth Noye.

By 1984 Noye had clocked up a number of criminal convictions for receiving stolen cars and had been given an eighteen-month suspended jail sentence for receiving and possessing a shotgun. But neither this apparently low-level villainy nor the profits from his legitimate building business could quite account for the lavish, ten-bedroom, mock-Tudor mansion Noye had built himself four years earlier on 20 acres of land near West Kingsdown, near Sevenoaks in Kent. The police decided to take a closer look, but it was to prove a fatal decision.

In January 1985, Detective Constable John Fordham was on surveillance duty inside the grounds of Noye's mansion. Noye attacked him with a knife and the unarmed detective subsequently died of stab wounds. Noye was charged with murdering Fordham, but the jury at his trial cleared him on a majority verdict, deciding that he had acted in self-defence.

It was a serious setback for Scotland Yard. But there had been one small shaft of light: a search of Noye's home had turned up eleven gold bars, hidden in various parts of the premises. Within a year Noye was back in court and, after an eleven-week trial at the Old Bailey, was convicted of conspiring to handle gold from the Brinks Mat robbery. As he was taken down to the cells he yelled at the jury, 'I hope you all die of cancer.'

Noye's arrest had also tightened the net on Palmer. Scotland Yard had sent a squad down the M4 to search his country home. As Detective Sergeant Tony Curtis later remembered, the raid produced unexpected results.

'When we raided John Palmer's house there were, in fact,

two bars of gold there that were still warm. They had just come from the smelter. Unfortunately, John Palmer wasn't in residence at the time. He had left earlier to go on holiday with his family.'

Palmer had fled with his wife and two children to Tenerife, then in its early years as one of Britain's favourite summer hotspots. The island, like the rest of the Canaries, fell under the administration of the Spanish government – a fact that made it rather more than just a holiday destination for the Palmer family.

In the 1980s and early 1990s Britain and Spain were at loggerheads over the issue of criminals on the run. Both countries accused each other of frustrating attempts to send wanted villains back home to face the music. As a result, the long-standing extradition treaty had been allowed to lapse.

These were the years in which major British criminals lived openly on the Costa del Sol – so openly, in fact, that it became known as the Costa Del Crime. Former Commander Roy Ramm was then the man in charge of the Metropolitan Police's most heavyweight investigative teams – the Flying Squad, Serious and Organised Crimes branch, the Fraud Squad and the Armed Response Units. For him and his colleagues, it was intensely frustrating that British crooks wanted for major crimes could sit back, sipping their beers in the sun, arrogant and untouchable.

'It was a real thorn in the side of the Yard, because here you had the likes of Ronnie Knight and the whole gangs of London villains who were hopping over to the Costa Del Sol and living the high life and flitting backwards and forwards and really running their criminal empires from the Costa Del Sol. This was not a retirement home. This was just the overseas office. And it was just outside the reach of the Yard.'

John Palmer thoroughly enjoyed being out of reach. As Ramm's detectives fumed – prevented from dragging him back to face charges of handling the Brinks Mat gold – television crews tracked him down to Los Cristianos, the island's tourist-trap centre. He grinned smugly as he answered their questions: 'I'm in no hurry to go back. I'll take my time and I'll go back when I'm ready and not when Scotland Yard's ready.'

It was to be almost eighteen months before Palmer was ready to go home, a year and a half in which – as we were to discover – he had been very busy indeed.

In late 1986 Britain and Spain were getting ready to sign a new extradition treaty – news that made the British villains living on the Costa del Crime distinctly nervous. Palmer saw the way the wind was blowing: the Canaries would be no safer than the Costas once the treaty was put in place. So he fled Tenerife for Brazil.

Scotland Yard knew to its cost that it was extremely difficult to prize wanted villains out of Brazil: the sorry saga of Great Train Robber Ronnie Biggs had been a salutary – and well-publicised – lesson in how not to extradite British criminals. The prospect of seeing John Palmer sunning himself on Copacabana Beach was not calculated to improve the position.

Unfortunately for Palmer, there was one small, technical problem: his passport was out of date. The Brazilian authorities duly refused him entry to the country. As a result, he had little choice but to return to Britain.

When he did arrive back in England he was charged with

handling the stolen bullion. Ramm, Curtis and the other members of the team were confident of a conviction. After all, hadn't some of the Brinks Mat gold been found in the makeshift smelter Palmer had built in his garden?

But throughout his career Palmer has had an uncanny knack of slipping through the fingers of the law. To general disbelief, when the jury returned their verdict, he was acquitted. Somehow he had convinced them that he had not known that the huge quantity of gold he was smelting had been stolen. That same evening, he stood in the driveway of his impressive mansion and once again held court for the press.

'I was smelting gold,' he told the assembled cameras with a straight face, 'but innocently.'

His admission that he had handled the bullion – and the brazen cheek of his successful defence strategy – earned Palmer the nickname that has stuck with him ever since: Goldfinger.

But, despite his impressive victory, John Palmer didn't linger too long in the Chiltern Hills. He quickly hightailed it back to Tenerife – and almost as quickly the reason became apparent.

From being a relatively small-scale dealer in precious metals – at least ostensibly – Palmer had somehow become the owner of vast tracts of land in Tenerife's tourist-friendly southern regions. Reports detailed an investment of £5 million in 450 timeshare villas, with an estimated potential sales income of £72 million.

Quite where the money had come from was a mystery. Palmer spread stories about borrowing an initial £30,000 stake from his brother, though that would hardly have covered the deposit on the £5 million he had seemingly invested. Ramm and Curtis were convinced that much of the Brinks Mat proceeds had been laundered through these Spanish property deals.

What Palmer did next was to be both his fortune and – ultimately – his downfall. It's also what earned him his place in this book and – almost exclusively, thanks to Palmer – turned an innocuous-sounding single word into universal shorthand for fraud. John Palmer discovered timeshare.

Timeshare began in the French Alps in the 1960s, when the owner of a ski resort marketed his new holiday destination with the catchy slogan 'Stop renting a room and buy the hotel'.

The idea took off almost instantly and the concept of selling the ownership of a property for a defined number of weeks per year was quickly embraced by developers worldwide.

John Palmer wasn't the first to tarnish the timeshare concept by crooked and fraudulent dealings, but he was the most organised and by far the biggest fish in an ever-growing pond. Throughout the 1980s and 1990s he expanded across the Canaries until he had established seventeen enormous timeshare resorts.

He also accumulated the trappings of an extraordinarily lavish lifestyle: a £2.5 million Learjet; a multimillion-pound yacht, the *Brave Goose of Essex*; two helicopters; a collection of classic cars and a chateau in France complete with its own golf course. The *Sunday Times* Rich List estimated his personal wealth at more than £300 million – greater even than that of the Queen.

Tenerife became his personal fiefdom. His timeshare empire accounted for a substantial proportion of the island's tourist trade, and he employed a small army of rapacious salesmen.

They quickly found that his was a name to conjure with in the eyes of any aspiring timeshare salesman. Working for John Palmer brought instant respect from smaller and rival outfits.

There was, of course, a reason for that. Palmer ran his empire by intimidation and violence. Intelligence collected by the Spanish National Police and the paramilitary Civil Guard began to show links between Palmer and his senior associates and protection rackets, extortion, death threats and violent attacks, as well as money laundering and working with the Russian mafia.

But, although the Spanish federal authorities were gradually building a bulky file on John Palmer, on Tenerife the local police seemed completely unconcerned by his increasingly brutal methods of getting his way.

In case after case of serious violence on the streets and in the shady nightspots of Playa de las Americas, Palmer's name was the almost universal common denominator. And many of these incidents involved a group of men identified as Palmer's 'security men'.

There were attacks with knives and baseball bats, cars were set on fire and properties smashed up. There were also stabbings and on one occasion a Briton was shot dead in a turf war between rival timeshare businesses. Other timeshare companies were forced to pay Palmer a hefty levy just to operate and protection money was demanded from bars selling sex and drugs.

If threats or violence from Palmer's henchmen did not work, they could call in two South American heavyweights known as 'the Sharks', who cruised around the resort in an ominous-looking black limousine.

One of Palmer's companies had sales offices in Russia

whose methods, according to a National Police report, 'used tactics more appropriate to a mafia organisation than to the rule of law'. Palmer himself often wore body armour.

And yet the police on Tenerife did nothing.

Meanwhile, the timeshare operation itself was developing into a ruthlessly criminal fraud, based on conning unwary holidaymakers into signing extortionate contracts for either worthless or nonexistent properties.

Anyone who has been to the Canary Islands in the past twenty years will have become all too wearily familiar with the techniques Palmer devised to gull his victims. They were so successful so quickly that they have been adopted by virtually every dodgy timeshare company since then.

He employed hundreds of street-level touts – mostly footloose Britons seeking temporary employment in the sun; they were instructed to use a series of bogus 'promotions' to lure holidaymakers off the street and into high-pressure sales meetings.

The touts variously promised the punters free champagne, cameras or children's gifts; they also handed bogus scratch cards, which purported to show that the lucky winners had won a major cash prize. All that was required to collect the money, camera, gifts or champagne was to step into a nearby office and listen for an hour or so to a presentation about the delights of timeshare ownership.

At these meetings, more senior salesmen told a series of barefaced lies to part the punters from their cash. The victims were tricked into believing the timeshares they bought could be rented out easily and would provide a lucrative income – 'so they could pay off the timeshare while watching television at home'. They were also promised that timeshares they already owned would be sold quickly at very attractive high prices by another company with which the timeshare people had a special arrangement. The salesmen even persuaded several hundred people to invest in timeshare apartments that had yet to be built.

And, like vampires returning to a suck blood from an existing victim, Palmer's operation went on to target some of those whom it had already conned. This group of victims – several thousand strong – were persuaded to join a resale scheme, operated by an ostensibly independent company, which involved selling or upgrading their timeshares 'at a fantastic profit'.

Among those taken in was Edward Jenkins, a Dunkirk war veteran and ex-professional golfer, who found himself paying for two properties, neither of which he ended up owning.

'They promised me the earth, so when I got home I sent them the amount they wanted per month, which was £500 to £700 for buying the new apartment. I thought it was the best bit of business I'd ever done in my life. It seemed too good to be true.'

Indeed it was. The independent company was, in fact, another branch of Palmer's empire. He was able to give it the façade of independence by creating a fantastically complex corporate web, which effectively disguised the ownership of all the resorts, sales companies and marketing agencies. Over a seven-year period, not a single resale was completed. Jenkins, like so many others, would end up losing everything.

Tens of thousands of holidaymakers were enticed to sink their life savings into Palmer's resorts and bogus resale schemes. And, as they did so, Palmer became ever more wealthy and ever more untouchable on Tenerife.

Property frauds are generally 'long cons': these require careful and patient planning to hook their mark at the end of an elaborate sting. After that, the con artist is careful to disappear before the scam is exposed.

Palmer's operation combined much of the sophistication of a long con with the rather less subtle characteristics of the short con – a process much more akin to white-collar pickpocketing. And so, while he built an entirely fraudulent empire on long-term false promises, he was quite happy to take a very direct approach to anyone who might complain.

Derek Bettridge was one of his senior salesmen and therefore benefited financially from the Palmer empire. He knew very well what his boss could be like. As he told *The Cook Report* in 1997, 'John is two people – without a shadow of a doubt, he is two people. One person is a good guy and the other person you don't really want to know. I don't think he has any control over it. That's just my honest opinion. I don't think he has any control on that at all.'

And Bettridge was quite happy to explain how Palmer maintained 'discipline' both with his staff and his customers. 'The word would go out, break their legs... This applied to customers also if they shouted too loud.'

Back in London, Scotland Yard was monitoring Palmer's growing empire – and Roy Ramm was becoming increasingly concerned.

'For me, John Palmer's relationship to violence was a very interesting trait of his character. We never saw direct evidence of him getting his hands bloodied and his fists scuffed. But there is no doubt that his empire in Tenerife was very largely enforced by violence. People working for Palmer broke people's legs. They maimed people and gave them injuries that will be with them for the rest of their lives.'

Which made it all the more extraordinary that no action was ever taken against him by the Tenerife authorities. Gradually, as they tried to piece together the evidence for a new case against Palmer, Ramm and his team came to understand why.

'We always had very grave concerns about his relationships with politicians and with police officers, once he was outside of the UK, and we were worried that our investigation may have been compromised on a number of occasions.'

And it wasn't just the fraud and the violence that had Ramm worried. In 1994 his teams had begun investigating the source of Palmer's seemingly endless funds, and had come to suspect that his burgeoning timeshare empire might be a cover for a drug money-laundering operation.

At *The Cook Report*, we were also interested in Palmer's activities and, after our paths had crossed, arranged to cooperate with the Metropolitan Police Special Operations Department. We agreed to steer clear of his timeshare activities, concentrating instead on the alleged money laundering. The question was how to devise a sting operation sufficiently sophisticated to encourage Palmer to demonstrate his money-laundering skills – and to do so with clearly illegal money.

No money is dirtier than that made in the illegal drugs trade, so we set about constructing a legally watertight – and, given his reputation, extremely convincing – undercover operation.

A few years earlier the programme had trekked through the steaming jungles of Burma's Golden Triangle to meet the world's most extraordinary heroin exporter – General Khun Sa. The general was then the source of much of the world's illegal heroin and had earned the nickname 'the Prince of Death'. In reality, he claimed he was a reluctant drug trafficker, who had been encouraged into the business by the CIA while fighting for the independence of the Shan peoples inside Burma. This was something Britain had promised prior to relinquishing control of Burma after World War Two, but had not delivered.

Once the American spy agency had finished using him for its own ends – it was said that the profits from drug dealing were used to pay for their illegal war in Cambodia – Khun Sa was left with no other option than to continue growing heroin to finance his own fight for a separate Shan State. He didn't appear to be spending drug money on himself, but had clearly spent a good deal of money on building schools and hospitals and an army to defend them. Bad, but not *all* bad – and we said so.

As a result, when we contacted him again to ask a favour, he was receptive. We asked if we could borrow two of his 'sales representatives' to front our sting operation on Palmer. Our reasoning was that Palmer would be initially suspicious of our undercover team – and that therefore they needed to be the real thing.

And so it proved: Palmer couldn't fault our Burmese friends and – captured by *Cook Report* hidden cameras – boasted of his money-laundering expertise and greedily agreed that, twice a year, he would launder around a $60 million worth of post-harvest opium profits for them. He also bragged that his commission rates were the best in the business.

'I can handle fifty million every six months. But I need time. I can't do it next week. I need time. I want to be clear with lawyers and everything, so that there is no problems.'

In return (and in addition to his fees for washing the dirty money), Palmer had an extraordinary request: he asked the Burmese if they could supply him with untraceable 'soldiers' to act as enforcers for him on Tenerife.

'You have people, yeah? So, if I have problems where I can't use my people you will give me some of your people to use, yeah? So if I want something done and somebody makes problems for me. You see, you're good in Europe. In England, you are good for me, rather than my own people. In Spain we are good and in France we're good and everywhere else we are good. In England it's a lot of pressure for us to use my own people. So if somebody is making problems, big problems, you can give me some men?'

We decided to confront Palmer in the tearooms of the Ritz in London – the perfect location, we thought, because that's where the Brinks Mat robbery had allegedly been planned.

We had done a little planning of our own too. *The Cook Report*'s arrival in the tearooms had been coordinated with police raids on all Palmer's UK addresses. As Palmer fled through the corridors of the Ritz, desperately trying to deny the evidence of his tape-recorded money-laundering boasts, Scotland Yard were taking away van loads of evidence relating to his entire empire.

The *Cook Report* investigation had confirmed all of Roy Ramm's fears about Palmer: here was a man running a vast and violent criminal empire – an empire stretching from timeshare fraud to international money laundering – and doing so with apparent impunity.

'The *Cook Report* film was a great exposé. It really demonstrated that this was not a bit of minor criminality. This was somebody quite clearly saying that he could launder millions and millions of pounds, criminally,' Ramm said.

It led Ramm to authorise one of the most far-reaching and costly investigations he had ever supervised: code-named 'Operation Beryk', it was to put Palmer and his empire under the most searching of microscopes.

'The programme was the springboard to the next section of our investigation,' he said. 'That involved a huge amount of surveillance – both here, Tenerife and in Spain.

'It really was a very, very in depth and detailed investigation that cost around £1 million. That's a great deal of money now and it was a lot more money back then in 1997. But I took the view that we had to start spending this kind of sum to get under the skin of serious organised criminals. Serious crime makes serious money – and that money goes into all kinds of other criminality.'

Still, it would take another five years before the Metropolitan Police got their man. In the meantime, Palmer was reported to be determined to extract revenge for our exposé.

We pieced together the events of the succeeding weeks from underworld contacts and the police. The word was that one of Palmer's lieutenants had apparently enlisted the services of a British-based criminal who, for £20,000, had agreed to kill me. He was picked up by the police in an entirely different connection and, in the course of trying to do a deal with the arresting officers, spilled the beans about what he claimed he had been contracted to do.

The briefing officer, having told me that the tariff on my life was £20,000, and having assured me that this particular potential assassin was now temporarily out of circulation, asked drily if I wasn't a bit miffed that the sum on offer was so low! After the story had appeared in the papers, Palmer denied any connection with the murder plot and issued a libel writ – which was never proceeded with. Nevertheless, on police advice, I stepped up our home security.

Palmer had also been reacquainting himself with old friends. In 1994, Kenneth Noye, the man who had passed Palmer some of the Brinks Mat bullion, had been released from prison. Unfortunately, within a year, he had let his temper get the better of him and in a widely reported 'road rage' incident had stabbed a motorist who had apparently cut him up at a motorway junction. The motorist died of his wounds and the Metropolitan Police were soon on Noye's trail.

Palmer possessed a private jet, and he wasn't going to let his old friend suffer the heat of yet another police investigation, so he cheerfully flew Noye out of the country. (Noye would eventually be caught, tried and convicted of the killing.)

Operation Beryk observed all Palmer's comings and goings. It also quickly spotted that the most efficient way of tackling their man was to go after the crimes for which witnesses were ready and willing to come forward. And that meant the timeshare scam.

Ramm said: 'It was a case of finding the most vulnerability. It didn't matter to us whether we took Palmer down for a serious assault or money laundering or anything else. We just wanted to get the best case on rock-solid evidence, and in the timeshare fraud that's what we knew we had.'

In fact, Palmer actually went on trial twice. In 1999 he and his business partner cum mistress, Christina Ketley, were charged with multiple counts of fraud.

But Palmer, defending himself, successfully argued that bad publicity linking him to a murder trial had prejudiced his case. As a result, the judge ordered that both he and Ketley should face a retrial.

The second trial opened late in 2000, with Palmer, Ketley and one of their associates facing charges of conspiracy to defraud. Over seven long months the court heard detailed evidence of how holidaymakers were systematically cheated out of vast sums. Both British and European timeshare customers fell victim to lies and false promises made to them in what prosecuting counsel David Farrer QC described as a 'slick, well-orchestrated and thoroughly dishonest sales operation'.

He went on: 'It involved high-pressure glib, untruthful salesmen who had been trained to latch on to the unwary – or even the wary. Customers were faced with complex, misleading paperwork and a confusing network of companies.

'These companies pretended to be independent of each other, but the companies each were all, in truth, controlled by one man – John Palmer.

'[His] victims were invariably couples. The majority of them lost thousands of pounds. They were of quite ordinary means, some with very modest incomes. Some were pensioners who like that sort of climate for their health.

'This was not an exotic fraud of finance houses or banks, but on people like any sitting in this court. It could be you or the person sitting next to you.

'Very many people learnt to their cost that there are no free lunches. A large number of ordinary people were systematically tricked into buying timeshare apartments in Tenerife. They were tricked into handing over large sums of money, which many could not afford to lose.'

Ramm and his team had done a very thorough job: their investigations had cut through the labyrinthine legal structure Palmer and Ketley had set up. They had also interviewed hundreds, if not thousands, of victims who all told the same story: Palmer's salesmen had promised either that timeshares they already owned would be sold quickly at premium prices, or that if they bought new these could be rented out easily and provide a lucrative return on their investment.

And every word had been a lie.

Palmer once again represented himself, claiming that he was the victim of a police vendetta: they had launched Operation Beryk only because they were still angry about his acquittal in the Brinks Mat smelting case. In what was an extraordinarily eloquent performance for someone with a reputation as an ill-educated near-illiterate, he strongly protested his innocence

'I have been portrayed as a gangster,' he told the jury. 'I am not a gangster or ever have been a gangster.'

But, however eloquent, Palmer's insistence on presenting his own defence – with all the tactical blunders that this involved – allowed Roy Ramm (under questioning from Palmer) repeatedly to tell the court that, in the eyes of Scotland Yard, the accused was much more than a mere conman.

'Our view is that you were a serious organised criminal trapped by his own words into admitting laundering money.'

The trial was one of the longest fraud hearings in British legal history and ended when the jury decided, after a record twenty-one days' deliberation, that, despite his protestations, John Palmer was very definitely a crook. He and Ketley were convicted of conspiracy to defraud. Palmer got eight years; Ketley an eighteen-month suspended sentence.

At the age of fifty-two, Palmer was sentenced to his first jail term in a criminal career spanning three decades. It should have been the end, but, in fact, it barely interrupted his business.

The court had heard that the timeshare scam had netted Palmer at least £33 million. And so, in April 2002, the Crown Prosecution Service served him with an official confiscation order for the sum of £33,243,812.46.

This money was to be handed over to the Treasury under the laws ordering convicted criminals to forfeit the proceeds of their crimes. Under these rules, none of this money could be used to compensate the people he had scammed, so a simultaneous order was made that he hand over £3.8 million to a sample group of his victims.

But Palmer's reputation as a crook so bent he could wiggle his way around a corkscrew was about to be reinforced. From his prison cell, he plotted a complex appeal against the confiscation order. In theory, it should have been no contest – an alleged illiterate against the very best legal minds in the government's service.

But, as he soon discovered, the legal brains trust employed by the CPS had managed to cock up the paperwork: they had applied for the order on out-of-date – and therefore inadmissible – forms. The confiscation was quashed, pending an appeal by the CPS.

In fairness to the CPS lawyers (and as a senior judge would subsequently rule) the forms were only very slightly out of date and the quashing order would, itself, have been quashed had the official appeal come to court.

Unfortunately the CPS made a second and fatal mistake: it failed to lodge its appeal inside the fourteen-day 'window'. As a result, Palmer was allowed to keep the £33 million he had stolen in the timeshare fraud. The law had made an ass of itself – and at Scotland Yard Roy Ramm and his team were furious.

'My instant reaction was anger. Complete incredulity. We were just dumbstruck that it could have happened. Here was £33,000,000 being returned to somebody who had been convicted of serious crime. Somebody who we believed to be in the world of serious and organised crime. We were immediately thinking, What can those funds be used to fund in terms of criminality? How might they be used to build a criminal empire? We were just astounded and absolutely devastated.'

Sadly, that was to be far from the last example of official incompetence. And each new example would greatly benefit John Palmer.

In 2003 solicitors acting for a group of 350 victims of his timeshare scam issued legal proceedings for compensation. Palmer was still in prison at the time, but all of his timeshare resorts were still running and earning big money. At their helm was Christina Ketley – Palmer's partner in crime.

A year later, the lawsuit was still grinding on, and according to Sandy Grey, head of the Timeshare Consumers Association, Palmer was doing everything in his power to avoid paying compensation. 'His conduct has been quite horrific and quite disgraceful. He's wriggled and squirmed at every opportunity to try and avoid paying.

'He had a massive structure of companies: the latest

information is that there were 122 companies all around the world which he had control over. And, of course, he's refusing to disclose either his control over them or their assets and it makes life very difficult for the trustees in bankruptcy trying to gather the money from the assets to identify the assets and then to sell them.'

But the victims and their lawyers stuck at it. And in 2004 they thought they had won a minor victory, when Palmer and Ketley each swore a statement – on oath – that Palmer's personal assets exceeded £22 million. That meant there would be enough money to compensate each and every one of them.

And so, when in May 2005 the High Court awarded these 350 victims an average of £11,000 each and ordered Palmer to pay their £1.4 million legal costs for good measure, his victims celebrated. The court even gave Palmer a date by which the compensation had to be paid: 24 May 2005.

For once Palmer seemed to accept his fate. He was nearing the date when he would be released from prison on parole, and so, when he failed to file an appeal against the compensation order, his victims assumed that he was trying to keep his nose clean and his release on schedule.

In fact, Palmer was simply playing a waiting game. He may not have appealed against the ruling, but he certainly didn't comply with it. Despite his stated wealth, there was no sign of the compensation.

As a result, bankruptcy proceedings were started against him. He didn't contest these either and was officially declared bankrupt by May 2005. There are many restrictions on what bankrupts may or may not do. One bars them from being company directors. Another requires them to turn over their assets to a trustee in bankruptcy, who will sell them off to pay the creditors. With no assistance from the man himself – or from Christina Ketley – Palmer's trustee began the complicated initial process of working out what these assets might be.

Over the ensuing months and years they identified all seventeen of the timeshare resorts and proved – despite there being not a single shred of company paper bearing his signature – that Palmer was their beneficial owner. But, before they could sell them off, the Spanish government stepped in. Many of the resorts had been officially 'frozen' both as payment for huge amounts in unpaid taxes and as part of a mysterious and highly complicated criminal case.

Spanish criminal proceedings are largely conducted under a bewildering blanket of official secrecy. It was not clear, therefore, what the case involved – or even whether Palmer was a suspect. But one thing was absolutely certain: the affected resorts could not be sold – and that meant the victims had no chance of getting their court-ordered compensation.

But, if the resorts couldn't be sold, there was nothing to stop them being run, and it soon became clear that it was pretty much business as usual for the Palmer timeshare companies. They carried on earning money from rentals and sales, and that income was paid into their company bank accounts. In turn, the companies paid wages to the staff who maintained them. And there was one person above all benefiting from the income: Christina Ketley.

Despite the fact that she had been convicted and sentenced for being a key player in the timeshare fraud, the Department of Trade had never got round to disqualifying her from running a company. So, when she went straight back to managing Palmer's timeshare empire, she was able to pocket the proceeds while the victims of their scam got nothing.

It was yet another official cockup – and one that Ketley exploited to the limit. In the course of our investigations in 2007 we discovered how much she was paying herself from the same timeshare businesses she and Palmer had used to fleece their victims: a cool £2 million per year.

Even seasoned Palmer experts such as Sandy Grey were astonished by the ease with which Ketley had been able to resume her very profitable life after a conviction over the world's biggest ever timeshare fraud.

'There seems to be no explanation as to why the government authorities have not banned Christina Ketley from operating a company and have actually allowed her to continue to run the same timeshare operation that operated the fraud. And it's quite wrong that she should be making a large amount of money from it, right now.'

Sadly, there was worse to come.

In August 2005 Palmer was released on parole. He returned to the luxury home he shared with Ketley in Essex. That home – Foxdown Cottage – was a huge, isolated and very well-protected house deep in a heavily wooded country park and completely surrounded by a substantial wooden fence. Gardeners tended its immaculate lawns; a private lake lapped against beautifully manicured shrubberies; security cameras and electric gates guarded the couple's privacy.

Solicitors for Palmer's trustee in bankruptcy valued Foxdown Cottage at £3 million – and no one had any doubt that it was purchased with the proceeds of the timeshare scam.

But, because it was ostensibly owned by a company that in turn was owned outright by Christina Ketley, it was apparently safe from Palmer's victims. Those we spoke to were – understandably – furious. Eric Dean, who had been taken for £4,000, summed it up: 'The effect it's had on me is, I would say, tremendous, because we could badly have done with the £4,000 we paid Palmer. And then to find that he's been living it up in a life of luxury where I've been suffering, well, I don't think he gives two hoots about people. All he's interested in is money, getting money off people. He couldn't care less who he gets it off.

'But I really blame the authorities – it doesn't make sense to me how he can get away with it.'

We felt the same. Especially when we located Palmer's 115-foot personal yacht – the *Brave Goose of Essex*, bobbing gently on the swell in Tenerife's Santa Cruz harbour. He had managed to hang onto it by telling the trustee in bankruptcy that it was worth no more than £100,000 – a sum too small to make much of a dent on the compensation he had been ordered to pay.

But, when we filmed it, the yacht positively sparkled. It looked like a great deal more than £100,000 worth – and, come to think of it, who was paying the full time Filipino crew who were assiduously scrubbing its gleaming decks? Or the harbour fees of more than €10,000 a year?

All in all, it wasn't a surprise to discover that official sale documents showed it to be worth well over US $1 million. At least, it wasn't a surprise to us.

Still, in theory, Palmer was not allowed to use it. One of the conditions of his release from prison on parole was that he stay inside the United Kingdom. No offender released on licence (as it is officially described) is allowed to leave the country without official (and rarely granted) permission.

And so we were rather taken aback when we received intelligence – later backed up by a sworn statement – that Palmer had been seen on Tenerife. The notion that John Palmer – with a still-standing criminal empire in the Canary Islands, not to mention his record of helping Kenneth Noye disappear during the road rage killing investigation – should be allowed to make trips to the heart of his empire was beyond belief, wasn't it?

We asked the Home Office – the government department responsible for parole. Had it given Palmer permission to travel? If not, would it investigate, since any proven breach of parole should have led to Palmer being recalled from the cosseting comforts of Foxdown Cottage to serve out the rest of his sentence in one of Her Majesty's rather less salubrious prisons?

The Home Office refused to discuss the matter but – by its own account – passed the information on to the parole board. Whatever the latter did, or did not do, it most certainly didn't drag John Palmer back to jail. Instead – and in yet another example of the charmed life of crime that he has enjoyed – it subsequently released Palmer from his parole.

To his thousands of victims – none of whom had received a penny in compensation – it was just one more slap in the face, the last of a succession of official cockups that had allowed Palmer to hang onto the millions he had made from his scams. John Davidson, an eighty-two-year-old from York, spoke for many of them.

'It is just really atrocious. It undermines us and makes us fools as far as the law is concerned. 'My £4,000 [loss] was chickenfeed compared to what some old folk lost. He took £60,000 from some, the life savings of some old people – he shortened their lives because of the stress they went through.'

Palmer's release from prison halfway through his eight-year term was bad enough, but his being completely freed from any restraints while he was treating his victims with such contempt was almost beyond belief.

John Plumpton, a seventy-five-year-old retired security guard from Bristol, who lost £5,500 in the timeshare scam, summed up the feelings of most of those still owed money: 'He should have stayed in prison until all his creditors were paid. If he had stayed inside, that would have put pressure on him to clear his debts. You shouldn't qualify for parole until you have complied with a bankruptcy ruling.

'On an optimism scale of one to ten about getting my money back, I am still on zero. I don't like the fact that he's now out of prison. He will wriggle, mark my words.'

And so we asked each of the three government departments – the Crown Prosecution Service, the Department of Trade and the Home Office – for an interview to explain how they managed to let Palmer and Ketley hang onto their ill-gotten gains and go on living the life of Riley. The response from each was the same: 'We never discuss individual cases.'

It seemed to encapsulate every lesson we had learned over more than thirty years of investigations: no matter how blatant the fraud, there was every chance that the legal authorities would somehow let con artists and scammers slip through their fingers – even when we had caught them bang to rights and on camera.

Within weeks of his release from parole, John Palmer was on a scheduled flight to Spain. After a pleasant day or so on the Costas, he boarded another scheduled flight to Tenerife.

His destination was no secret. This was John Palmer's

homecoming and Tenerife was abuzz with rumours about his reclaiming the sprawling criminal enterprises that had grown, apparently organically, from his original timeshare fraud. So widespread, numerous and profitable are these scams that the British Office of Fair Trading has a squad of investigators desperately trying to keep up with each new permutation.

And then the unthinkable happened.

Within minutes of leaving the plane at Tenerife's southern airport, John Palmer was collared by Spanish police. The man who had once boasted of having much of the island's law enforcement and many of its politicians in his pocket found himself abruptly handcuffed and bundled onto a waiting flight to Madrid.

News of the arrest flashed around the world. It quickly emerged that it had happened on the orders of Spain's most celebrated investigating magistrate, Judge Baltasar Garzón. And the judge plainly meant business.

'He [John Palmer] is wanted by the court for being the suspected leader of an international criminal group based on the island,' a police spokesman said. 'The multiple criminal activities carried out by this gang included timeshare fraud, money laundering, credit-card fraud, threats, crimes against people's physical integrity and freedom, trafficking drugs, falsifying passports and possession of weapons.'

For good measure, the police also levelled a telling rebuke at the British government: Palmer, they alleged, had continued to run his criminal empire while serving time behind bars in an English prison.

From that moment in July 2007 – other than a formal Spanish police estimate placing Palmer's overall wealth at around €600 million – the story disappeared under the stifling blanket of Spain's judicial privacy laws. As we write, the case has been officially classified as 'top secret'.

Of John Palmer's whereabouts all that is known is that he sits – on apparently indefinite remand – in a jail cell in Madrid. If he is convicted, he faces spending the rest of his life behind bars.

But, in the meantime, Christina Ketley, his mistress and partner in the world's biggest ever timeshare fraud, continues to run his empire and enjoy the considerable fruits of their collective con.

And their victims? Not a penny piece of compensation has been paid, despite a forest of court judgments. You could be forgiven for concluding that crime does pay.

AFTERWORD

There is – as we said at the beginning – a certain guilty pleasure to be taken in the story of a good con.

And, because the lives of the masters of the art form are so truly extraordinary, perhaps what prompts that pleasure is some sort of vicarious thrill-seeking: there, if we did but have the brass nerve and the lack of remorse, might go many of us.

But, for the all fun to had from the stories of Gregor McGregor, Philip Morrel Wilson, Peter Foster and the like, there is always a dark side to these 'super-scams': people get hurt.

Often the victims of confidence tricks get lost or forgotten in the drama of the tales. And yet they are often completely ruined – their lives shattered, their homes, savings, families and self-respect frequently lost.

We hope that in this book we have not lost sight of them,

nor the pain and misery they have endured. In some of the stories we have told, these men and women have sought our help – as journalists – to publicise and hopefully put an end to the scams that have fleeced them.

They do so, in general, because the law has a nasty habit of not helping them. Fraud – particularly the sort of cons and scams that steal relatively modest sums from a large number of victims – has a depressingly low priority in police forces up and down the country.

It is perceived as less important than other modern problems – be they knife crimes, drugs or even traffic management. Somewhere, hidden in the subliminal reasoning behind these priorities, is the persistent myth that the victims must have been in some way complicit in the con, that they must have been trying to get something for nothing.

It's not a view borne out by the facts and it is emphatically not a view we share. We therefore dedicate this book to those who have been fleeced; and we urge British police forces to pay much more attention to complaints about con artists, swindlers and fraudsters – however charming or extraordinary they may seem.

Because if they don't, tens – possibly hundreds – of thousands of future victims will be caught in their schemes and summarily relieved of their savings.

BIBLIOGRAPHY

Abagnale, Frank W, with Stan Redding, *Catch Me If You Can*, Grosset and Dunlap, 1980.

Connel, John, and Douglas Sutherland, Fraud, *The Amazing Career of Doctor Savundra*, Hodder & Stoughton, 1978.

Fehrenbach, T R, *The Gnomes of Zürich*, Leslie Frewin, 1972.

Knight, Curtis, *Jimi: An Intimate Biography of Jimi Hendrix*, W H Allen, 1974.

Maurer, David, *The American Confidence Man*, Charles C Thomas Ltd, 1974.

McDermott, John, with Eddie Kramer, *Hendrix: Setting the Record Straight*, Time Warner, 1994.

Nash, Jay Robert, *Hustlers and Conmen*, Evans & Co., 1976.

Nash, Jay Robert, *The World Encyclopaedia of Organised Crime*, Headline Books, 1993.

Naylor, R T, *Wages of Crime: Black Markets, Illegal Finance, and the Underworld Economy*, Cornell University Press, 2004.

Rose, Colin (ed.), *The Confident Tricksters*, Topaz, 1977.

Shapiro, Harry, and Caesar Glebbeek, *Jimi Hendrix: Electric Gypsy*, William Heinemann, 1990.

Sifakis, Carl, *Frauds, Deceptions and Swindles*, Checkmark Books, 2001.

Smith, Sarah, with Kate Snell, *Deceived*, Orion Books, 2007.

Tigue, John J, and Thurston Clarke, *Dirty Money*, Simon & Schuster, 1975.

Note: We have also made liberal use of online newspaper archives; particularly those of the *Telegraph*, *Daily Mail*, *Independent* and the British Library.

NOTES

INTRODUCTION

1   In the original form of the Spanish Prisoner Scam the con artist tells his victim that he is in correspondence with a rich and powerful man who has been imprisoned in Spain under a false identity which he (the prisoner) dare not reveal for fear of repercussions. The con artist dupes his victim into putting up ever more money to secure the prisoner's release, generally on the promise of financial reward or marriage to the man's beautiful daughter just as soon as he gets out of jail. The con ends only when the victim is relieved of all his money. Today's Nigerian 'Advance Fee' frauds are direct descendants of this vintage con.

CHAPTER 1

2   Adolf Hitler, *Mein Kampf*, 1925.

3   *Die Zeit ohne Beispiel*, 12 January 1941.

CHAPTER 3

4   All the quotations from Wilson that follow in this context are excerpted from his testimony to the McClellan Committee during September 1973.

CHAPTER 4

5   An *anstalt* is an entity that has no members, participants or shareholders and no identifiable beneficiaries. With minor exceptions, it is free to conduct all kinds of business, including nontrading activities such as holding passive investments, in which case it is not required to submit annual audited accounts. It does not carry the legal background (and baggage) of restrictive common-law interpretations, and is virtually opaque to outsiders.

6   *Lanka Times*, UK profiles.

7   This and following quotations are taken from court transcripts, *R v. Savundra*.

CHAPTER 5

8   Harry Shapiro and Caesar Glebbeek, *Electric Gypsy*, William Heinemann, 1990.

9   Curtis Knight, *Jimi: An Intimate Biography of Jimi Hendrix*, W H Allen, 1974.

10   John McDermott with Eddie Kramer, *Hendrix: Setting the Record Straight*, Time Warner 1994.

11   Estimates vary, but one source puts the figure for the Hendrix share at around $100 million at today's rates.

CHAPTER 6

12   Frank W Abagnale with Stan Redding, *Catch Me If You Can*, Grosset and Dunlap, 1980.

13   *Ibid.*

14   *Ibid.*

15   Address to National Automobile Dealers Association Convention, 12 February, 2006.

16   *Ibid.*

17   *Ibid.*

18   Abagnale with Redding, *op. cit.*

19   Address, *op. cit.*

20   ABC Radio interview, 17 March 2000.

CHAPTER 7

21   *Daily Telegraph*, 20 June, and *Independent*, 22 June 1995.

CHAPTER 8

22   ABC, *Australian Story*, October 7, 1999.

23   *Ibid.*

24   'When Make-Believe Maketh the Man', *Sun-Herald*, 11 February 2007.

25   ABC, *op. cit.*

26   *Ibid.*

27   *Sunday Mirror*, December 2002.

CHAPTER 10

28   Arthur Daley was a nattily dressed and rather dodgy character played by George Cole in the British TV comedy drama series *Minder*